Labour Shortage and Economic Analysis

Warwick Studies in Industrial Relations

General Editors: G. S. Bain and H. A. Clegg

Also in this series

Shop Stewards in Action
Eric Batstone, Ian Boraston, and Stephen Frenkel
British Employment Statistics
N. K. Buxton and D. I. MacKay
Trade Unionism under Collective Bargaining
Hugh Armstrong Clegg
Union Growth and the Business Cycle
George Sayers Bain and Farouk Elsheikh
Social Values and Industrial Relations
Richard Hyman and Ian Brough
Industrial Relations in Fleet Street
Keith Sisson
Industrial Relations and the
Limits of Law
Brian Weekes, Michael Mellish,
Linda Dickens, John Lloyd
*Social Stratification and Trade Unionism**
George Sayers Bain, David Coates, Valerie Ellis
*Workplace and Union**
Ian Boraston, Hugh Clegg, Malcolm Rimmer
*Piecework Bargaining**
William Brown
*Disputes Procedure in Action**
Richard Hyman
*The Docks after Devlin**
Michael Mellish
*Race and Industrial Conflict**
Malcolm Rimmer

*PUBLISHED BY HEINEMANN EDUCATIONAL BOOKS

Labour Shortage and Economic Analysis

A Study of
Occupational Labour Markets

Barry Thomas
David Deaton

BASIL BLACKWELL · OXFORD

British Library Cataloguing in Publication Data

Thomas, Barry
    Labour shortage and economic analysis. — (Warwick studies in industrial relations).
    1. Labour markets — Great Britain — Case studies
    1. Title   2. Deaton, David   3. Series
    331.1'2'0941   HD 5767

    ISBN 0–631–18310–8

Typeset by Preface Ltd, Salisbury, Wilts.
Printed in Great Britain by
The Camelot Press Ltd, Southampton

Contents

Contents

List of Figures

List of Tables

List of Abbreviations

AEC	Association of Education Committees
AEF	Amalgamated Union of Engineering and Foundry Workers
AESD	Association of Engineering and Shipbuilding Draughtsmen
AES	Aero Electrical Systems (*pseudonym*)
AFP	Associated Farm Products (*pseudonym*)
ATCDE	Association of Teachers in Colleges and Departments of Education
AUEW	Amalgamated Union of Engineering Workers
BTC	British Transport Commission
CAD	Computer-Aided Design
CFE	Civil Flight Enterprises (*pseudonym*)
CODOT	Classification of Occupations and Directory of Occupational Titles
DATA	Draughtsmen's and Allied Technicians' Association
DE	Department of Employment
DES	Department of Education and Science. Before 1964 it was known as the Ministry of Education, but the abbreviation DES has been used throughout.
DW	Durbin–Watson Statistic
EEF	Engineering Employers' Federation
EITB	Engineering Industry Training Board
EPA	Educational Priority Area
ESN	Educationally Sub-Normal
FEDC	Federation of Engineering Design Consultants
GLC	Greater London Council
GMT	General Machine Tools (*pseudonym*)
GNP	Gross National Product
ILEA	Inner London Education Authority

LEA	Local Education Authority
LP	London Planemakers (*pseudonym*)
LT	London Transport
LTB	London Transport Board
LTE	London Transport Executive
MLH	Minimum List Heading
NACTST	National Advisory Council on the Training and Supply of Teachers
NAS	National Association of Schoolmasters
NBC	National Bus Company
NBPI	National Board for Prices and Incomes (*see* PIB)
NC	Numerical Control
NCOI	National Council for the Omnibus Industry
NJIC/ (RPTI)	National Joint Industrial Council for the Road Passenger Transport Industry
NUT	National Union of Teachers
OECD	Organisation for Economic Co-operation and Development
OME	Office of Manpower Economics
OMO	One-Man Operation
ONC	Ordinary National Certificate
PER	Professional and Executive Recruitment
PIB	Prices and Incomes Board (*see* NBPI)
PSV	Public-Service Vehicle
PTA	Passenger Transport Authority
PTE	Passenger Transport Executive
RTITB	Road Transport Industry Training Board
SBG	Scottish Bus Group
SIC	Standard Industrial Classification
TASS	Technical and Supervisory Section
TGWU	Transport and General Workers' Union
THC	Transport Holding Company
UKAPE	United Kingdom Association of Professional Engineers
UM	United Missiles (*pseudonym*)

Editors' Foreword

The University of Warwick is the major centre in the United Kingdom for the study of industrial relations. Its first undergraduates were admitted in 1965. The teaching of industrial relations began a year later in the School of Industrial and Business Studies, and it now has one of the country's largest graduate programmes in this subject. Warwick became a national centre for research into industrial relations in 1970 when the Social Science Research Council, a government-funded body, located its Industrial Relations Research Unit at the University. The Unit has a full-time staff of about twenty and undertakes research into a wide range of topics in industrial relations.

The series of *Warwick Studies in Industrial Relations* was launched in 1972 as the main vehicle for the publication of the results of the Unit's projects. It is also intended to disseminate the research carried out by staff teaching industrial relations in the University. The first six titles in the series were published by Heinemann Educational Books of London, and subsequent titles have been published by Basil Blackwell of Oxford.

This volume by Barry Thomas and David Deaton is concerned with an important aspect of the working of labour markets. It comprises studies of the way employers of draughtsmen, school teachers, and bus drivers respond to labour shortages. These studies of diverse occupational labour markets are combined by the use of a theoretical framework which stresses the way in which employers seek information, and the mechanism by which they choose between alternative courses of action. General insights into labour-market behaviour are derived from this approach. The authors argue firstly that the traditional economic postulate of 'the firm' acting as a single decision-maker fails to account for many of the features observed in the markets studied, and that a firm's decision-making structure is a crucial part of the explanation of the adjustment process. Secondly, they argue that non-wage adjustments, such as a reduction in hiring standards or a curtailment of output, are often so important that economic models which tend to ignore them or to assign them very little weight are open to challenge. Improvements in labour-market policies and advances in the economic theory depend on a deeper and more realistic understanding of labour-market behaviour. This study helps to further this understanding.

George Bain
Hugh Clegg

Preface

This volume is the result of a research project undertaken at the SSRC Industrial Relations Research Unit between 1971 and 1975. The aim of the project was to examine the responses of employers to shortages of labour. Our interest in labour shortage arose from the fact that comparatively little is known about how labour markets operate and how individual firms react to particular labour-market conditions facing them. One of the more important problems which has been neglected in the empirical literature is the analysis of the variety of adjustments which are used in response to disequilibrium, and the implications of these different adjustments. It is this problem which we tackle in our study.

One of the immediate difficulties we faced was the inadequacy of the conventional theory of cost-minimizing behaviour subject to constraints. It was difficult to make it operational for our particular purpose, and our case studies soon revealed that this theory did not by itself explain and predict the behaviour of firms. We have therefore had to consider other theories and have indicated some possible lines of synthesis.

This study has depended on the co-operation of a great many people and organizations. We must express our sincere thanks to those officials of the TASS (AUEW), the TGWU, the NUT and other unions, various employers' associations, government departments and local authorities, and numerous employers in the engineering and road passenger transport industries, who gave us their time and help. Their willingness to answer our questions, provide data, and comment on our work has been invaluable. We are also indebted to Margaret Morgan and Valerie Jephcott for their statistical assistance, to our secretary, Connie Bussman, who typed several drafts of the manuscript, and to Judith Carver for her painstaking editorial work. We have had many helpful discussions with

Preface

our colleagues at Warwick University in the Centre for Industrial Economic and Business Research and in the Industrial Relations Research Unit. Our greatest debt is to William Brown, Rodney Crossley, and Donald MacKay. Our work has benefited enormously from their detailed comments on earlier versions of the manuscript, and we are grateful to them. They do not of course bear any responsibility for the remaining shortcomings.

Barry Thomas
David Deaton

1

Introduction

1. The Study of Labour-Market Adjustments

This study deals with a central aspect of the way labour markets work. It examines employers' responses to shortages and surpluses of labour.

Understanding the adjustment processes at work in the labour market is of interest from many points of view. Individual workers are obviously deeply concerned about such matters as the level and stability of employment and pay, and these will be partly determined by the way employers behave when faced with imbalances of labour supply and demand. More generally, the type of adjustment which is used may affect the way in which labour resources are allocated and how 'efficiently' labour markets operate, and these matters are relevant for the discussion of policy issues. Furthermore this problem is of considerable significance from the point of view of economic theory.

Much of the literature assumes that 'adjustments of demand and supply of manpower will, normally, take place through the price mechanism' (Ahamad and Blaug, 1973:314). However, a good deal of evidence suggests that price adjustments are only part of a large range of possibilities, and that in some markets, or at certain periods, non-price adjustments predominate. In this study we take a general view of managerial policies. Whereas other studies have investigated such variables as pay, the level of recruitment activity, or hiring standards in isolation, our emphasis is on the whole programme of adjustments which managements adopt and on the inter-relationships between different responses. Our aim is to identify and classify the responses to see whether conventional labour-market theory has not merely oversimplified but has got the emphasis wrong as well.

There are many processes relating to the sale, purchase, and pricing of labour services,[1] involving many different agents — individual job seekers and job holders, individual buyers, various institutions and groups with collective interests, and the government. The behaviour of each of these must be considered if we are fully to understand adjustments which take place. This study, however, is concerned primarily with just one set of such agents: the employers. Any analysis of adjustments must start with them for, though their actions may be shaped by union behaviour and by government policy, it is management which must take the initiative in reacting to a shortage of labour and attempt to deal with it. Taking no action is equivalent to the conscious acceptance of certain consequences, such as a reduction in the rate of output. Unions or informal workplace organizations may try to exploit shortage situations and may react defensively to certain types of management response, but unlike management, they are not obliged by the existence of a shortage to change their behaviour or expectations. We shall therefore concentrate on management behaviour and tend to regard unions as acting as a constraint on it, though such a view is certainly not meant to imply any judgment on the legitimacy of union goals which differ from those of management.[2]

In recent years there has been a marked growth of state intervention in the labour market both at the micro-level in the form of the legislation on training, redundancy, taxes and subsidies, programmes of job creation, and the improvement of information and placement services, and at the macro-level in the form of counter-inflation policies. Consideration of the adjustment process is relevant for policy matters in two ways.

In the first place there is the problem of measuring certain crucial variables, such as excess demand for labour, which are used by policy-makers. What is measured or proxied in available statistics may differ from what is theoretically relevant. Unemployment and vacancy statistics, for example, may not be a good guide to the level of shortage or surplus as a source of pressure for wage or other adjust-

1. MacKay *et al.,* for example, argue that 'there is a large number of processes, each of which is important to the efficient operation of the economy and each of which is imperfectly understood. These concern, *inter alia,* wage structure and wage determination; labour turnover; labour mobility within and between plants; personnel and manpower policies relating to manpower forecasting, selection, training, redundancy and labour "hoarding"; and the role played by agencies such as the public employment exchange' (1971:19).
2. On this point we adopt the standpoint of those industrial sociologists who see management *as making its decisions within a complex set of constraints which include employees,* consumers, suppliers, government, the law, the local community, and sources of finance' (Fox, 1973:192; our italics).

ments. Latham and Peel (1974) show that unemployment is only a good proxy for excess demand for labour services if excess demand for hours is zero, and MacKay and Hart (1974) argue that current un-employment levels may not accurately reflect inflationary wage pressure if a substantial part of the initial adjustment to increases in the demand for labour takes place within internal labour markets and only subsequently in the external market.[3] Hence, policy based on external labour-market indicators is likely to misjudge major turning-points, and any corrective action may not be relevant to the current situation. The form of the adjustment is thus important. It was in fact a major part of the counter-inflation strategy of the 1960s and early 1970s to encourage non-wage adjustments. This was certainly the philosophy of the PIB and later the Pay Board, which argued that, where a widespread labour shortage is apparent, wage increases may be ineffective and internal sources of supply should be considered. Improvements in efficiency to secure manpower savings were therefore advocated.[4]

Second, in the field of manpower policy it is essential to analyse the complex labour-market and employment environment if the impact of manpower programmes is to be predicted,[5] and this requires consideration of how employers behave in response to different market conditions. In the case of manpower forecasting and manpower planning, there are many assumptions made concerning labour quality, the level of labour under-utilization, the man–hours mix, and factor substitution, which often underestimate the extent to which these factors may be varied, and so limit the usefulness of the exercise.[6]

In addition to the relevance for policy-makers and for individual workers, the study of the nature of the adjustment process is at the heart of much theoretical discussion. The reappraisal of Keynes has been especially concerned with comparing the allegedly conflicting

3. They therefore used U_{t+1} as the unemployment variable, rather than U_t or U_{t-1} as an explanatory variable in their wage determination equations.
4. See Pay Board (1974a: para. 49), and (1974b: para. 52) for consideration of the problems in measuring shortages and in interpreting such figures as do exist. We might also note at this stage that, where heavy use is being made of temporary adjustments, these may actually be concealing a shortage position in the sense that it does not show up in measured indicators.
5. See Holt *et al.* (1973: 64).
6. Doeringer and Piore (1971:207) argue that 'present techniques of manpower planning . . . inevitably underestimate the capacity of the private sector to effect adjustment.' They see this occurring largely through the internal labour markets where there are continuous changes in job design and required worker charac-teristics.

postulates of Keynes and Marshall on the relative speeds of price and quantity adjustments.[7] Adjustment processes are thus of interest on a broad level, but despite the slowly growing literature it remains true that 'we know very little about how a labour market operates and very little about how individual firms react to particular labour market conditions facing them' (Robinson, 1968:115).

This is an area where *a priori* theorizing is, by itself, rarely sufficient to provide realistic insights into behaviour, and the purpose of this study is therefore to take an initial step towards developing a theory of choice of adjustments by analysing the responses which are made by employers with labour imbalances. This involves analysis of the nature of shortage (or surplus) itself, an extensive catalogue of the possibilities open to firms, and an examination of how the particular characteristics of the plant and the labour-market environment determine the adjustments.

Ultimately our interest is in what happens at the market level, but the correct place to begin a study of adjustments is at the level where the decisions are actually made. We shall argue that organizational and institutional factors are sometimes crucial in determining the particular adjustments chosen, and this necessarily means that a substantial part of the explanation of the choice of instruments depends on employer-specific factors. Particular local and historical circumstances must therefore be combined with other structural and environmental factors, such as the nature of the product market, in developing an understanding of adjustments.

It is only by investigating employers' behaviour in a particular market context that we can discover the policies adopted and the factors which mould those policies.[8] We use case studies of three markets — bus drivers, school teachers, and draughtsmen — as an empirical basis for the analysis. In the following section we give reasons for the choice of these particular markets and describe the methods of study.

2. Methods

The Level of Aggregation

There has been a lot of work at the industrial and aggregate levels, often relying heavily and sometimes exclusively on statistical material, which has contributed to our knowledge of labour

7. See Leijonhufvud (1968) and Davidson (1974).
8. This assumption underlies all empirical studies of labour markets. See, for example, MacKay *et al.* (1971: 35).

markets. An essential complement to such work, however, is an examination of the micro-level, which is the focus of this study.

It is at the micro-level that adjustment decisions are generally made. Decisions on hiring and firing are frequently made at firm or plant level, though the discretion allowed locally on such things as hiring standards or rates of pay may be determined by parent companies or other higher-level decision centres,[9] and in some cases such as the teachers' market almost all the important decisions are taken nationally. In the analysis of the teachers' market it is therefore appropriate to pitch the study at a national level, but this is the exception and it is usually more appropriate to concentrate on a lower level.

Often the relevant evidence can only be gathered at these lower levels. It will for example be argued throughout this study that internal political factors, the structure of the decision-making machinery, and the particular history at plant level often have a bearing on the type of adjustment used. Empirical work at this level also has the advantage of allowing a more satisfactory interpretation of statistics which are occasionally used in a cavalier manner in more highly aggregated studies. It is only at the micro-level, for example, that problems of occupational classification become apparent or that the worth of official vacancy statistics can be appraised.[10] We would certainly not wish to deny the importance of aggregate statistical studies but we feel the need to indicate their limitations.[11]

The Choice of Markets For Study

The choice of draughtsmen, teachers, and bus drivers as markets for study was based on two sets of reasons; first, the reasons for

9. See Rees and Shultz (1970) for some interesting hypotheses on how the degree of discretion at plant level may determine such things as the form of wage payments. It is also worth noting at this stage that the Rees and Shultz study has been supported by MacKay *et al.* (1971) in emphasizing, contrary to expectations from theory, the importance of plant or establishment variables in explaining some labour-market phenomena. Others, notably Doeringer and Piore (1971), have shown the relevance of internal labour markets, all of which suggests the importance of the micro-level in analysing labour-market behaviour.

10. See Chapter 5 on draughtsmen for a discussion of some of the problems which arise in interpreting and compiling statistics of numbers employed in different occupational categories. Changing job titles and plant-level reclassifications present severe difficulties. Chapter 3 on bus drivers shows that the level of vacancies notified to employment exchanges often bears little relation to the number of posts the employer is trying to fill.

11. For an extreme viewpoint see Routh (1973) who argues that statistical series may do more to confuse than illuminate since the statistics themselves are taken as reality.

choosing to define labour markets in occupational terms, and second, the reasons for the choice of these particular occupations.

There are many ways of defining a labour market. A distinction can be drawn between internal and external markets,[12] and the latter have been defined in terms of geographical locations, occupation, and industry. Local labour markets are defined in terms of the generally acceptable commuting distance and the extent of the information network, both of which vary considerably between occupations. The geographical basis forms a necessary but not sufficient condition for delimiting a market, for it would be absurd to suppose that individuals or firms were in the same market solely because of geographical proximity. Though it is often statistically convenient to define labour markets industrially, this dimension provides neither a necessary nor a sufficient condition for a market boundary. In occupational terms many problems arise because there is often, as we shall show in the case of draughtsmen, a continually changing job content but this definition nevertheless forms a suitable basis for the purpose of this study.[13]

None of the three bases mentioned — geographical area, occupation, and industry—forms a sufficient basis by itself for defining a market.[14] This recognition that we have no entirely adequate definition of a labour market must, however, give way to at least a provisional acceptance of some working definition if we are to

12. Doeringer and Piore (1971) define an internal market as an administrative unit such as a plant or firm *within* which the pricing and allocation of labour takes place and is largely governed by administered rules and procedures.

13. In principle it is possible to delimit a market occupationally, in terms of postulated values of elasticities. Bunting (1962) makes use of cross-elasticities. (Where the cross-elasticity of demand is large and positive the two occupations may be regarded as being in the same market. If the cross-elasticities were infinite, then the occupations would be identical.) The problem of defining occupations revolves around the fact that there are two sides to the market. The market process is one of matching *workers* with *jobs*. Demand-side occupational classifications are usually based on the job content of the work which people do, whereas supply-side classifications generally rest on the skill level, education, or even prestige level of the worker. In practice most occupational classifications, such as the Registrar General's, operate with a combination of job classification and the attributes of workers. Cain *et al.* (1967) attempt to develop criteria for classifying occupations which take explicit account of the two sides of the market. More importantly, the occupational structure itself may be as Crossley (1973), following Tinbergen, has pointed out, an artefact of the market.

14. In the last resort, it is in practice usually agreed that the definition is a matter of arbitrary convenience based on such factors as data availability. See, for example, Goodman (1970). In some studies, such as Robinson (1968), the market frontiers are virtually treated as an endogenous variable.

proceed at all. We have adopted an occupational basis of definition, though for empirical purposes some geographical delimitation has been necessary, and it so happens that each of the occupations chosen for study falls into a single industry.[15]

The use of occupationally defined markets is justifiable for several reasons. First, in Routh's words, 'employers do not buy labour as such; they buy the services of fitters, bricklayers, clothing machinists, nurses, teachers, or typists and it is by occupation that rates of pay are fixed.'[16] When a firm is contracting or expanding its labour force, it usually involves changes in specific occupational groups rather than proportionate changes in all occupations. Second, on the supply side, there is evidence that workers tend to think in occupational terms — people tend to present themselves for employment in an array of skill groups. Third, occupationally defined labour markets have received comparatively little attention in this country in the more recent empirical studies, which have focused on local and plant-level labour markets, and to a lesser extent on industrial or regional labour markets.

In a study of this scale the problem has been one of weighing the advantages of in-depth analysis against those of achieving insights through comparison. Since labour markets differ considerably in their characteristics, comparisons are valuable if any general theory is ever to be developed. We are well aware that our decision to examine three markets scarcely provides a sound basis for generalization, but it does permit some interesting comparisons without sacrificing all important detail.

In our choice of the particular occupations it is apparent that the occupational basis of defining a market holds up best for more highly skilled groups, since the greater the investment in training the greater is the occupational attachment; and two of the three occupations chosen belong to the highly qualified white-collar labour force. It is conceptually and empirically convenient to study a well-defined group with a high degree of homogeneity. Bus drivers

15. Teachers are all in education, bus drivers in road passenger transport, and draughtsmen in engineering. Thus draughtsmen, for example, working in architectural and town planning departments of local authorities are excluded.
16. Routh (1965:51). An alternative view has been expressed by Raimon (1953:181): 'The first thing one notes in examining present-day hiring is that much of it is conducted on a non-occupational basis, i.e. specific occupational experience is not essential in the background of applications for many industrial jobs, particularly for the mass of semi-skilled machine operations and assemblers' (quoted in King, 1972:15). The strength of this alternative view depends on the level of skill. It is less applicable for more highly skilled occupations.

fall into this category, and so do teachers.[17] Draughtsmen are less well defined though this permits the study of some interesting forms of adjustment which are not apparent with the other two occupations. One of the ways in which employers have responded to certain labour-market situations is by changes in job content and job titles. These adjustments are relevant in the case of draughtsmen, where there is a proliferation of job titles and a lack of standardization in job content across different industries and plants.[18]

It is desirable to select occupational markets which have exhibited some pronounced imbalance of supply and demand so that responses can more easily be observed. Teachers and busmen are occupations which have for many years been characterized by shortages, and draughtsmen work in a market which is more volatile than these and which has indicated some of the characteristics of surplus in recent years.

No adequate typology of labour markets exists at present which would indicate what are the principal structural and institutional characteristics of different markets and how these affect behaviour,[19] and the selection of characteristically different markets has therefore been somewhat arbitrary. The teachers' market study

17. Teachers are a well-defined occupation though it is shown in Chapter 4 that there is some heterogeneity in the teaching force.
18. The Rees and Shultz (1970) Chicago study originally included draughtsmen in their list of occupations for study but dropped them because of problems in defining the occupation. Loveridge (1972) argues that who is defining the occupation, and for what purpose, may be important; e.g. it was found in the LSE study of technicians that several employers awarded technician and technologist status to those who aspired to it, as a sop to the administrative needs of the EITB.
19. There have been several criteria put forward as bases for distinguishing between different types of labour market. One of the most important is in terms of mobility characteristics. This has sometimes been in general terms such as Cairnes's (1874) non-competing groups, or Doeringer and Piore's (1971) dual labour-market hypothesis, and sometimes in terms of the type of mobility, such as Kerr's (1954) distinction between craft and industrial mobility. It has also been linked with level of training, as in the case of those who distinguish a number of markets ranging from the markets for professional workers to those for casual workers, e.g. Freeman (1972) and Levitan *et al.* (1972), and with the boundaries of the market as set by managerial influence, e.g. Dunlop (1966). Other bases for classifying markets are the supply characteristics in terms of its elasticity, e.g. Ulman (1973), or control over supply as in Phelps's (1961) unionized–non-unionized scheme. The transfer from the product market literature of the monopoly–perfect-competition continuum has often been used, e.g. Lipsey (1966), and also whether economic or institutional forces determine pay, as in Lester's (1952) classification of markets where 'competitive', 'anti-competitive', etc. forces are dominant. Other writers have classified markets on the basis of prevalent ideologies or values, e.g. Caplow (1954), or on the basis of the central processes as in Kerr's (1950) distinction between job and wage markets.

deals with a highly qualified white-collar occupation in a not-for-profit public-sector service industry, and here administered features and the way they affect the adjustments are given special attention. It is a market which has experienced very rapid growth. Draughtsmen are a white-collar group in the private sector where there has been a change in the nature of the job and there is some fluidity in the market boundary itself. The problem of unemployment amongst draughtsmen is also explored. There has been a long-run decline in the demand for draughtsmen and an increase in the demand for closely allied technicians. Bus drivers are, by way of contrast, a semi-skilled blue-collar group which has the unusual feature of being in a declining industry which has experienced labour shortages.

The Method of Study

Much of our evidence is of a descriptive or qualitative kind. This is largely because hard statistics which would permit rigorous testing of hypotheses were rarely available on a comparable basis over a sufficient number of organizations, or over a long enough period of time. For many purposes, however, qualitative evidence is of prime importance in understanding the complex decision processes at work at the micro-level. Wherever possible we have collected statistical data but they are rarely robust enough to support strong conclusions and tend to be used as illustrative material.

In the case of the bus drivers' and draughtsmen's markets, we made considerable use of case studies. Eighteen transport undertakings were visited for the busmen. The studies differed greatly in depth, ranging from single interviews with the general manager or other senior officer to more intensive studies where there was an opportunity to see a large number of people representing management and union interests and to analyse detailed records of the undertaking. In addition, a number of organizations associated with the passenger transport industry were visited. Most of the transport undertakings operated in a limited geographical area, and much of the analysis is therefore at a local labour-market level, where the employer is often a near-monopsonist.

Similar methods were adopted for draughtsmen, and case studies of a number of plants in ten different engineering firms were supplemented by case-study material prepared by other researchers and by contacts, sometimes over a lengthy period, with several organizations having an interest in the employment of draughtsmen. The most important of these was the AUEW (TASS). The market for draughtsmen is less closely tied to local labour markets than that for bus drivers, and the analysis thus ranges more widely and includes consideration of the national position at one extreme and internal labour markets at the other.

In the case of bus drivers, an attempt was made to cover undertakings which differed in size, traffic-operating conditions, local labour-market environment, and ownership, and in the case of draughtsmen we tried to cover employers operating in a variety of product markets. In neither case, however, can we claim to have used a scientific sampling procedure. The scale of the study did not permit any rigorously stratified sample but the range of employers is wide enough to illustrate some of the major differences to be found within these markets.

The limitations of relying on interviews as a major means of acquiring information about decisions which have been made, and the circumstances giving rise to such decisions, are well known and need not be recalled here.[20] We have therefore been cautious in using the interview material especially where corroborative evidence is lacking, but we doubt whether feasible alternative techniques would yield greater insight.

In the case of school teachers, the analysis is almost exclusively in national terms. This is because the structure of the education industry is such that many of the major decisions which affect the demand for and supply of teachers are taken at national level, despite the fact that the responsibility for the provision of education rests at local level.[21] For this reason, more reliance has been placed on the use of officially published statistics of the national position than in the case of bus drivers and draughtsmen. The use of these statistics has been supplemented by interviews with LEAs, unions, and other organizations.

The teachers' study also differs from the other two in that it is more concerned with a particular period of history — the two

20. Swann *et al.* summarized the problems of all researchers using such techniques. 'Interviewing is essentially a detective game. A wide variety of facts and impressions are collected (sometimes these conflict) and the ultimate aim is to piece them together to produce a coherent picture of what happened' (1974: 16–17). This can be difficult since the willingness and ability of those interviewed to analyse their own actions and the structure and workings of the labour markets in which they operate vary greatly. There are also the problems that memory involves reconstruction as well as recollection and that some information gained in interviews may be unintentionally misleading through differences in the meanings assigned to particular events.

21. See Chapter 4 for a discussion of this split and the reasons for concentrating on the national level.

decades up to 1970. There is by no means exclusive attention given to this period, and some of the recent interesting developments in this market are examined, but the main analysis is of responses to shortages which were most severe in the 1950s and 1960s. There are now signs that the overall shortage has been eliminated.

2

A Theoretical Framework

1. Introduction

In this study we are concerned with explaining the adjustments made by employers to their internal labour imbalances, and to the state of the external labour market. It is a major shortcoming of economic theory that there is no theory of adjustments to disequilibrium, and we do not therefore have a ready framework for analysing the type of behaviour in which we are interested. Fisher has noted that

economic analysis, *per se*, does not prescribe through which avenues adjustments are to be secured and one cannot maintain *ab initio* that it should not proceed to some degree through interdependence with other labour, factor or commodity markets. (1971: 99)

If, for example, responses to imbalances in the labour market take place through product markets via output or inventory changes, then a general equilibrium approach may be appropriate. This, however, by-passes many of the detailed considerations which may be relevant for the understanding of particular markets. Kaldor has condemned general equilibrium theory on the grounds that

in the rarefied world of Walrasian perfection where markets are continuously in equilibrium, the question of how the market responds to 'disequilibrium' does not arise because all such 'disequilibria' are ruled out — all equilibrating adjustments are assumed to be instantaneous, either because changes are timeless or because all changes have been perfectly foreseen. (1972:1247)

Since we live in a world of change and uncertainty, where time brings new knowledge, the importance of the lack of a generally accepted body of theory on disequilibrium behaviour is difficult to exaggerate.

Much of the purely theoretical work which does exist seems to abstract from virtually all the essential characteristics of any real-world labour markets. On the other hand the existing empirical work scarcely adds up to a coherent body of knowledge of adjustment processes at work.

A satisfactory model of adjustment should have a discussion of the rules which market participants follow when out of equilibrium, a description of how a market system in which individuals follow these rules works, and a convergence theorem.[1] This study deals with the behaviour of employers in disequilibrium with respect to their employment and thus focuses primarily on the first of these three components. The following chapters discuss how employers behave when faced with labour shortages, and the present chapter sets out a framework of analysis. The second part of the ideal adjustment model — consideration of how *markets* operate — is approached via a study of individual firms. Some comments on the market-level implications of our findings are given in the concluding chapter. There is also, in the final chapter, a brief discussion of the stability implications of the adjustment processes which we identify, which relates to the third part of the ideal model referred to above.

The plan of this chapter is as follows. In the rest of this section a number of basic distinctions and concepts are reviewed. Section 2 indicates the wide range of possible options open to employers when deciding on the type of adjustment, and this is followed in Section 3 by a detailed examination of the inter-relationships between shortages and adjustments with a number of hypothetical examples presented. Section 4 states the cost-minimizing hypothesis which provides a foundation for the discussion in the empirical chapters.

It is useful at the outset to make a number of basic distinctions: the most important is that between stocks and flows.[2] For expositional convenience at this stage we shall assume that there is no variation in the average number of hours worked per employee so that the number of employees is the only variable affecting the flow of labour services. This assumption is relaxed later. A firm experiences a *stock balance* when the desired and actual stocks of labour (E_i^* and E_i) are equal. *Flow balance* for the firm is achieved when there is no change

---

1. See Rothschild (1973).
2. This follows the helpful framework put forward by Holt (1970), Holt and David (1966), Mortensen (1970), and others in which the labour market is viewed in terms of the interaction of various stocks and flows.

in the stock position over time (i.e. $\Delta E_i^* = \Delta E_i$). This occurs when the change in the actual stock of employees, which is the inflows of labour less the outflows over the relevant period, is equal to the change in the desired stock of employees. In the simple case where there is no change in the desired stock over time, the flow balance is merely the equality of inflows and outflows.[3] It is evident that stock and flow balances need not coexist. A flow balance may accompany a stock shortage, stock surplus, or stock balance. If there is a stock shortage and a flow balance then the same absolute level of stock shortage persists.[4] The relationship between stocks and flows is shown in Figure 2.1.

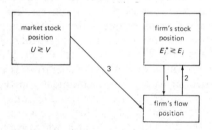

FIGURE 2.1. THE RELATIONSHIP
BETWEEN STOCKS AND FLOWS

If a firm experiencing a stock shortage tries to correct it by attempts to increase hires or reduce quits, the flow position is altered. This is shown by arrow 1. Changes in the firm's flow position have a direct impact on the firm's stock balance as indicated by arrow 2. Apart from this two-way relationship, the firm's position is also affected by a number of other factors, the most important of which is the external market position,[5] shown by arrow 3. Any stock imbalance in the market as a whole will transmit itself to the firm via

3. The inflows can be thought of as hirings, including transfers into the occupation from other parts of the organization. The outflows comprise dismissals, retirements, quits, deaths, layoffs, and transfers out of the occupation to other jobs in the firm.

4. Flows will never in fact be zero for all firms even if each firm has stock balance, since the *market* flow position (not shown in Figure 2.1) includes those entering and leaving the market and the labour force.

5. Internal factors, apart from those corrective actions shown by arrow 1 in Figure 2.1, may also affect some of the flows. Sociological studies of labour turnover, for example Gowler and Legge (1973), have shown that quits from any firm may vary quite independently of external market conditions, so that a firm may be experiencing a wastage problem even if there is excess supply in the external market.

the flows which the firm experiences. For example, even if an individual firm starts off in a position of stock and flow balance, it may find that excess demand in the market as a whole (the stock of job vacancies, V, exceeding the stock of unemployed workers, U) causes higher quits from the firm and greater difficulty in hiring. This may eventually produce stock imbalance in the firm. The more sensitive the firm's flow position to the external situation, the more the firm is likely to respond to the market situation.

There is no reason why each firm should experience the same extent of shortage and some may even have a stock surplus when there is a shortage in the market as a whole, but in such circumstances the typical firm will be experiencing a shortage.[6]

The firm is interested ultimately in its stock position, that is, whether it has the desired quantity of labour. This study concentrates on the behaviour of the enterprise in response to stock shortage,[7] but the flow position can be important. Those members of the enterprise with responsibility for production may be primarily interested in the stock balance and only concerned with the flow position in so far as it affects the stock balance. But the flow position may be of more direct concern to those responsible for recruitment. For example, even if the firm enjoys stock balance, the recruitment officers may have to make adjustments to external market conditions as they are felt through the firm's flow position. Such responses may be more or less instantaneous, such as the placement of additional advertisements, and these may go virtually unnoticed by production managers. Indeed, in large organizations, where there is a split between production and personnel departments, one department may claim that there is no shortage while another claims to be responding to a shortage by, say, increasing recruitment costs.[8]

The importance of the decision-making process has been stressed by Vincens and Robinson (1974), who argue that firms are

6. Where there is a market surplus (unemployed exceeding vacancies), it is perhaps more likely that the typical firm will experience balance, rather than surplus, but this depends on the empirical relationship between unemployment and labour hoarding.
7. In Chapter 5 there is some discussion of employer responses to surpluses in the case of the market for draughtsmen, and see also pp. 27–9.
8. The extent to which responsibility for recruitment and selection is divided between personnel and production departments will depend on factors such as the organizational principles adopted, the size of the flows, and the skill level. Where there are large numbers and less skilled groups involved, personnel departments will usually have major responsibility. For senior specialist posts within the organization, the personnel department will have little influence in recruitment decisions.

organizations composed of different interests which are not always mutually consistent. Different parts of the organization may press their own sectional interests with the result that the overall objectives of the enterprise become distorted or contradictory. Shultz, in one of the more perceptive empirical studies, found that the role and activities of the personnel department varied with the degree of tightness of the labour market and that the personnel department was not only the prime originator and administrator of non-wage responses, but also took the initiative in pay changes (1962:121).

Our focus on the behaviour of firms is not meant to imply that sellers of labour are unimportant. Responses to particular market states will be made by sellers as well as buyers. Variations in the stock imbalance in any labour market are likely to cause individual sellers of labour services to vary their labour-force participation and mobility patterns.

The relationship between stock and flow balances and how adjustments alter these is shown in Figure 2.2. This is a highly simplified illustration. A much more detailed discussion of these relationships appears in Section 3 of this chapter.[9] Figure 2.2 shows that in the period $t_0 t_1$ there is both stock and flow balance. The actual level of employment (E_i) is the same as the desired stock (E_i^*), and this stock balance is preserved because the inflows and outflows of labour also balance. Thus the level of E_i neither rises nor falls. At time t_1 let us suppose there is a sudden increase in the desired stock of employees. This causes a stock shortage, shown by the gap between E_i^* and E_i. In the absence of corrective action or any exogenous changes, the flow position continues as before, and during the period $t_1 t_2$ there is stock shortage and flow balance. At time t_2 let us imagine that the firm takes positive action to reduce the stock shortage, say by raising pay. This will reduce subsequent outflows and increase inflows; the rising E_i line during the period $t_2 t_3$ shows a net inflow. Over this period there is therefore neither stock nor flow balance.

Suppose the pay increase were just sufficient to eliminate the stock shortage and this was achieved by time t_3. There would be no need for further adjustments, and after t_3 there is once again both stock and flow balance.

In this example we have implicitly assumed that there were no exogenous changes, so that the flows into and out of the firm changed only when the firm took positive action in response to shortage. Any change in the market levels of unemployment and

9. In this example we assume that demand (E_i^*) exceeds supply and that actual employment (E_i) is governed by the supply of labour.

16

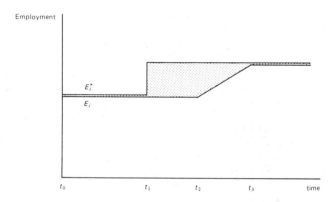

FIGURE 2.2. AN EXAMPLE OF ADJUSTMENT TO
SHORTAGE

vacancies would be likely to affect the firm's flows. The only positive
response to shortage, in this example, was on the supply side. Had it
been on the demand side, say by capital substitution, then E_i^* would
have fallen.

During the whole of the time $t_1 t_3$ there was stock shortage, either
because no positive adjustment was made or because the adjustments had not had time to produce the required effect.[10] This means
that various residual adjustments, such as the unintended failure to
meet production targets, must have taken place to bridge the gap
between E_i^* and E_i. These are represented by the shading in Figure
2.2.

2. The Range of Adjustment Instruments

Empirical work on local labour markets and on the markets for
particular occupations has revealed an extremely wide range of
measures open to management for dealing with shortages, and it has
been shown that a variety of responses are adopted. Several studies
have revealed that overt wage changes may play only a minor role in

10. The period of inaction, $t_1 t_2$, may be due to various information and decision lags.
Firms may want confirmation that the sudden rise in E_i^* is not just a transient
phenomenon before deciding on a course of action. The adjustments they adopt
may be temporary or permanent in character. See Section 3 below.

responding to shortage,[11] and that of the other possibilities the most commonly observed have been attempts to expand the sources of labour supply and to vary the quality of labour hired.

Efforts to increase the inflows of labour appear to be common. These may take the form of more vigorous recruitment in the external labour market, more extensive search, and employing people previously considered unsuitable. Hiring standards are thus important, and most studies have shown them to be a prominent variable. Sometimes changes are easy to observe, as when there are falls in explicit measurable hiring standards, but in other cases it may be more difficult to judge, as when standards of discipline or expectations of individual performance are gradually reduced. It may even be that recruitment officers deliberately inflate their quality evaluation of new employees in order to preserve wage structures where specific qualifications are required to achieve certain wage levels.[12]

In order to understand the choice of instruments it is necessary to know what instruments are rejected as well as those which are chosen, and in this section, therefore, we describe the range of possible adjustments and the way in which they are constrained. Throughout this discussion we shall consider adjustments to shortage. Some consideration of adjustment to surplus is given in Section 3 of this chapter.

Instruments and Operands

The various instruments can be grouped according to their mode of impact or operand. For example, some instruments such as cutting output will have an impact mainly on the demand for labour services whereas others, such as a policy of later retirements, will reduce the outflows of labour. The various operands can be conveniently grouped into four types, namely:

(1) the reduction of desired total man-hours;
(2) increasing the average hours worked per employee;
(3) reducing outflows of labour; and
(4) increasing inflows of labour.

Type 1 is the only one which relates to the demand side and covers those responses to shortage which reduce the desired labour input,

---

11. Some of the earliest empirical studies which stressed non-wage adjustments were those by Lester (1954a) and (1954b). Since then there have been many others, varying greatly in their style. On the one hand are those which have painstakingly collected detailed data and attempted statistical analysis, e.g. Rees and Shultz (1970), and on the other are those which rely on impressions from a more casual sort of empiricism, e.g. Robinson (1968).
12. See, for example, Franke and Sobel (1970).

measured in total man-hours. The other types of operand concern the supply side and cover those responses which increase the input of man-hours. They comprise increases in average hours worked per employee (type 2) and increases in the number of employees. The latter may be accomplished by reducing the outflows of labour (type 3) or by increasing the inflows of labour (type 4).

An extensive list of instruments grouped according to their operand is given in Appendix A. Instruments which affect the desired total man-hours are comparatively straightforward and do not require comment. In the case of the type 2 operand, increasing hours worked, it may be possible simply to authorize more overtime if employees are willing to work longer. There may, however, be a supply constraint in which case instruments such as increasing overtime payments may be necessary to induce workers to supply more hours.[13]

There are many different flows into and out of an occupation in any plant, and many of the instruments which are relevant for the type 3 operands (reducing outflows) are also relevant for type 4 operands (increasing inflows). Pay increases, for example, are likely to affect both. Outflows comprise deaths, dismissals, retirements, voluntary quits, and transfers out of the group to other parts of the organization. In the case of inflows, we can distinguish four different employment states from which labour can be drawn: those employed by the organization, those employed elsewhere, those unemployed, and those outside the labour force. In each case, available labour may or may not meet the current hiring standards, so there are eight pools of labour. It is likely that an employer will use different strategies to attract labour from these different sources.

Many of the instruments designed to affect the type 4 operand are devices to increase inflows by tapping existing pools of workers who are prepared to accept employment if offered. This may mean providing extra training or perhaps altering entry requirements. An example of the latter adjustment was those bus undertakings which relaxed a policy of having only male drivers.[14] Alternatively, an instrument may be designed to increase the actual *size* of the potential inflows, rather than merely realizing more of the potential

13. Increased overtime payments will only increase the number of hours supplied by any individual if the substitution effect outweighs the income effect.
14. If an organization decides to take on women for a job from which they were previously excluded, one would expect the number of female applicants to rise, but this does not mean that the size of the potential inflow has increased, merely that the size has become apparent to the firm. The number of applicants is not necessarily a good guide to the size of the potential inflow.

inflows which already exist. Increases in pay or improvements in working conditions are the prime examples of this type of instrument.

The wide range of instruments available is apparent from the table in Appendix A — some are specific to one operand and some affect a number of different operands. Appendix A lists the instruments as pure types but in practice there may be a high degree of interdependence. Some instruments are substitutes for one another and others are best viewed as complements or as mixtures of theoretical possibilities. One rarely sees, for example, an instrument that can be termed pure capital substitution. When capital replaces labour this tends to involve job redesign which allows the use of less skilled labour, or the speeding up of routine work so that an employee spends more time on the skilled part of his work.

Constraints

Most instruments are subject to a variety of constraints. Constraints vary in their degree of rigidity; some are immovable, others can be overcome, usually at some cost. We have not mentioned a budgetary constraint because we see cost as playing an important role in the choice of instrument, and with few exceptions all instruments involve a cost. Many of the constraints mentioned are self-explanatory such as legal or contractual obligations or those imposed by government policy. Those which we have called 'organizational' are constraints imposed on one section of management by other parts of the organization,[15] and those referred to as 'fairness' constraints indicate that the use of an instrument, such as pay, is governed by considerations of what is fair.[16] Technical constraints may mean that the production function limits the use of capital substitution, or that indivisibilities limit output curtailment.

Unions, by which we mean any collectivity of the organization's employees inside or outside the group in question, or their representatives, impose important constraints on management's choice of

15. See Schultze: 'There are political opportunity costs to any decision, just as real as the economic opportunity costs. Because values conflict among different groups and among themselves, securing the agreement to pursue one line of action most often reduces the opportunity to pursue other lines of action' (1968: 45). He was writing of central government decision-making but this analysis is applicable to large organizations generally.
16. See Vincens and Robinson (1974:108) and the comments of MacKay *et al.* (1971: 400), on the complexity of plant wage structures. Folk (1970) observed that the combination of custom and fairness and problems with internal differentials tended to make salary increases bottom of the list chronologically.

instruments. Union interests often differ from those of management, and unions will rightly seek to protect these interests by preventing management from exercising unilateral control over all aspects of the employment relationship. Thus a concern with employment stability and security may appear as opposition to uncontrolled subcontracting, resistance to redundancy, restrictions on part-time workers or dilutees or women, or opposition to capital substitution. The concern with conditions of work and levels of pay may lead to union attempts to control working arrangements, such as restricting the flexibility of schedules in the case of bus drivers, or implementing minimum levels of overtime work. Our empirical work suggests that the instruments on which unions impose tightest controls will vary between occupations and organizations, but the reasons why unions choose to constrain the use of some instruments rather than others is an interesting question in its own right and lies outside the scope of this study.[17]

Some of the union constraints, like most of the technical ones, limit the range of possible instruments open to the organization. In other instances they may make an adjustment more costly or more inconvenient to apply. In the case of pay, for example, the union may press for the use of this instrument rather than any other, but it may also oppose any sectional pay adjustment and so make this instrument a more expensive one to use. Sometimes union behaviour will ensure that one instrument can be used only as a complement to another. Included under this would be the union succeeding in re-ordering the priority with which instruments are used, as in the case of the draughtsmen's market, for example, when drawing office subcontracting may only be acceptable to the union where the firm is engaged in a good deal of search activity.

Thus the effect of constraints is not simply one of limiting the range of possibilities from which adjustment instruments are chosen. In some cases the constraints change the extent to which an instrument achieves the desired goals.

3. Inter-Relationships Between Shortages and Adjustments

In this section we develop a framework for analysing the interrelationships between shortages and different adjustments. Such a

17. Even the industrial relations literature does not tackle this question, though Flanders (1967) does discuss changes in the range of subjects covered by collective bargaining.

framework is helpful for disentangling some of the problems of definition and measurement which confront those undertaking empirical research, and there are two problems in particular on which it throws some light.

The first is the use by public-sector industries of a formal establishment figure. Since these establishment figures usually differ from the level of demand for labour, measures of shortage which relate to establishments have been criticized as being unrealistic.[18] A second problem is that it may not be possible to observe directly an *ex ante* shortage. One can see only the outcomes of situations and it may be that the use of certain types of adjustment instrument conceals a serious shortage situation. This 'suppressed disequilibrium' is analogous to the inability to recognize a critical balance-of-payments situation from *ex post* figures where certain types of 'unsatisfactory' adjustment, such as import restrictions, have been used.[19]

Norms and Shortages

When we refer to a shortage of a certain type of labour, this statement is not made in the abstract. We mean that the demand for labour of a specified minimum quality at some specified wage exceeds the supply of that labour at that wage. If the minimum acceptable quality of labour is lowered or the wage increased, then demand and supply could balance. Hence, before measuring the extent of a shortage one has to specify the ruling wage rate and the required quality of labour. When employers talk of a shortage of a particular kind of labour, they have some idea of the normal wage which is paid for that type of labour and the normally acceptable quality of labour. We shall term these values, on which the measurement of supply and demand depends, norms.[20]

There is, in reality, a large number of norms assumed when the

---

18. For example, the NBPI Report No.16 argued, in the case of busmen, that 'Establishment figures necessarily reflect a historical pattern of services and are therefore a very uncertain measure of staff shortage' (para. 61).
19. See Tew (1965: 59–61) for a discussion of suppressed disequilibrium.
20. The notion of norms which we shall use extensively is implicit in much of the empirical work. Metcalf (1973) for example suggested that in the market for university teachers hiring standards were inversely related to excess demand, and Corry (1973) has expressed this particular hypothesis in terms of norms in the form

$$M^k_{Norm} = F(D^k - S^k) \qquad F' < 0$$

where M^k_{Norm} is the normal skill requirement for the kth type of labour and D and S are demand and supply.

concept of a shortage is considered, in addition to wages and labour quality. The extent of staff advertising, the length of the working week, working conditions, the severity of the dismissals policy, the level of productivity, and the production technique will all affect the supply of labour and the demand for it. Thus the *ex ante* demand and *ex ante* supply can only be determined with respect to a given set of norms, which may be specified explicitly or implicitly. This means that it is realistic to talk of a shortage, in the sense of *ex ante* demand exceeding *ex ante* supply, only if all the norms are stated. Simple definitions of shortage in terms of the excess of demand over supply at the prevailing wage level fail to recognize this.

It is useful to distinguish between formal norms and working norms. The formal norms are those which the organization formally recognizes. These may represent 'ideal' standards or targets as in the case of the use of a desired pupil–teacher ratio in education, or the length of the scheduled working week in bus operation, or the ideal nursing standards in the health service. These formal norms, which relate almost exclusively to the demand side of the market, are the values from which establishment figures are calculated. The working norms represent those values which are in fact adopted by the organization and which, together with certain exogenous factors, such as the state of the external labour market, determine *ex ante* demand and supply. The working norms take account of such things as financial constraints and union agreements, whereas the formal norms may not, and this may give rise to differences between the establishment figure and the demand. This is typically the case in the public sector.[21]

It is clear that *ex post* demand must equal supply in the sense that the quantity of labour bought must equal the quantity sold. When there is an *ex ante* shortage a number of outcomes are possible. There may be a conscious decision to alter a working norm such that the *ex ante* shortage is eliminated. However, where working norms are not so revised, the necessary *ex post* equality means that the actual value of some adjustment instrument diverges from the working norm. Such a divergence may take the form of a positive

---

21. See, for example, the discussion in Chapters 3 and 4 on bus drivers and school teachers. A similar distinction can be seen with the demand for draughtsmen, though here this is rarely formalized. There is an economic level of labour requirements for the optimal rate of development of a firm's products or for the technical level to be met on a specific project. Sometimes labour demand is less than this for financial reasons, where the firm is required to make an annual profit. This divergence tends to create surpluses rather than make the shortage less than the shortfall from establishments.

response or simply an unintended adjustment such as the failure to produce the desired output. This latter form of adjustment arises when deliberate attempts to adjust to the shortage fail, and these are referred to as residual adjustments. When we talk of positive adjustments we must be careful to distinguish between those which eliminate the shortage and those which merely suppress it. To do this we make an explicit distinction between permanent and temporary adjustments.

Permanent and Temporary Adjustments

Adjustments which are introduced on a permanent basis are implemented with the intention that they should not be removed. Sometimes permanency is a feature of the instrument itself in that it may be impossible, costly, or very difficult to reverse. This is seen in the case of pay increases where institutional constraints prevent reductions in pay. Although it may be possible in some cases to deduce permanency from the constraints which are operating, frequently the permanence of an adjustment can only be identified by studying the intentions of management. One has to assess whether a working norm has in fact changed. Thus any impact which a permanent adjustment has on the shortage will continue to be felt in subsequent periods. A successful permanent adjustment will eliminate or reduce the *ex ante* shortage. Other adjustments are used on a temporary basis only — at the time of their introduction the intention is to remove them at some future time. For example, a raising of the retirement age or the acceptance of dilutees may be regarded as emergency measures which the organization does not want to accept permanently.

Unlike a permanent adjustment, a temporary adjustment does not alter any working norm. Adherence to the same working norm means that a state of disequilibrium is created in the divergence between the actual value of the adjustment instrument and the working norm. This acts as a stimulus, albeit a muted one, for a further adjustment. The *ex ante* shortage remains. A temporary adjustment will thus only suppress an *ex ante* shortage and reduce the reliance on residual adjustments. Such temporary adjustments are likely where permanent measures take time to implement and where the organization is very uncertain about the outcome and merely wishes to try out an unknown instrument without committing itself to its permanent use.

In fact, some of the instruments which are introduced on a temporary basis may become permanent. This may happen where employers are experimenting with an untried instrument which proves to be extremely beneficial and is thus adopted permanently, and more interestingly, where there is some unforeseen ratchet present. Such unexpected non-reversibility may explain why some apparently erroneous adjustments take place — an instrument which is intended as temporary may become custom and practice and hence difficult or costly to reverse. The widespread use of overtime working may partly be explained in these terms.[22] It is worth noting at this stage that, where the use of the same *residual* adjustment is prolonged, this may become an accepted form of adjustment. For example, in the passenger transport industry, one residual adjustment is that some services are not run. If a shortage continues and the non-running of services becomes a regular feature, then the employer may decide to make a cut in scheduled services 'in order to use existing resources rationally'. In such cases the actual value of the output becomes a working norm. (And, if the establishment figure is cut to correspond to the new schedules, then we can say that the formal norm for output has changed.)

The timing of the effect of any instrument may not coincide with the timing of its use. Instruments may have an effect outside the periods in which they are used.[23] For instance, a reduction in hiring standards or an increase in recruitment effort may be used for a single period, but by affecting the flows in that period it will affect the stock position in subsequent periods.[24] The effect in the later periods is likely to be one which decays. Even permanent adjustments may have an effect which decays, though this will normally be because it is overtaken by changes in exogenous factors. The effect of a given permanent increase in pay, for example, may diminish over time. Finally, we may note that some adjustments may only become effective after a time-lag. However, the fact remains that the *ex ante* shortage can be measured by the size of the residual adjustment necessary if all temporary adjustments currently in use were removed.

An Illustration of Adjustment to Shortage

The process of adjustment just outlined can be illustrated by the following example. We shall assume that there is no change in any of

22. See W. Brown (1972).
23. An investment model would take into account differences in the timing of costs and benefits of any instrument. The normal discounting process gives different weight to different periods. See Section 4.
24. It is possible, however, that changes in the composition of the stock may have a feedback to the flows. For example, current alterations in hiring standards may change the characteristics of the stock and may affect wastage in subsequent periods.

the exogenous variables, and that the initial position is one where the firm is experiencing a stock shortage and a net outflow of labour. This situation is characteristic of a firm which has a very high wastage rate and finds difficulty in recruiting, both of which are likely if there is a shortage in the external market. If there is no permanent adjustment (i.e. there is no change in any of the working norms) then the gap between *ex ante* demand and supply must be covered by temporary and residual adjustments. The net outflow of labour means that the stock shortage is growing over time, as shown in Figure 2.3,[25] in period $t_0 t_1$. The extent of the residual adjustments, say lost output, is shown by the diagonally shaded area. Up to time t_1 this is the same as the *ex ante* shortage because no temporary adjustments are in use.

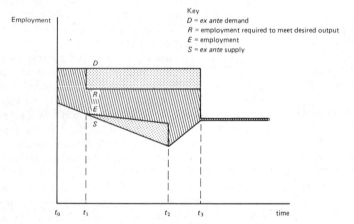

FIGURE 2.3. THE ELIMINATION OF SHORTAGE

At t_1 suppose there is a temporary adjustment on the demand side, say the use of sub-contracting, which reduces the level of employment required to meet desired output below *ex ante* demand. There is also a supply-side temporary adjustment, say an increase in the retirement age, which raises actual employment above the *ex ante* supply.[26] This position continues until t_2 at which time we suppose

25. The use of straight lines in this diagram is merely for simplicity of exposition. Clearly the impact of an adjustment may depend not only on the size of the adjustment but also on the number of employees. Thus, if the percentage quit rate is constant, the number of quits declines as employment falls.
26. Whether employment will continue to fall, or remain constant, or rise depends on the size of the quit rate and the numbers affected by the changed retirement age.

that the firm reverts to its former retirement age, and two further adjustments are made, an increase in pay and an increase in the recruitment activity. The pay increase is seen as a permanent adjustment and the recruitment campaign as a temporary one. The combined result of these changes is to cause a net inflow, and employment thus increases. Indeed the *ex ante* supply also increases.[27] The reversion to the previous lower retirement age causes a sudden drop in employment at time t_2, since there will be an accumulated stock of workers over the new retirement age who now all retire at once. Let us suppose that the pay increase was sufficient to produce flow balance, and that the additional recruitment improves the position further to produce a net inflow shown by the rise in employment and *ex ante* supply. By time t_3, the stock shortage has been reduced considerably and we assume that the recruitment campaign is ended, leaving a flow balance, and that in response to the persistent residual adjustment there is permanent demand-side adjustment in the form of capital substitution which lowers the *ex ante* demand and produces both stock and flow balance and no further residual adjustment.

Adjustments to Labour Surplus

Adjustment to shortages and surpluses are not entirely symmetrical. The asymmetry arises from the fact that, in some surplus situations, instruments may be used as ends in themselves rather than simply as means of achieving or maintaining a stock balance, and also from the asymmetry of the constraints. For example, attempts to respond to a stock surplus by cutting overtime or by short-time working would probably be resisted by unions, whereas increases in hours as a response to shortage may actually be encouraged by them.

Apart from reducing hours, adjustments to stock surpluses may involve changes in the demand for labour through the acceptance of a lower working norm for productivity in the form of planned labour hoarding, through work-creation policies, or increases in stocks of finished goods. Alternatively, adjustments may be designed to

---

27. That the *ex ante* supply increases through a temporary adjustment appears to contradict what has been said previously about temporary adjustments merely disguising an *ex ante* shortage. However, the removal of this temporary adjustment would have no effect on the current *stock* shortage. What the temporary adjustment disguises is the underlying flow balance.

increase the outflow of labour through redundancy, early retirement, the firmer application of dismissals policy, the inducement of
higher quits, or the transfer of staff elsewhere.

Figure 2.4 illustrates some possible responses to labour surplus.
The starting-point is assumed to be a stock surplus shown by the fact
that employment is greater than the demand. In this case there will
be a residual adjustment in the form of unintended labour hoarding.
We shall also assume that there is initially some 'make-work' policy
in operation. In the period $t_0 t_1$, the level of employment falls through
natural wastage, and demand is also shown as falling since we
suppose that the ability and willingness to create work decreases. At
t_1 the firm has exhausted its work-creation policy and it introduces
short-time working. This has the effect of both increasing wastage
(hence a more rapid fall in the employment level) and reducing the
supply. The stock surplus continues, though declining, and at t_2 a
redundancy takes place which greatly increases the rate at which the
employment level falls.[28] This action by the firm further reduces the
supply. By t_3 the redundancy is completed and net wastage continues
as before, at which time it is also assumed that product market
changes result in a further fall in the demand for labour. After t_3 net
wastage continues as before, until t_4 when stock balance is achieved
as shown by the equality of the numbers employed and the demand.
The unintended labour hoarding is eliminated. After t_4 the stock
balance continues, implying that any wastage is offset by recruitment.

Throughout the period of time shown in Figure 2.4, it can be seen
that there is an excess supply of labour to the firm over the employment level. In this situation there is a queue of applicants — it arises
when there is an excess of unemployment over vacancies in the
market as a whole. It is a situation to which the firm might react independently of its internal stock position.

Suppose we start with an internal stock balance and a queue of
applicants, as shown after time t_4 in Figure 2.4. In this situation,
where the flow of suitable applicants for jobs exceeds wastage, the
firm may remain passive and simply recruit sufficient labour to
replace outflows, or it may try to take advantage of the situation by
selecting only the highest-quality applicants and it may even raise
formal hiring standards. There may even be a possibility of reducing
wages as long as any consequent increase in wastage and reduction in

28. If the entire redundancy took place at one instant, employment would show a
    sharp step down. Here it is assumed that the redundancy is phased continuously
    until its completion.

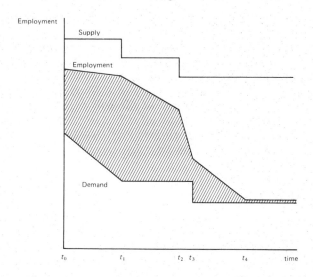

FIGURE 2.4. THE ELIMINATION OF SURPLUS

applicants were small enough still to leave the firm with a flow balance. However, because of the fixed employment costs incurred in training, recruitment, and selection of staff, a firm may try to reduce its wastage even when leavers can be easily replaced.

It is apparent from this analysis that responses to shortage and surplus may not be symmetrical. A stock shortage and a net outflow of labour pose similar problems for the firm, and both give rise to similar responses. However, a firm which has an internal stock surplus and a queue of applicants (reflecting a market surplus) may react in different ways to these two phenomena. In order to preserve internal stock balance, a firm does not have to eliminate a queue of applicants but it does have to eliminate any net outflow of labour.

4. Cost-Minimizing Behaviour

The diversity of responses to shortages which have been observed in practice and the variation between occupations and between different localities for the same occupation have made explanation in terms of some generally applicable theory difficult. Indeed some studies have been content to describe the various instruments and have made virtually no attempt to account for the particular type of adjustment used.[29]

A plausible *a priori* hypothesis is that enterprises are cost minimizers in their adjustment behaviour. The idea of some form of cost minimizing runs through much empirical work,[30] notably that by Doeringer and Piore (1971) who argue that, where different instruments will achieve the same result, the alternatives can be ranked in a cost hierarchy and the enterprise will, subject to various constraints, adopt progressively more expensive adjustments within this hierarchy as the size of the adjustment required increases.

The Relevant Costs

The cost-minimizing idea can be expressed in static terms by supposing that a given quantity of labour services can be achieved by various combinations of different types of labour outlay. Wages and search costs, for example, can be substituted for each other to some extent to provide a given quantity of labour services and, assuming a continuous trade-off between them, the cost-minimizing combination can in principle be determined.[31]

Presenting the cost-minimizing hypothesis in these static terms, however, ignores the time element which, as the examples of adjustment in the previous section show, is an essential feature of the choice of adjustments.

The deficiency can be partly overcome by adopting an investment-type approach where the costs of the various possible sets of adjustment are discounted over time. Besides emphasizing the time dimension and hence allowing for the fact that instruments vary in

29. See, for example, Martin and Wilson (1969) who discuss many changes in response to shortages of policemen — advertising, salary changes, capital substitution, reduced physical standards (in terms of minimum acceptable height and eyesight), etc. — but offer no clue as to why the particular mix and sequence of instruments were chosen.

30. MacKay *et al.*, for example, concluded after a thorough examination of behaviour in local labour markets that although decisions concerning wages and employment are 'never solely determined by a strict evaluation of costs and benefits . . . when one advances beyond the description of a particular set of events . . . these assumptions . . . help to explain and predict some aspects of such behaviour' (1971:387). A different example is Metcalf's (1973) study of university teachers which showed that the usual responses to excess demand in particular faculties were varying the normal skill/age requirements and adopting a permissive attitude towards moonlighting rather than raising pay, which Corry (1973) has interpreted as universities selecting the *apparently* cheapest strategies.

31. For such a model, where the usual tangency solution applies, see Devine (1971). The optimum combinations of men and hours per man have often been presented in a similar manner.

the number of periods in which costs are incurred and effects felt, we can within this framework handle interdependence between instruments[32] and the constraints which were listed in Section 2 above.

By postulating that the firm tries to minimize the discounted value of its total cost stream, we can see the process of adjusting to labour shortage as part of the overall problem of achieving optimal production.[33] However, we shall only be directly concerned with these broader questions when they have an impact on labour costs.

In order to make the problem tractable and to concentrate on the labour-adjustment decision, we shall adopt two sets of simplifying assumptions. Firstly, we take the desired quantity[34] and quality of output and the tastes of producers with respect to the method of production as given. Secondly, non-labour costs are ignored or assumed to be constant, unless they are incurred in process of adjusting to imbalances of labour or reducing labour costs.

The cost plan of the firm comprises two broad types of cost. The first of these is the cost of using various positive supply-side and demand-side instruments. The cost of an instrument is normally the stream of financial outlays resulting from its use at a particular level. This is easy to envisage in the case of a stream of wage costs or of a recruitment campaign, but there are costs associated with other forms of adjustment which involve no direct financial outlay. The costs of reduced hiring standards, for example, may appear as reduced productivity, poor time-keeping, higher absenteeism or turnover, or reduced quality of output. The bench mark for measuring such costs is the working norm for these variables. Thus, if hiring standards are abnormally low, then the resulting higher-than-normal absenteeism will be counted as a cost. We must also include the levels of employment and hours per employee in the cost functions. Besides being adjustment variables, these act as a kind of scale factor in determining the costs of many of the instruments.

The second type of cost is that of residual adjustments. This will typically be in the form of operating at less than desired rates of output, but also includes the cost of operating at less than the desired quality of output or violating tastes with respect to production

32. See Abraham and Thomas (1973), especially chapter VII.
33. See Vickers (1968) for some exploratory ideas on how an integrated optimization analysis for the enterprise as a whole might proceed.
34. The assumption that desired output is given for all future time periods is unrealistic but facilitates the development of this theoretical framework. In the course of the empirical chapters it is relaxed when, for instance, we consider the effect of increases in product prices on product demand.

methods. Thus both positive and residual adjustment costs are included in the sum to be minimized.

The firm's expected cost plan over time will depend on the strategies adopted. Each time the firm changes the value of one or more of its adjustment instruments then the cost plan will change. As an illustration, suppose that a decision is taken to alter the value of some instrument. The cost plan relating to this decision may lie above the existing (no change) cost plan for a few periods, but if the adjustment is effective in reducing labour shortage the new cost plan may fall below the existing one. This later fall may be due to the achievement of increased levels of production, improvements in the quality of output, or reduced operating costs. Figure 2.5 shows this hypothetical position.

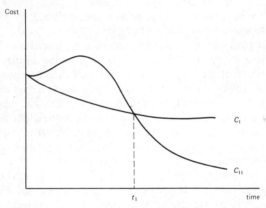

FIGURE 2.5. THE COSTS OF TWO STRATEGIES

C_I represents the cost of the existing strategy with no change in the values of the variables, assuming no exogenous changes. C_{II} is the cost plan given a change in one or more variables.

The Choice Problem

The firm is concerned to choose the plan which minimizes the discounted present value of the stream of costs associated with any plan.[35] There will be an infinite number of cost plans since there is an

35. i.e. it wishes to minimize

$$\int_0^T C(t)e^{-rt}dt$$

where C is costs, r the rate of discount, and T the time horizon.

infinite number of changes in the variables which can be made. Each adjustment instrument can be altered by differing amounts and can be employed for differing time periods. Because of the complexity of the adjustment process it is not possible to deduce simple rules for finding the optimal cost plan. The employer has to conduct his search for the optimal cost plan by comparing a succession of pairs of possible cost plans.

In some cases, one cost plan may be unambiguously lower than another. Where, however, two cost plans cross, identifying which is the cheaper depends on the shapes and positions of the curves and also the time horizon and the rate of discount. An example of this is the choice of whether to incur adjustment costs in order to secure a reduction in future costs.[36] This problem can be handled in our

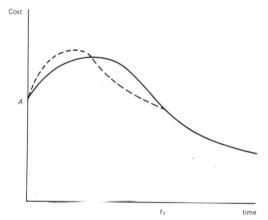

FIGURE 2.6. THE IMPACT OF ADJUSTMENT COSTS

framework if we think of the firm being at point A in Figure 2.6, and faced with alternative cost plans embodying, as they do, *all* the costs from making any change. The broken line and the solid line both achieve a similar result after about t_1. If the time horizon is beyond t_1, the strategy represented by the broken line is preferred at low rates of discount and that represented by the solid line at high rates of discount.

If the firm had perfect information and access to cost-free calculations, it would continue to make comparisons between pairs of

36. This is a question raised in most of the employment function literature. See, for example, Nadiri and Rosen (1973: Chapter 1).

cost plans until all the alternative possibilities were exhausted and the optimal plan found. However, since the acquisition and evaluation of information requires time and money, the firm is faced with the problem of determining how much information to seek and how to narrow down its options to a feasible few.[37] In seeking information, an optimal stopping rule could be formulated in terms of equating the expected marginal benefit from a further unit of information acquisition with its marginal cost. It is reasonable to assume that the cost of evaluating alternative strategies depends partly on how much they differ from the present strategy. Strategies which involve minor departures from the present position and which do not involve the use of previously untried instruments, or new ranges of values of known instruments, are likely to be easier to evaluate and thus are more likely to be chosen. There will therefore be a tendency to adopt adjustments which involve relatively minor departures from the present position.

The process of decision-making which we have in mind is one where the decision-maker is faced with the problem of choosing the best cost plan, and this decision is continually under review. At any time, changed circumstances, or new knowledge which suggests that the firm has a better feasible cost plan to pursue, will result in the adoption of the more desirable plan from then on. The actual time path which a firm follows will therefore be one in which there is switching between cost plans. Even if the firm stays with one cost plan, its path over time may differ from that which it initially envisaged if the cost plan had been incorrectly foreseen.

Some Other Factors

There are a number of factors affecting the choice of adjustments which must be considered within the context of this cost-minimizing framework. In particular we are concerned with the role of constraints, the impact of uncertainty, the effect of the external market, and the situations which stimulate the firm to make adjustments.

In Section 2 the importance of constraints was noted, and we must recognize that the firm will not have complete freedom to choose its optimum cost plan. Some constraints impose limits on the use of certain adjustments and can be expressed mathematically as equalities or inequalities between the values of adjustment instruments. Other constraints can be regarded as imposing additional costs on the use of certain adjustments. For instance,

37. See Horowitz (1970), especially 338, for other related questions which it has to deal with.

many union controls can be overcome by the firm incurring sufficient costs in the form of a productivity deal. Thus the distinction made by Doeringer and Piore (1971) between highly constrained and less highly constrained instruments can easily be translated into the cost-minimizing framework.

There are several aspects to the problem of uncertainty. In its loosest form it merely acknowledges that costs are often extremely difficult to measure. This has been noted in many empirical studies and has caused some authors to be deliberately vague in their discussion of cost, as when Robinson for example refers to 'the backwash of repercussions of the actions of the firm . . . [being] relevant to the decision as to which particular policy the firm should adopt'.[38] The degree of uncertainty surrounding different cost paths may differ and the analysis should therefore be in terms of risk-adjusted values of the cost plans.

The cost plans of the firm will be dependent, *inter alia*, on the external market situation. When a firm, for example, is enjoying a net inflow of labour, given the existing values of its adjustment instruments and the state of the market, it may see its best strategy as 'doing nothing'. However, if the external market changes, new plans may then be required.[39]

It is important to consider what stimulates a firm to seek a new cost plan. Earlier we assumed that the rational decision-makers continually have cost plans under review. If firms are satisficers rather than strict cost-minimizers they may not continually reappraise their position. It is perhaps only when profits become seriously squeezed and the economic viability of the firm is threatened that a firm will be induced to seek a better cost plan. The emergence of a labour shortage may act as a stimulus which triggers a firm into action, since the existence of a labour shortage is an explicit signal that there may be better cost plans. Labour shortages rarely go unnoticed by firms experiencing them, and they will be aware that some costs, the residual adjustments, are directly attributable to the shortages.

38. (1968:134). The point is vividly brought out by imagining the real-world situation where chain reactions of costly consequences of certain actions may be triggered, e.g. Gowler and Legge's (1970) 'regressive spiral'. Under such circumstances it is difficult to pin down expected costs.
39. This makes the problem more difficult. In making initial decisions the decision-makers must take the values that are expected to prevail up to the time horizon, though Tinsley has shown that, where there are non-stationary parameters, 'under certainty equivalence the stochastic optimisation procedures are equivalent to the deterministic rules' (1969: 26).

Predictions and Implications

In its crudest form, the model outlined states that a firm will choose its cheapest cost plan. However, because information acquisition and decision-making are themselves costly, this statement is subject to qualification. Thus the search for alternative cost plans is likely to be limited rather than exhaustive, and most adjustments will tend to involve small departures from the existing arrangements rather than major changes. To some extent this qualification allows us to make certain predictions. We would suppose, for instance, that when a reduction in shortage can be achieved in several alternative ways, each of which is familiar to the firm, the cheapest strategy will be chosen. Where the cost of one strategy is unambiguously lower than any other, the choice is straightforward. If, on the other hand, cost plans cross, the choice will depend on the rate of discount and the time horizon. A high rate of discount or a near time horizon will lead to a preference for cost plans which are more favourable in earlier rather than later time periods.

There is likely to be considerable uncertainty affecting cost plans. This takes two forms: uncertainty about the precise effects of certain instruments, and uncertainty about future states of the labour market and the product demand. The first type of uncertainty is likely to lead to the use of instruments which are tried and familiar,[40] though there may also be a certain amount of learning by doing[41] as the firm acquires information about instruments and their effects through using them.

Uncertainty about future product and labour-market conditions is likely to lead to a different sort of caution — a preference for reversible or temporary adjustments.[42] The firm which is uncertain about whether a labour shortage will correct itself in the near future will tend to treat it as a temporary phenomenon rather than commit itself to a higher set of costs in the longer term. The greater the uncertainty the greater the preference for reversible adjustments is likely to be.[43]

40. We are here arguing that habitual behaviour is a rational response to uncertainty. There may be other, organizational, reasons for preferring habitual behaviour. See Chapter 6.
41. The length of time the firm has been in the labour market and, more particularly, the time over which it has had to deal with labour-shortage situations may be an important determinant of its knowledge.
42. Shultz (1962) argued that the reversibility of many non-wage responses injects an element of flexibility in a firm's adjustments. For a more general development of this point see Arrow (1974).
43. If the firm behaved as a rational player in a game-theory model, we might expect it to adopt a mixture of instruments in the face of uncertainty rather than pursue a single-instrument form of adjustment. Indeed, the cost-minimizing model outlined here is suitable for adaptation into a game-theory framework.

5. Summary

In this chapter we have outlined a theoretical framework with which to analyse the question of how firms react to a shortage of labour. We postulate that the firm adopts those adjustments which minimize its costs. However, this basic hypothesis requires elaboration in the light of a number of factors which complicate the adjustment process.

Firstly, there is no single stimulus to which firms react. Though we emphasize the adjustments which are made in response to a stock shortage of labour, the flow balance may act as additional stimulus or it may modify the adjustments made to the stock shortage. Moreover, firms may also react to the problem of increasing costs even in the absence of a shortage.

Secondly, the firm has at its disposal a wide range of adjustment instruments which are subject to a variety of constraints from different sources. Thus the firm's knowledge of its alternative courses of action and their effects is far from perfect. Moreover, the different instruments affect the shortage in different ways. Indeed, we can distinguish four types of instruments according to the operand affected: there are those which affect the demand for labour services, those affecting the number of hours worked per employee, those affecting outflows, and those affecting inflows. Several adjustment instruments affect more than one operand.

Thirdly, it is necessary to distinguish between permanent and temporary adjustments. Temporary adjustments merely disguise the extent of the underlying shortage because they are designed to be removed after a certain period of time. The existence of such instruments makes the measurement of shortage difficult particularly when the distinction becomes blurred. However, the main complication of temporary adjustment is that firms faced with uncertainty may prefer them to permanent adjustments. This is something which the framework must accommodate.

These three factors are relevant to the specification of the cost-minimizing model. In particular they mean that formalization and the derivation of rules for reaching an optimum, though possible, do not justify the complexity involved. They also make necessary an explicit consideration of the time dimension.

The model is therefore set up in terms of discounted cost-minimization. Included under the notion of cost are the financial costs of making adjustments, the costs to the organization of the constraints imposed on adjustment instruments, and the costs of residual adjustments such as lost output. In a world of perfect knowledge, the firm

37

would continue to search for the cheapest set of adjustments until all alternatives had been considered. But, because information is not freely available to firms, their search for the optimal adjustment will be severely limited.

The framework permits consideration of problems such as un-certainty, constraints, and the various stimuli to which firms react, and it enables us to derive some implications about the behaviour of firms. The empirical chapters will assess the usefulness of the frame-work outlined mainly by examining three questions.

First, there is the question of the weights which have to be attached to the arguments in the cost function. This will involve assessing the importance which firms attach to such goals as achieving the desired product quality and quantity, and also the areas in which constraints increase the costs of using particular instruments.

Second, we examine how firms search for their best strategy and ask whether they can be said to continue searching until the marginal cost of additional search is equal to the marginal benefit derived from it. We are concerned also with what stimulates firms into considering alternative courses of action and the impact the external market has on this process.

Third, we will consider the accuracy of the cost-minimizing model. In particular we ask if it provides the best way of dealing with constraints and the firm's various objectives, and whether it can adequately explain the outcomes of the complex decision-making process of a large organization.

3
Bus Drivers

The market for busmen is one where shortages have been large and persistent and where a number of major attempts have been made in recent years to eliminate them. The first section of this chapter describes the structure of the road passenger transport industry and some of the important changes which have taken place. This is followed by an examination of the nature of labour shortages in this market in Section 2, and then by a discussion of the various adjustment instruments and their inter-relationships in Sections 3–10. Much of the discussion relies heavily on material from a number of case studies of transport undertakings which varied in their size, operating conditions, and local labour-market environment. Altogether, eighteen studies were carried out and the various undertakings, with the exception of LT and London Country Buses, have been given a pseudonym.[1]

1. The Road Passenger Transport Industry

By far the major part of the work of the road passenger transport industry is the operation of stage carriage services. Contract work —

---

1. The names used for municipal undertakings are Newcaster, Hamborough, Fishport, Easthampton, Granchester, and Waring. There was also one Passenger Transport Authority which is simply referred to as the PTA. The company-sector undertakings, all subsidiaries of the NBC, have been given names with the suffix 'bus' except for London Country which goes by its real name. The names used are Alphabus, Betabus, Gammabus, Deltabus, Lambdabus, Thetabus, and Townbus. The last named is an indication that the operations of this particular undertaking were concentrated in a single large town and in that sense it was more akin to the municipal undertakings rather than the company undertakings. Two large independent companies, which engaged mainly in excursions and tours but operated some stage carriage services, have been referred to as Snow's Coaches and Clement's Coaches. LT goes by its real name.

in particular the provision of works and school buses — accounts for the bulk of the remainder of the industry's output, while express services, excursions, and tours are of little numerical importance.[2]

The industry is concentrated in the public sector but it is useful to distinguish the subsidiaries of the NBC and the SBG from undertakings which are owned by local authorities.[3] The distribution of the industry according to the type of operator is shown in Table 3.1 which also indicates that there is a considerable variation in the size of operation ranging from LT and the PTAs down to the 5,000 independent operators. Most of our attention will be confined to the public sector which is responsible for virtually all the stage carriage work.

Generally public-sector bus undertakings are set a financial objective, which may be to cover operating costs or to provide some surplus to cover depreciation of capital, and are required to run an adequate public service. Often, however, these formal objectives conflict and the goals of the undertakings may tend more towards maintaining output or to keeping costs down. As a broad generalization the NBC subsidiaries are subject to tighter financial control than those undertakings which are responsible to local authorities. It was certainly the experience of London Country Buses that the NBC was more revenue-conscious than LT and that the former was less able to finance a deficit. Moreover, local-authority subsidies are more restrictive in the company sector. The provision for subsidizing specific rural services affects the companies much more than the urban-based municipal undertakings and PTAs, which may receive a general subsidy from the rates.

The system of licensing routes means that bus undertakings are

2. The vehicle miles operated in 1972 were distributed as follows: stage carriage 72%, contract work 20%, express services 5%, excursions and tours 3% (source: *Passenger Transport in Great Britain, 1972*).
3. Under the 1947 Transport Act the BTC acquired most of the major private companies, except the British Electric Traction Company. The 1962 Transport Act transferred the BTC holdings to a new Transport Holding Company which was to manage them as if 'engaged in commercial enterprise'. LT, which had been part of the BTC, was made independent, as the LTB, but in 1970 was transferred to the GLC. The latter change was part of a major reorganization which took place in the industry as a result of the 1968 Transport Act. Under the Act the privately owned British Electric Traction interests were acquired by the THC and the NBC was set up as a new holding company for bus interests (except those to be looked after by the SBG). A number of PTAs were also established to provide an integrated transport system in the major conurbations. The NBC has, in its short life, undergone several reorganizations. At present there are three divisions, each of which are units of financial accountability. In 1970, when LT went to the GLC, London Country Buses were transferred to the NBC.

TABLE 3.1
STRUCTURE OF THE ROAD PASSENGER TRANSPORT
INDUSTRY, 1972

	Operators	Vehicles	Staff			
			Drivers	Conductors	Other	Total
LT	1	6,053	11,997	8,518	13,611	34,126
PTAs	4	6,145	10,517	4,493	9,937	24,947
NBC and SBG	56	24,240	37,025	17,392	30,550	84,967
Local authorities	68	10,025	17,413	8,908	14,982	41,303
Other	5,107	26,351	19,558	2,791	12,931	35,280
Total	5,236	72,814	96,510	42,102	82,011	220,623

SOURCE: *Passenger Transport in Great Britain, 1972.*

monopolists on the routes they operate. However, they are not necessarily monopsonists. People with driving skills may offer themselves to many employers other than bus and coach operators, and even within the bus industry we find cases of two or more operators sharing the same territory. This happens typically where the services run by a municipal undertaking and a company providing inter-town and rural services overlap. Bus undertakings tend to recruit from their local labour market,[4] but PTAs and other large undertakings cover areas which comprise several different local labour markets.

There has been a fall in the demand for bus services in the post-war period and a corresponding growth in car ownership.[5] However, the

---

4. In periods of severe recruitment difficulty the employer's area of search may be extended. In general it is the norm to recruit from the local labour market and any extension of search can be seen as a deviation from the norm.
5. This can easily be seen from the following figures:

Passenger Miles '000 million

	Public-Service Vehicles	Private Road Transport	Other Public Transport
1952	50.1	37.9	24.2
1972	34.2	223.5	22.4

SOURCE: *Passenger Transport in Great Britain, 1972.*

NBPI Report No. 16, Chapter 3, discusses other reasons for the fall in demand such as increased fares.

relationship between these two trends is not one of simple causation. A fall in the demand for bus services reduces an undertaking's revenue and whether this is met by a reduction in service, increases in fares, or a fall in the relative wages of busmen creating a labour shortage, car usage tends to increase. In addition, an increase in car ownership may lead to traffic congestion and hence unreliable services which paradoxically reinforce the preference for private transport. Thus some bus undertakings find themselves locked into one or perhaps two vicious circles.

However, the fall in demand from bus transport has not been uniform over different types of service. The demand for peak-hour services has fallen less than the demand for off-peak services,[6] while the amount of contract work has been rising.[7] The severity of the general fall in bus traffic and the rising costs led some observers to conclude that 'the bus industry in Britain . . . is now in the early 1970s going through the most severe crisis in its history' (Thomson and Hunter, 1973: 266). But it seems to have been a crisis that has been largely overcome, and recently there has been considerable optimism in some quarters of the industry which suggests that the decline in passenger traffic has finally been arrested and an upturn has begun.[8]

A fall in labour productivity has resulted from an inability to run down the labour force in line with the fall in passengers.[9] There was a drop from about 50,000 passengers carried per employee in 1958 to about 40,000 in 1968.[10] More sophisticated measures of productivity confirm the decline.[11] As well as a rise in the input of man-hours per unit of output, there has also been an increase in the effort input in the sense that the bus driver's job has become more demanding in

6. See NBPI Report No. 16, 6.
7. Compare footnote 2 with Thomson and Hunter (1973: Table 5.1).
8. A number of individual transport undertakings have claimed a turning-point has been reached, and see the NBC *Annual Report* for 1972, especially para. 29.
9. British Rail, on the other hand, has been able to do this. This is partly due to the technology of the bus industry. The bus is a relatively small unit (with a maximum carrying capacity of about 75, unlike a train) which means that there is a high proportion of operating staff to ancillary staff.
10. Thomson and Hunter (1973:300). The equivalent figure for 1972 was 38,183 passengers per employee. Clearly OMO has not offset the decline. Indeed, for 1972 the number of passengers carried per employee (excluding conductors) was 47,188, which shows that even with complete OMO there would have been a decline in the number of passengers per employee.
11. See for example Deakin and Seward (1969) who calculated a measure of output per *total* factor input, and Wabe and Coles (1975) argue that there was a decline in labour efficiency in the 1960s (as measured by the growth in crew costs of a marginal bus in terms of man-weeks at the basic rate).

terms of the fatigue and strain of driving in congested urban areas, and the added responsibility of OMO.

There have been few changes in technology which have allowed substantial improvements in the operating position. The use of special bus lanes and tidal bus flows,[12] attempts to smooth peak demand,[13] and variations in the size of buses have so far made little impact. However, improved vehicle design has reduced the physical effort required to drive a bus — a factor which has been important in allowing the growing use of female drivers. A major part of the attempts to increase productivity has been the introduction of OMO though this has met with very varied success.

2. Shortage

The Measurement of Shortage in the Bus Industry

Two problems arise when measuring shortage in the bus industry. First, establishment figures, which are a common means of stating labour requirements in the public sector,[14] tend to be misleading measures of demand. Second, the extent of a labour shortage may be concealed by the use of temporary adjustments.

The demand for bus drivers will depend on desired output, the presumed length of the working week, and labour productivity,[15]

---

12. This means that buses returning from peak-hour journeys go by the shortest possible route and with limited stops.
13. There is a demand for a large number of peak-hour buses and drivers in relation to the non-peak period, and the size of the fleet and the number of drivers required is governed to a large extent by the size of the peak. The peak may be smoothed by the introduction of discriminatory pricing for peak and off-peak services, and by encouraging staggered work and school hours.
14. Fishport was the only public-sector undertaking in our survey which did not set an establishment figure, but it was under pressure from the union to do so. The absence of an establishment figure gave the undertaking a certain flexibility — it had dismissed several bad timekeepers under the guise of a redundancy. Neither of the two independent companies set establishment figures. The reason for this was that their output depended directly on the demand for their services without the intermediary of scheduled mileage.
15. The measure of labour productivity which translates mileage into driving hours will vary according to the speed of the bus and hence the traffic density. However, it also subsumes such factors as scheduling efficiency and the peakedness of the service. In undertakings which had a large peak, establishments reflected the drivers required at peak time rather than total mileage. In Newcaster, the evening peak was accentuated because of schools and works closing around the same time. This meant that establishments were set according to the needs of this particular day. Thus, the constancy of labour productivity only holds for an unchanged distribution of services over the week.

43

with an additional provision to cover sickness, absenteeism, and holidays. However, the actual demand often differs from the establishment figure which is set because the latter is calculated on the basis of notional values of these variables which reflect neither the real state of affairs nor what management would consider to be the norm. It is convenient to call the values of the independent variables which determine the establishment figure, formal norms, and those on which actual demand is based, working norms.

The discrepancy between establishments and labour demand is immediately apparent from an examination of the presumed length of the working week. About half the undertakings in our survey based their establishment figures on the length of the scheduled week which was between 40 and 43 hours. In practice these undertakings anticipated that staff on average would work significantly longer than the scheduled week and so required fewer busmen than the establishment figures suggested. Thus the working norm was usually in excess of the formal norm for hours. However, the origin of the working norm for hours varied in different undertakings. In Hamborough it stemmed from the local agreement which laid down a basic working week of 48 hours, whereas the establishment was calculated from the formal norm of 40 hours. In other undertakings, in particular LT, there were informal agreements at some garages to guarantee a certain amount of overtime. Gammabus followed this practice in the main, but in one garage hours were controlled unilaterally by the platform staff. Here, management alleged, high levels of overtime were maintained through the men driving away new entrants by being unpleasant to them.'The situation at Townbus on the other hand was more akin to unilateral management regulation of hours. The manager thought it cheaper to work longer hours than take on extra staff and deliberately sought to recruit the type of person who likes to work long hours. Here both the formal and working norms were 50 hours.[16]

In a number of undertakings, however, the working norm was not easy to deduce. This happened when, because of shortage, overtime was always available and the question of recruiting up to establish-

16. Betabus provided an interesting example of these diversities within one undertaking. In the larger depots, management sought to work to a 40-hour week because overtime was considered costly. In the smaller outstations the formal and working norms could be up to 60 hours because the employment of an extra driver reduced the average hours per driver below 40. In one depot there was an agreement to provide overtime by having no provision for sickness and absence, whilst in others the establishment figure had not been reached and an equilibrium model applied.

ment level had not arisen. The typical management attitude to such a situation was to adopt an equilibrium model of the hours/employment choice. For instance, a Newcaster manager said, 'If we ceased to provide overtime some men would drift away and restore the need for it.'

The most common divergence between working norms and formal norms was seen in the setting of the provision for sickness, absenteeism, and holidays. Most undertakings increased the required number of duties by 10 per cent (or sometimes 20 per cent) to arrive at the establishment figure. In these cases the provision was just a rule-of-thumb mark-up applied uniformly throughout the undertaking and over the year. Such a practice can result in a situation similar to that found in Easthampton. In the spring, there was a severe notional shortage but because of low sickness and holidays the actual shortage was only slight. In two of the larger and more heterogeneous NBC subsidiaries, Betabus and Gammabus, the absence and sickness provision varied between garages according to local need. However, in the main urban depot in Gammabus, the formal provision still underestimated the working provision resulting in a surplus over the establishment level. It was in LT that the formal provision most accurately reflected need. This varied over the year according to a five-year historic average of sickness and absence rates. The holiday provision was based on information about holiday allocation from individual garages. The desire for accuracy was carried further. Because sickness and absenteeism were greater amongst women, the provision for conductors was an average of male and female absence rates weighted by the current sex distribution of conductors. But, with the exception of LT, working norms for the provision are not accurately reflected in formal norms.

There was a tendency in undertakings for the establishment to cover only the scheduled services and omit requirements for private hire. It was also customary for private hire and contracts with the LEA to be reduced when there was a shortage. This suggests that actual output will exceed the formal norm for output when labour is abundant, but will tend to approach the formal norm as a labour shortage appears. But what happens to the working norm (and therefore *ex ante* demand for labour)? There is no *a priori* answer because the distinction between temporary and permanent adjustments depends on managerial perception of the situation. Some municipal undertakings were resigned to the fact that they could only take on a certain proportion of the LEA's contracts, whereas a number of NBC subsidiaries showed an awareness of the extra private hire work they could do if labour were available. As a crude generalization, one can say that to relinquish contractual work is a permanent adjustment for a municipality and a temporary adjustment for an NBC subsidiary, but the correlation is by no means perfect. Other considerations are as important, in particular the availability of buses and the administrative capacity for dealing with unscheduled work.

Hence, because the divergence of formal norms from working norms means that establishments differ from demand,[17] it might seem appropriate to use vacancies statistics rather than the shortfall from the establishment figure as a measure of shortage. But while the shortfall from establishments may reflect the extent of shortage *vis-à-vis* demand at any instant, the level of vacancies will tend to reflect future requirements. For Holt and David (1966), vacancies are composed of three elements: the current shortfall from requirements, the expected change in requirements, and the expected wastage. However, few undertakings allowed for all three components. LT, for instance, adjusted for impending cuts in the establishment due to OMO (in the case of conductors), seasonal changes, and reductions in service. They did not allow for increasing requirements or expected wastage. Thus the vacancy figure could be equal to or below the shortfall. In fact it was nearly always below this because shortfall included those in training whereas vacancies did not. In a couple of undertakings the vacancy figure included a provision for expanding requirements and expected wastage, but this practice was not common.

In short, one has to take care in the interpretation of both vacancy and establishment figures. We would not, however, go as far as the Pay Board (1974b) which suggested that these difficulties make the measurement of shortage impossible. It is the second problem, that of the disguised shortage, which makes measurement nearly impossible, and to this we now turn.

Whatever measure of labour demand is used, it is normal to subtract from it the level of employment in order to derive the size of the shortage. However, we are really interested in the extent of the

17. Although formal and working norms diverge, this does not necessarily mean that demand differs from establishments. Establishments sometimes presume that scheduled hours cover scheduled services and that overtime will be used to cover private hire work and duties which are left vacant by absenteeism or sickness. Thus London Country's establishments were based on a five-day week with an allowance for known sickness but no cover for short-term absence. The intention was to recruit up to establishment level though in practice there were some local variations. Here demand was coincident with establishments because the divergence between the formal and working norms for hours was offset by a counteracting divergence in output norms.

Shortage

shortage which exists when working norms are being adhered to. If some temporary adjustment increases the level of employment, the extent of the underlying shortage is disguised but not alleviated. A good example of this was seen during the Second World War when LT recruited women conductors 'for the duration of the emergency' with the intention of sacking them when the market returned to 'normal'. But, because an all-male platform staff was the working norm, the underlying shortage remained. In fact LT turned out to be so dependent on its women conductors that this temporary adjustment became fossilized into a permanent one. Here again it is not easy to distinguish between a temporary and a permanent adjustment — working norms can only be deduced from the attitude and actions of those holding them.

While we have concentrated on the overall stock shortage, this need not be the problem of greatest concern. Sometimes the geographical distribution of the shortage is more important. Moreover, for some parts of an organization, net wastage is a greater problem than any stock position. Indeed the same objective stimulus may have different meanings for different actors, and this may be important in explaining the action taken.

The Causes of Shortage

To discuss the causes of labour shortage in the abstract would be a futile activity. Instead we are concerned with a number of inter-related and specific questions: what factors have been instrumental in affecting the level of shortage, what causes do employers attribute to shortages, and why do they persist?

The simplest way to test for the factors affecting the level of shortage is by regressing a measure of shortage on possible explanatory variables. This was done for LT. The level of driver shortage was regressed in turn on measures of all drivers' relative pay, crew drivers' relative pay, and the local unemployment rate. In each case the coefficient had the expected sign, but was not significant at the 10 per cent level. The only significant result in this form of regression was achieved when driver shortage was regressed on local vacancies.[18] This gave

$$X(DR) = -2.85 + 0.799 \ VM. \qquad R^2 = 0.273$$
$$(-0.57) \quad (2.87) \qquad\qquad DW = 1.50$$

18. $X(DR)$ is the percentage shortfall from establishment and VM is the absolute number of male vacancies in the area measured in thousands. The equation was run on quarterly data from 1967 I to 1972 IV. The t-statistics are given in brackets.

This result must be considered unsatisfactory from the point of view of the low coefficient of determination. Results for cross-section analysis of these relationships in LT were no better. Local unemployment (from the 1971 Census of Population) was regressed on shortage by garage. This gave a significant positive correlation, contrary to expectation, for drivers and no significant relationship between local unemployment and conductor shortage. The PTA data limited us to a cross-section analysis of shortage on pay by garage. This yielded no significant result.

There are problems in taking the level of shortage as the independent variable. It discounts the possibility of lagged effects — no matter what the level of staff previously, the relative pay or state of the labour market will determine the level of shortage. Secondly, any demand-side changes are ignored in the model. For these reasons it is more appropriate to seek an explanation for the variations in wastage and recruitment.[19]

There is a temptation to attribute shortage to high wastage, low recruitment, or a combination of both. This has led to difficulties. For instance, the Phelps Brown Report said: 'The main cause of the difficulty in filling the establishment in London Transport has been a high rate of wastage of existing staff . . . [approximately 20 per cent per annum] . . . this is a high rate of turnover for a public service where special qualifications and training are required, and long term employment has been normal in the past' (1964:13). The PIB contradicted this: 'In London, where it is said there is a shortage of labour, the figures which are available suggest the labour turnover among drivers and conductors is not high' (NBPI Report No.16, 1966:13). The difference between these two statements does not reflect a large decline in wastage between these two reports, but rather the use of different comparisons.[20] Today many managers in LT attribute a more important role to wastage than recruitment in an explanation of shortage, yet it is evident from LT's data that the shortage grew worse between 1971 and 1973 more through the fall in recruitment rather than through a rise in the quit rate. It would seem that observations about whether recruitment or wastage is 'responsible' for the shortage indicate the main concern of managers rather than the objective position. Often this area of concern reflects the position of a manager in the organization and his responsibilities.

19. The results of wastage and recruitment equations tell us more about the impact of OMO than the causes of shortage — they are therefore reported on p. 70, footnote 73.
20. Wastage was high in comparison with LT standards but low if compared with other employers.

Similarly, there was a tendency for the people we interviewed to volunteer what they saw as the cause of their shortage. In the majority of undertakings which were experiencing a shortage, a great deal of emphasis was laid on busmen having to work shifts.[21] Though most employers assigned some role to local labour-market conditions, only in a few cases was any importance attributed to pay. The immediate reaction of economists to such attitudes is that they do not explain the reasons for a shortage persisting, as wages should rise to compensate for disadvantageous aspects of the job. Moreover, to attribute a role to shiftwork in emergence of a shortage requires the postulation of a *growing* dissatisfaction with shiftwork and not simply a dislike of it.[22] It is, however, worth taking a more tolerant view of such attitudes because in doing so some interesting ideas emerge.

The study was conducted during a period of incomes policy but this is not the reason for pay being discounted as a compensation. Very few undertakings (and only some of LT's managers) took the view: 'If only we could get round the incomes policy we could cure the shortage.' To a certain extent there was an implicit notion of a fair wage for busmen and that it would be wrong to pay above this to compensate for other factors. These attitudes may be reinforced by the problem of declining revenue. As Arrow and Capron (1959) point out, 'in any market when there is a relatively sudden and dramatic change in either demand or supply which results in large price increases, we may find complaints of a "shortage" while people get used to the fact that the price has risen significantly.' Perhaps the decline in passengers has had a similar effect on the willingness of bus companies to pay the market wage.

That employers attribute a cause to a shortage of labour is an important datum in its own right. If the problem of shortage is analysed as stemming from dislike of shiftwork, this may carry implications for the way management tries to adjust to shortage. There did not, however, seem to be many major attempts to eliminate shiftwork, the notable exception being Alphabus which achieved this by

21. This assessment of shiftwork as being the cause of shortage seems to be based on observation of the behaviour of leavers. A number of managers said that the leavers were tending to go to jobs which did not pay better but where shiftworking was not required. If this is the case, it might explain the importance of the labour-market variable in the quit-race equation (see p. 70): when labour demand in a market rises, quit rates increase not simply because there are more vacancies *per se* but because there are more vacancies with better conditions.
22. This certainly did not result from shiftwork becoming less widespread elsewhere. NPBI Report No. 161 shows that the proportion of manual workers working shifts rose from 12.5% in 1954 to 24.9% in 1968.

severely reducing weekend and evening services (see Appendix B). Such an adjustment is severely constrained by public attitudes, the unions, and the organizational effort required. LT followed the implications of its attributed cause in a rather curious way. It considered shiftwork to be a major cause of shortage and therefore sought to introduce substantial payments for unsocial hours. These payments are not seen as a pay increase to attract more people into transport but rather as an explicit compensation to busmen for having to work uncongenial shifts.[23]

Possible Adjustment Instruments and Constraints on Their Use

Before looking at the ways in which bus undertakings have adjusted to shortages of labour, it is useful to consider how the list of possible adjustment instruments outlined in Chapter 2 are translated into practical measures that can be used in the bus industry. To do this we consider the various constraints which affect the adjustment instruments.

Constraints can affect the adjustment process in two main ways. First, an instrument may be rendered inapplicable, costly, or in conflict with some other objective by the presence of a constraint. Second, constraints may create interdependencies between instruments either by the formation of a joint instrument, or by ensuring that certain instruments are only used as complements.[24] Thus the undertaking does not face a set of independent instruments from which it can freely choose the best adjustment, but it has a number of strategies it can use where each strategy may involve manipulating one or a number of adjustment instruments.

Certain features of the bus industry impose *technical constraints* upon the range of possible adjustments. Inventory changes are not permissible to any great extent as one cannot impose changes in the travelling arrangements of passengers. Capital substitution in the form of increases in the size of buses is limited by the physical aspects of bus routes. However, the existence of crew-operated buses and the availability of fare-collecting aids make OMO a possible adjustment to a shortage of busmen. But, as we shall see, this does not fall neatly

23. This was the situation when fieldwork was carried out in 1973–4. Since then there has been a substantial increase in basic rates.
24. There are, of course, pairs of instruments which have to be used as complements in any market. For example, although advertising and increasing wages may be seen as alternative ways of increasing labour supply, it is usually necessary to advertise before a wage increase affects recruitment. Also a reduction in hiring standards is often accompanied by an increase in training in order to maintain output quality. Moreover, increasing the opportunity for overtime increases average earnings as well as the flow of labour services.

into the framework of possible adjustments which was outlined in Chapter 2.

Financial consideration will be important in the choice of instruments, but in some instances it is useful to talk of a *financial constraint* ruling out particular possibilities regardless of whether the ultimate choice of adjustment is made on strict or loose cost-effectiveness grounds. There are *legal constraints* on the hours which bus drivers can work, on who can drive a Public-Service Vehicle, and the extent to which an undertaking can sub-contract work. It would be a mistake to consider legal constraints as ruling out certain adjustments entirely — they impose a moral disincentive together with the threat of sanctions. *Incomes-policy constraints* and *non-poaching agreements* must be considered as similar in this respect to legal constraints.

Other constraints act more to influence choice than limit it. The *organizational* structure imposes constraints of this nature through national or company-wide agreements and by the impact of other departments on the decision-maker. The *supply* situation and the earnings paid in the local labour market will have some bearing on the choice of adjustments, as will the extent to which instruments have already been employed. Various external bodies have an influence in particular areas. Local councils and other pressure groups may influence the extent and distribution of scheduled services, the RTITB can withhold its grants where training schemes do not conform to its rules, and the Traffic Commissioners can affect the choice of adjustments by their ability to veto applications for fare increases.

But perhaps the most important, and also the most complex, are the constraints imposed by the trade unions to which employees belong. These may arise from the union's participation in joint regulation or sometimes from unilateral control. Union constraints may prohibit the use of certain instruments, but often they merely make an adjustment more costly. The impact of the union varies between undertakings and also in some instances within a single undertaking. This was particularly noticeable in a heterogeneous undertaking such as Betabus, where the depots varied from the large city garage with tight union control to the small rural outstations where the union presented management with no problems. In addition, the unions have tended to ensure through collective bargaining that OMO and other increases in productivity are only permitted in return for increases in pay. This means that there is yet another side to OMO as an adjustment instrument and that increasing productivity is rarely permitted as an independent instrument. It should also be noted that a union constraint is not static, in that management may try to negotiate constraints away or seek to amend a collective agreement.

The effect of these various constraints on the range of possible instruments is mostly on the demand side. The undertaking is left with relatively few ways of reducing the demand for busmen which do not involve simultaneous action on the supply side. Inventory adjustments and pure capital substitution are not possible, while increases in productivity are linked with increases in pay. A reduction in output remains as almost the sole independent adjustment on the demand side.

On the supply side, virtually all the adjustments listed in Chapter 2 can be used in response to a shortage of busmen. The impact of the various constraining forces is mainly on the cost or suitability of the instruments. Very rarely do constraints restrict the range of supply-side adjustments or cause them to be used only in conjunction with other instruments.

Thus, in choosing between adjustment instruments, management is influenced by a number of internal and external factors which are usefully considered together as constraints. These may limit the range of possible instruments, make instruments more costly to use, impose a moral obligation on management, or simply make life difficult for a management employing certain instruments. Constraints, however, can in some cases be removed but such action is, according to our framework, the use of a further adjustment.

3. Pay

Since the road passenger transport industry is labour-intensive, pay is one of the major costs. In this section the pay of busmen is considered as an instrument for adjusting to shortages. An increase in pay is likely to reduce a shortage by reducing quits and by increasing the size of some of the potential inflows. However, an undertaking's main sources of new drivers tend to be drivers employed elsewhere, and its own conductors. In both these cases the existence of traditional differentials and national agreements may inhibit the extent to which pay can be used as an adjustment instrument.

The question of whether pay is an appropriate instrument to reduce shortages has been the subject of a number of reports on the bus industry. The Phelps Brown Report which examined LT pay and shortages over the period 1955–63 concluded that 'the fluctuations in the extent of the shortage of staff for the buses provide evidence that the recruitment and wastage are affected by the relative level of busmen's pay.'[25] The report argued that the shortage of staff was due to inadequate pay,[26] and went on to recommend an increase in relative pay for London busmen which was intended to bring the labour force up to the establishment figure.

Two years later the PIB (NBPI Report No.16) noted that the pay increase recommended by the Phelps Brown Report had reduced neither wastage nor the level of shortage. Indeed the PIB argued that any such pay increase would fail to re-distribute labour because it would be matched by other employers granting similar increases. This argument rested on the assumption that the shortage of labour was *general* and that LT was a pay leader whose increases would always be followed by others.[27]

There was thus some dispute over the question of whether or not a pay increase is an effective adjustment to shortages of bus crews. A slightly different question, but one which is more directly relevant for the purposes of this study, is how far various undertakings have attempted to use pay to reduce shortages. Before trying to answer this question it will be useful to outline the negotiating machinery in the industry.

It is apparent that the area covered by negotiations usually differs from that of the labour-market pressures which produce the shortage. Most busmen have their pay set by national agreement and supplemented through a company agreement, as shown in Table 3.2. Hence the ability to adjust pay in response to *local* labour-market pressures may be constrained by national or company agreements and also by union attempts to preserve or narrow certain differentials.

The three principal negotiating groups are LT which negotiates directly with the TGWU, the NJIC, which covers most of the

25. (1964: para 83). The evidence is less conclusive than the report supposed. Its conclusion was based on a visual impression of graphed data. However, when the data from the report are used in regression analysis, the basic rates of drivers relative to other groups are not significant in explaining drivers' wastage. Thus wastage does not seem to be affected by relative rates. However, when recruitment is regressed on relative wage rates, using Phelps Brown's data, a significant positive relationship is found.

26. In fact, no significant relationship could be found in regression analysis between driver shortages or driver vacancies as the dependent variable and relative pay as the independent variable.

27. LT may indeed set the wage of drivers in the area and hence not be able to increase pay relative to other drivers. It is the biggest single employer of drivers in London, employing over 10% of all professional drivers in the area.

Bus Drivers

TABLE 3.2
NEGOTIATING MACHINERY OF BUSMEN
(Figures show % of Males affected by different types of Agreement)[a]

	Bus and Coach Drivers	Conductors
National agreement and supplementary company agreement	50.0	48.2
National agreement only	37.4	51.0
Company, district, or local agreement only	8.1	0.8
No collective agreement	4.5	0.0

SOURCE: *New Earnings Survey* (April 1973).
NOTE: a. The *New Earnings Survey* classifies the LT agreement as a national one.

municipal undertakings, and the NCOI which covers the NBC subsidiaries and a few independent companies. There are close links between these three groups both in terms of the timing and size of settlements and in the type of argument used.[28]

The difference in the basic rates between the company and municipal sectors is negligible, but the rates in LT exceeded those in both the provincial sectors by about 38 per cent in 1973.[29] However, the difference in earnings between London and the provinces is considerably less than this as Table 3.3 shows.

The table also shows that there are slightly higher earnings in the municipal sector than in the company sector. This might be construed as support for claims that the municipal-sector managements have been 'softer' than those in the company sector because they lack autonomy and professionalism and have a lower degree of accountability in terms of profit levels. However, this earnings differ-

28. See Wilson Report (1965: paras. 28, 93, and 103), and Clegg (1970: 211–12 and 221–2). A recent example of how strategies which are successful in one sector are soon generalized is the award of a shift allowance for the NJIC group, which is now paid throughout the industry.
29. The differential between LT's basic rates and those in the provinces had widened from 10 to 15% in the period 1955–65. Since the 1950s the gap between NJIC and NCOI rates has not been more than 1%. During the 1960s the charge of 'leap-frogging' was made (e.g. see NBPI Report No. 16, para. 56). This led to a proposal in the Wilson Report (1965: para. 118) that the negotiating machinery of the municipal and company sectors should be merged. Initially the PIB did not favour this suggestion (see NBPI Report No. 16, para. 57) but later it supported the idea (NBPI Report No. 50, para. 68).

TABLE 3.3
AVERAGE WEEKLY EARNINGS OF BUSMEN, APRIL 1973[a]

	Earnings (£)	Hours
LT	41.4	48.7
Municipal undertakings	39.4	50.0
Company undertakings	38.2	50.5

SOURCE: *New Earnings Survey*.
NOTE: a. These figures are not strictly comparable because they relate to workers covered by agreements and thus include inside staff in the municipal and company sectors. However, the average earnings of male bus drivers for each agreement were given in the 1971 *New Earnings Survey* and the rank order is the same.

ential can be seen simply as reflecting the more acute labour-market pressure in urban-centred undertakings.[30]

The differential between drivers' and conductors' pay is surprisingly narrow. Both in terms of rates and earnings it is around 5 per cent, though in recent years with the introduction of OMO a much wider gap is appearing between conductors and OMO drivers.[31]

There also arises the question of whether pay is increased in response to shortages of labour. An examination of basic rates shows that over the last decade drivers have had percentage increases which have been similar to the increases in the index of average basic rates for male manual workers. A more appropriate comparison is to use earnings data and see whether relative earnings have increased over time as a result of the shortages. Unfortunately suitable earnings data are not available to make such comparisons, though there is some weak evidence for LT which suggests that shortage

30. Wilson Report (1965: para. 121) reported the argument of the company sector that the municipal employers were in a position to subsidize their operating costs out of the general rate fund. Thomson (1971) noted that the municipal sector was less cohesive and was thus less well placed to resist union pressures. In terms of operating goals there appears to be little difference now between the subsidiaries of the NBC and many municipal undertakings (i.e. breaking even and providing a surplus to cover capital requirements). The difference in goals which does exist is reflected more in the commitments to maintain the level of service, and the readiness to negotiate productivity deals.
31. See pp. 85-8, for a discussion of the relationship between conductors' and drivers' markets.

levels are associated with relative pay increases.[32] We therefore rely on cross-section evidence when dealing with this question and approach it at two levels, first by looking at differences between undertakings and, second, at differences between garages within undertakings.

Though national agreements impose some constraints on the ability to vary pay in accordance with local conditions, they have not prevented the emergence of substantial differences in earnings between different operators. For example, the highest-paying undertakings in our sample had gross weekly earnings 66 per cent above the lowest for OMO drivers, and 74 per cent for crew drivers.[33] The question arises as to whether these variations in earnings reflect responses to different levels of shortage in different undertakings. The range of earnings is partly accounted for by variations in hours. Indeed it is argued in Section 4 that varying the number of hours worked is one of the principal ways of adjusting pay.

There is generally a close correspondence between local labour-market conditions and weekly earnings levels. The earnings of drivers tend to be in line with local earnings of semi-skilled workers, though in virtually all cases this is achieved by working longer hours.

---

32. This can be seen from the following regressions of LT quarterly data from 1967 IV to 1972 II:

$$CP_t/CP_{t-1} = \underset{(39.76)}{0.955} + \underset{(1.80)}{0.00345X(DR)_t} \qquad R^2 = 0.146 \\ DW = 2.91$$

$$CP_t/CP_{t-1} = \underset{(57.82)}{0.972} + \underset{(1.61)}{0.00300DV_t} \qquad R^2 = 0.120 \\ DW = 2.66$$

where CP is the scheduled pay of crew drivers deflated by the DE monthly index of average earnings, $X(DR)$ is the percentage shortfall from driver establishments, and DV is the number of driver vacancies expressed as a percentage of the number of drivers employed.

These results are weak though the expected positive signs appear. Seasonal dummies were added to test whether this association was due to the coincidence of the timing of the settlement and the period of most acute shortage but these were not significant at the 10% level. Indeed the addition of dummies tended to increase the significance of the shortage variables.

33. The figures were:

	OMO Drivers	Crew Drivers
Highest	£55	£48
Lowest	£33	£27.50

These figures are unstandardized for differences in hours worked and are not strictly comparable in that they relate to different pay weeks — though all are in the last half of 1973. Nevertheless they do demonstrate the wide range.

There were two cases amongst our sample undertakings where drivers' earnings were below prevailing local earnings levels for semi-skilled work, and here the shortages of busmen were relatively high. These were Newcaster and one of the depots of Lambdabus, and in both cases local earnings levels were very high on account of large car plants in the area. Townbus was also situated in a car-producing area but here earnings had been raised, as part of a productivity deal, to a level comparable with those in the local vehicle plants and the shortage of labour had been reduced considerably.

Attempts to meet the variations in local labour-market pressures have imposed some strain on both the national pay agreements, even though the NJIC agreement permits some variation in the basic rates between undertakings. 'Deviation' payments were added to the basic rates in certain municipal undertakings in recognition of local shortages of labour,[34] but in some cases these supplementary payments were insufficient to allow undertakings with acute shortages to use pay as an adjustment instrument to the extent that they wished. This led to the expulsion or voluntary withdrawal of a number of undertakings in high-paying areas.[35] The development of company-level bargaining since the end of the 1960s has given operators more scope to respond to local shortages with pay increases.

The position of individual undertakings constrained by national agreements is repeated at a lower level where company-wide rates apply to garages with different local labour-market conditions. Different companies have pursued different strategies in these circumstances. In Lambdabus, for example, the company rate is insufficient in one particular area to match earnings at a local motor works, and shortages of labour remain heavy in that particular depot. In Alphabus, on the other hand, the company wage levels have been pitched high enough to eliminate shortages at every

34. There were a number of other minor payments such as long-service, safe-driving, and good-conduct allowances which produced variation in rates. The PIB in its 1966 earnings survey found that these additional payments varied from as little as 5p per week to £1 at Luton and £1.57 in Coventry — both the latter being in high-wage areas.
35. For example, Newcaster was expelled from the NJIC in 1966 for an agreement which gave a basic rate of £18 compared with the prevailing rate of £12 per week, but it was still unable to compete with the local motor industry. Hamborough was also expelled in 1966 for consistently paying above the NJIC rate. Voting on the NIJC was not on a proportional basis and some of the large operators claimed that this meant that the rates were set by a large number of small undertakings which did not experience severe labour-market pressures.

garage with the result that at some of the smaller garages in rural areas there are earnings considerably in excess of what is justified on the basis of local labour-market pressures. Presumably the costs of eliminating and the costs of accepting a shortage, between which there will be a trade-off, differ in the two samples quoted. There are, of course, some variations in the earnings between different garages in Alphabus and this is largely achieved through variations in the level of hours worked at each depot.[36]

One aspect of pay not so far discussed is the composition of earnings. There are a number of allowances,[37] variations in the terms of which can produce substantial differences in earnings even though the same basic rates are in force.[38] In some cases it is through the manipulation of these allowances that various constraints on pay increases have been overcome. In recent years the best example of this is seen in the implementation of shift pay.[39] This was awarded on the understanding that it should not count as part of the basic rates for the purposes of enhancement. It has, however, now been generalized to all busmen's agreements and in some cases (e.g. LT) has now been consolidated into the basic rates.

Apart from the constraints of operating under company-wide or national agreements there are other factors which constrain the use of pay as an adjustment to shortages. The major one is incomes policy. Over the last decade this constraint has probably affected busmen's pay more than that of many other occupations. Indeed, there was intensive examination of the bus industry and its labour

36. See Appendix B.
37. These included long-service increments (though these have now been abolished under the NJIC and NCOI agreements), special rates for OMO, graded bonuses for operating in urban areas, allowances for spreadovers, early and late duties, shiftwork, weekend work, and a variety of bonuses for accepting OMO and for changed working practices. In the last five years there has been a strong movement towards the consolidation of these various rates into a single basic rate. Some managements have favoured this on the grounds that it regularizes payments and thus facilitates the easy calculation of labour costs, though it has been strongly opposed by some undertakings in our sample, on the grounds that a uniform rate for all duties reduces the incentive to work less agreeable duties. A consolidated basic rate implies higher overtime payments since there is a bigger base for enhancement. Consolidation is thus a means of increasing earnings though in some undertakings e.g. Lambdabus the overtime premia have been reduced so that enhanced rates do not increase labour costs.
38. For example, in a few undertakings spreadover duties are paid through from signing on to final signing off, though this is not generally the case. The TGWU is now seeking wider implementation of this.
39. In November 1972, shift allowances were introduced equal to 10% of the basic rate following the Clegg arbitration award. These were paid on a daily basis. It has been increased to 12½% in the 1974 NCOI Agreement.

problems during the 1960s by the PIB. The readiness of governments to take a stand against busmen, when imposing incomes restraint, has been attributed by Thomson to the fact that busmen 'have high public visibility but little significant influence on the output of the manufacturing and export sectors' (1971:390). A particularly turbulent period in industrial relations occurred in 1967 when a negotiated pay increase was frozen for twelve months.[40]

In general, pay has not been used aggressively as a means of reducing shortages but defensively in the sense of setting earnings levels comparable with those prevailing in the local labour market.[41] Indeed our survey indicated an attitude prevailing amongst the managers of bus undertakings that it was neither necessary nor appropriate to increase pay in response to shortage unless the earnings of busmen were seriously out of line with local earnings. Such attitudes are understandable if, as it appears, the elasticity of supply is sufficiently low to make small changes in pay ineffective in reducing shortages.[42]

Even in Alphabus and Townbus, where major increases in pay enabled substantial and permanent improvements in the staffing position, the aim was to bring busmen's earnings into line with local industry. After many years of persistent shortages Alphabus raised pay dramatically in return for various productivity provisions relating to flexibility, the use of part-timers, and the elimination of 'restrictive practices'.[43] This had a pronounced effect on both recruitment and quits which swiftly eliminated the shortage. However, the

40. This is well documented in Thomson (1971), Thomson and Hunter (1973), Balfour (1972), and see NBPI Reports Nos. 16, 50, 56, 63, 69, 78, 85, 95, 96.
41. Fieldwork was concluded before the post-Phase-three LT settlement which took effect in August 1974. This increased basic rates by between 12.8% and 14.5%. It is difficult to deduce from the deal itself whether it should be classed as an aggressive use of pay or if it merely anticipates future price rises.
42. Two assertions which illustrate this attitude were made by senior LT managers: 'The problem is conditions . . . when a man is away in the evenings the wife gets a boyfriend'; and 'After a man is fairly comfortably off, he starts to want better conditions out of a job rather than more money.' See Section 2 for a discussion of the attribution of causes to shortage situations.
43. We use the term 'restrictive practices' not because we concur with its emotive connotation but simply as a matter of convenience. We have stated earlier that we would adopt a pluralistic frame of reference in preference to a unitary approach and as Fox has said: 'Like conflict, restrictive practices and resistence to change have to be interpreted by the unitary frame of reference as being due to stupidity, wrongheadedness, or out-dated rancour. Only a pluralistic view can see them for what they are: rational responses by sectional interests to protect employment, stabilise earnings, maintain job status, defend group bargaining power, or preserve craft boundaries' (1966: para. 50).

pay change required was non-marginal and caused severe financial problems for the undertaking. Townbus provides a similar example. Chronic shortages were experienced until 1967–8 when a new management team was brought in with a brief to rectify the situation. A productivity agreement with the union was drawn up which for the first time put the undertaking's weekly (not hourly) earnings on the same level as local engineering factories.[44]

These examples of pay increases linked to productivity agreements emphasize the fact that the decision to increase pay is not independent of other instruments. Financial considerations and the structure of national agreements make large pay increases difficult to justify unless they are earned by increased productivity. Conversely it is difficult for an undertaking to increase productivity unless it is paid for by increases in pay. The adjustments made by Alphabus and Townbus were certainly effective, but because pay was used in combination with other instruments, namely tighter schedules, introduction of OMO, and the elimination of controls on entry and the utilization of manpower, it is impossible to say which instrument had the greatest effect.

There are thus a variety of constraints which prevent the exclusive use of pay as an adjustment to shortages in the bus industry. The presence of incomes policies, national and company-wide agreements, and the belief in low elasticities of supply mean that non-wage adjustments have an important role to play and it is to these which we now turn.

4. Hours

Overtime working is widespread in the bus industry. According to the *New Earnings Survey*, the average weekly hours worked were 51.0 for drivers and 51.1 for conductors in 1973 compared with 46.7 for all male manual workers.[45] These figures are, however, highly aggregated and there are considerable variations in hours worked between undertakings; amongst our sample of undertakings the average weekly hours worked varied from about 42 to about 60

44. In 1968 average weekly earnings in local engineering plants were £38 compared with £23 for the bus undertaking, but in 1973 they were both about £55 per week (for very different hours).

45. It is usual for busmen to work overtime. The *New Earning Survey* figures show that, in 1973, 86.1% of conductors worked overtime, 84.3% of bus and coach drivers, 84.8% of those covered by the NCOI agreement, 86.4% of those covered by the NJIC agreement, and 68.0% of those covered by the LT agreement.

hours. Typically, busmen work one rest day per week plus a few additional hours overtime,[46] and it is such a regular feature in many undertakings that it is incorporated into the basic duty rosters.

However, overtime levels amongst busmen have fallen slightly over recent years,[47] as a result mainly of restrictions on the length of hours a driver may work which came into force with the 1968 Transport Act. These set a fairly rigid upper limit, which was relaxed in 1970, but even before then several undertakings adopted a fairly liberal interpretation of the regulations.

Our main concern in this section is with the way hours worked are adjusted in response to labour shortage. We start by considering how the cost-minimizing employer might be expected to vary his employment–hours mix, and then consider the extent to which this model is confirmed by our observations.

A cost-minimizing model of the firm's desired hours–employment mix can be constructed whereby the demand for overtime depends on the cost of overtime hours relative to the fixed cost of employing extra workers. If diminishing returns to hours and employment are assumed, a tangency solution prevails,[48] and if positive adjustment costs are assumed, temporary fluctuations in product demand are met by temporary movements in hours rather than by a permanent increase in the work force.[49] However, such a model relies on fluctuations in output to generate changes in hours, and is therefore inadequate for predicting movements in hours in the bus industry where output tends to be constant over the cycle.[50]

In order to predict how the cost-minimizing employer adjusts hours in response to a shortage of labour, we have to build a supply constraint into this model. One possible way of doing this is to make the supply of employees dependent on the wage rate with an elasticity which varies with local labour-market conditions. However, this would be unnecessarily complicated and somewhat unrealistic. Because wage adjustments are highly constrained and also permanent, the main alternative adjustment to hours in a

---

46. This has caused some disgruntlement, e.g. one branch secretary in LT is quoted as saying 'if you want overtime, you have to give up a complete rest day, which is hardly overtime in the real sense of the word' *The Record* (January, 1974).
47. NBPI Report No. 50, Table 1, shows that the average weekly hours of busmen in July 1967 were 53.7.
48. This is shown by Brechling (1965).
49. For a survey of these models see Fair (1969).
50. There has been a secular decline in the demand for bus services as shown in section one, and there are usually seasonal fluctuations in demand, but both these are distinct from the cycle.

tightening labour market is an increase in recruitment costs. We can assume therefore that, as the market tightens, an elastic supply of labour is only forthcoming with increased recruitment expenditure. This increased recruitment expenditure enters the model as an increase in the fixed costs of employing workers and thus induces the cost-minimizing employer to meet a shortage with an increase in the amount of overtime working.

However, the evidence of our case studies was that hours form a much more complex adjustment instrument than this model supposes. In fact, the level of hours may be used as an adjustment to shortage in two ways. More overtime working will increase the flow of labour services from a given stock of employees, and it may increase the size of the stock itself if recruitment and wastage are dependent on *weekly* earnings. The structure of hours will also be relevant as an adjustment instrument. The peakedness of the demand for bus services[51] necessitates a very uneven flow of labour services required during the day and over the week but there are various ways of meeting the problem. The morning and evening peaks can be covered either by overtime working at peak periods, by the employment of part-time workers at the peaks, or by working split shifts (sometimes called spreadovers) which cover the peaks with a rest period in between.[52] Weekend services can be covered by scheduled duties, rest-day working, or part-timers. The choice of which working pattern to adopt depends partly on the pattern of services but there is a certain scope for the undertaking to adjust the system of duty scheduling in response to shortages of labour. Thus an undertaking may try to reduce quits by providing a more attractive structure of hours. However, it should be noted that the structure of hours also affects the earnings of bus crews through the various additional payments for Saturday and Sunday working, spreadovers, and early and late duties.

It would be theoretically possible to adapt the above cost-minimizing model to allow for the dependence of labour supply on the overtime levels provided by the firm.[53] However, it would result

51. The size of peak tends to be greater in urban areas and is therefore more of a problem for municipal undertakings than for companies.
52. It is usual for some split duties to be worked but we found cases (e.g. in Easthampton, before the 1970 productivity agreement) where all the peaks were covered by overtime.
53. Despite its general acceptance in the theoretical literature, the notion that the supply of workers to the firm is dependent on available overtime is rarely incorporated into models of the determination of hours. Fair is an exception to this. In his model of the demand for hours paid for, he employs an unemployment variable 'on the hypothesis that in tight labour markets an added

in a highly complex model. While one can envisage ways in which a firm in the real world approximated to the basic model, it is difficult to see how a firm with imperfect knowledge would even approximate to the behaviour which the amended model depicts.

In fact, the implications of a labour supply which varies with the amount of overtime available are somewhat different from that described by the cost-minimizing model. Hours are not increased in response to shortage through an explicit decision to change the hours–employment mix. Rather, overtime becomes available when staff who leave cannot be replaced quickly given the existing terms and conditions. Thus hours are increased as a temporary adjustment before any decision about permanent adjustments can be made. Then, if the new level of overtime exceeds the cost-minimizing level, other adjustments should take place which increase employment and reduce the availability of overtime. However, many undertakings displayed a reluctance to search for the cost-minimizing combination of hours and employment, fearing that any reduction in overtime levels would lead to increased wastage. They saw themselves as being governed by supply conditions and were happy to cling to the nearest available 'equilibrium'. Hence, the knowledge that an increase in overtime working increased the supply of labour could not be exploited in the way the cost-minimizing model predicts. Because the elasticity of supply with respect to hours was unknown, the fact that it was positive led to caution and a certain rigidity in the level of overtime working.

In addition, the controls which unions sometimes exert on the level and structure of hours worked are important. There is rarely any formal agreement to provide voluntary overtime work though there are a number of informal agreements and controls on recruitment which may be designed to provide a minimum level of overtime work. The tightness of such control as is exercised varies considerably between undertakings, and there is sometimes an element of custom and practice which produces a ratchet effect on hours. This implies that, though hours are increased as a temporary adjustment,

---

inducement to keep workers from looking for other jobs is to keep the number of hours paid for per worker high while in loose labour markets less of this kind of inducement is needed'. Fair's results confirm this hypothesis, indeed they indicate 'that labour market conditions have more of an effect on the short-run demand for hours paid for per worker than on the short-run demand for workers' (1969: 154). If our quantitative data on hours were better, we would have tested Fair's model. It should be noted, however, that his incorporation into the model of the dependence of labour supply on hours does not reflect cost minimization but merely a behavioural reaction.

the new level may become accepted as a working norm. Controls on the structure of hours, and in particular the proportion of total duties which are spreadovers, also vary greatly. Amongst our sample undertakings some had faced a complete ban on spreadover duties, whereas others were permitted by an agreement with the unions to have an unlimited number. In many cases there has been a relaxation of controls on spreadovers, as part of local productivity deals (e.g. Easthampton used to have no spreadovers until its productivity agreement in 1970), and this has sometimes permitted tighter schedules to be introduced. Most productivity agreements cover the structure of hours in a more general way than just provisions on spreadovers, and in some cases this is central to the agreement. This is clearly seen in the case of Alphabus, described in Appendix B, where Saturday and Sunday rest days were introduced and weekend work covered, to a large extent, by part-timers.[54]

This leaves us with the question of the extent to which the variations in hours worked by bus drivers can be explained. The data available to us were in two forms: a short time-series for LT, and some cross-section data for the undertakings in our survey and across garages in Alphabus.

For LT, the drivers' hours variable was regressed on driver vacancies (DV) for biannual data between 1967 and 1973. The result was as follows:[55]

$$\text{Drivers' hours} = 43.63 + 0.0726DV \qquad R^2 = 0.082$$
$$(8.59) \quad (1.46) \qquad\qquad DW = 1.93$$

The coefficient on driver vacancies was significant at the 10 per cent level. This indicates that hours are adjusted in response to labour shortage. However, the low coefficient on vacancies suggests that the adjustment is small, and the low coefficient of determination suggests other factors are dominant in the determination of hours worked.

The cross-section evidence which is cited in Section 3 and Appendix B suggests that hours vary with local labour-market

---

54. Many undertakings have now introduced Sunday rest days and some others are attracted by the pattern of Monday–Friday working found in Alphabus, though in other undertakings, such as LT, it has been ruled out on the grounds (often unsubstantiated) that it would not be possible.
55. Using vacancies as the independent variable provides a better test of the hypothesis that hours are increased in response to shortage than does the use of 'shortfall from establishment'. If the latter variable were adopted here, it would be possible to interpret the equation as high hours creating a high notional shortage.

conditions, so that average earnings of busmen can be aligned with the local earnings of semi-skilled workers without departing from the uniform rates laid down in the national agreement.

In conclusion, we can say that hours have been adjusted in response to shortage, both directly, as a means of increasing labour services from a given stock of employees, and indirectly as a means of keeping weekly earnings at a level comparable with what is paid in the vicinity. Though the direction of movement in hours is consistent with the predictions of a cost-minimizing model, it is clear that a simple cost-minimizing model ignores many factors which can only be explained with reference to a more behavioural type of model.

5. One-Man Operation

One of the major features of the bus industry over the last decade has been the increased use of OMO. The conversion of a service to OMO can be an instrument of adjustment to shortage either directly through a saving in manpower or indirectly because cost savings allow the payment of higher rates of pay. Alternatively, OMO may be introduced to provide a cost saving *per se*.

Certain types of work, such as excursions, tours, and private hire, have never required a conductor, but in stage carriage work OMO has become prominent only since the mid-1960s. Almost every stage carriage operator has introduced some OMO but the proportions differ markedly. In a few cases, such as Fishport in our sample, there is 100 per cent OMO, and some undertakings hope to achieve 100 per cent operation eventually, but in others the target is considerably less than this, especially where problems have been experienced.

Reasons for Introducing OMO

When OMO is introduced as a device to eliminate a shortage of conductors, it can be regarded as a form of factor substitution, but when it is used as a response to driver shortages the mechanism by which the shortage is to be eliminated is more involved. Firstly, it is a means of increasing pay since higher rates are paid to OMO drivers, and we may suppose that, even though this is for more exacting work, it will reduce wastage and increase the flow of applicants. Secondly, there is a change in the nature of the driver's job and this is also likely to affect the supply of drivers. However, there are conflicting pressures here — the job becomes more 'interesting' with a higher degree of responsibility and contact with the public, but it also involves greater strain on the driver. Thirdly, OMO may reduce driver shortages by providing a pool of potential drivers from conductors who are no longer required.

The basic reason for introducing OMO is to secure an increase in labour productivity. Sometimes this is seen as a way of combating labour shortages — following the recommendations of the PIB reports on the bus industry — but often the aim is simply to reduce costs. Although the most common reason given by our sample undertakings for introducing OMO was to reduce costs, the timing of many conversions led us to the view that labour shortages were an important stimulus to change.

The extent of OMO in any undertaking, and the speed with which it is introduced, depend on an evaluation of the expected gains and costs and the constraints which operate.[56] The increase in vehicle costs is normally offset by savings in labour costs. The vehicle costs to the undertaking have been held down by a system of bus grants designed to stimulate investment in new buses which are suitable for OMO, and these grants have acted as a major incentive.[57] Though labour costs are usually reduced there may be substantial additional labour costs associated with the introduction of OMO. These include not only a premium for OMO drivers but also an acceptance bonus.[58]

Constraints on OMO

There are many constraints on the introduction of OMO. Legal restrictions limiting the size of buses which could be operated solely by a driver applied until 1966 when double-deck operation was permitted. This relaxation, combined with pressure from the PIB for greater efficiency, led to much greater use of OMO in the late 1960s.

56. Generally, the stimulus for introducing OMO comes from management, sometimes as a response to outside pressures such as those from the PIB. Unions have invariably treated OMO as a major bargainable issue and, as early as 1959, the TGWU drew up a set of conditions which included the following: there should be no redundancy, limited seating capacity, no standing passengers, additional allowances for signing on and off, and the routes concerned should be uneconomic.

57. The 1968 Transport Act included provision for the Minister of Transport (now Secretary of State for Environment) to make 25% grants to bus operators providing stage carriage services towards the cost of buying buses of an approved type. In 1971 the grant was raised to 50%.

58. Acceptance bonuses were in most cases consolidated into the basic rate at the end of the 1960s, and special rates were introduced for OMO drivers to replace the percentage addition to crew rates. The acceptance bonuses are generally payable to all staff in a garage where there has been an acceptance of OMO.

Despite the lifting of legal restrictions there are still limitations, in the form of union controls[59] and physical constraints,[60] on the type and size of bus which may be used for OMO. The most important constraint on the rate of introduction of OMO outside London is the availability of vehicles. The delivery of new, suitably equipped vehicles and the rate at which existing ones can be converted have limited the spread of OMO in almost every undertaking in our sample. Other constraints which have been found in different undertakings are traffic congestion,[61] fare structure,[62] the extent of training capacity,[63] and problems with ticket and cash-handling equipment.[64]

Initial resistance to OMO by the unions has now almost everywhere been overcome through productivity deals which have provided acceptance bonuses and a share, usually at least half, of the savings. There are, however, many controls exercised by the unions which can have a major impact on the pace of introduction and the extent to which the aims of introducing OMO are met. In undertakings where tight controls are enforced, there are likely to be

59. In Granchester, for example, where the union resisted OMO until 1970, a number of standee buses (which accommodate 17 standing passengers and are designed for OMO) had to be operated as crew buses because of lack of union agreement.
60. In the case of LT it was said that the distribution of OMO across garages was governed not by labour-market factors but by physical limitations of the routes and the size of bus garages. This was confirmed to some extent by the result of regressing the proportion of OMO in 1973 on the percentage driver shortage in 1968 by garage, $X(D68)$.

$$OMO = 41.02 - 0.118\,X(D68) \qquad R^2 = 0.012$$
$$(5.70) \quad (-0.86)$$

The lack of any significant result here suggests that labour-market factors were not very important in influencing the distribution of OMO. Similarly in Newcaster OMO conversion was determined by physical factors. The undertaking had purchased several larger-capacity buses but these were the only ones it had with a front entrance. As it proved necessary to use these bigger buses on the heavily used routes which were unsuitable for OMO, the rate of OMO conversion was less than that allowed by the supply of vehicles.
61. In heavily congested areas, especially central London, OMO buses may not be feasible because of their size and slower speeds. See Fidler (1974) for an analysis of the determinants of boarding and alighting times.
62. In some undertakings, simplified fare structures have had to be introduced.
63. LT gave priority to training crew drivers and sometimes this meant holding up the training of driver/operators.
64. This is a major problem in LT where OMO is not being taken beyond 50% until the mechanical reliability improves.

longer running times,[65] increased signing on and signing off times, no conductor redundancy, no mixed (crew and OMO) operation of routes,[66] no non-OMO work for OMO-designated drivers,[67] selection for OMO training on the basis of seniority, control over the type of ticket-issuing equipment and bus design, and a very high proportion of all savings accruing to platform staff. Needless to say, there is great diversity of practice between different undertakings.

OMO as a Cost Saver

The two objectives of OMO introduction, it was suggested earlier, are cost savings and the elimination of labour shortages. These will be dealt with in turn. Cost savings are in most cases small[68] (so the managements in our survey alleged) despite the fact that labour costs account for a high proportion of total costs. The degree of measurement and control over estimated savings does, however, vary. In Hamborough, for example, 70 per cent of operation was OMO before serious attempts to measure savings were made, and LT does not make any direct measures of savings for the purposes of wage determination. This is rare and it is the usual practice to sign productivity agreements at the outset of OMO introduction, and some estimates of savings are made at that stage and monitored subsequently.

The cost savings which are actually achieved depend on a number of factors, one of the most important being the severity of those constraints on the introduction of OMO, which were described above. Perhaps the most successful conversion programme was in Fishport which moved from under 10 per cent OMO to 100 per cent in just

65. It is usual for longer running times to be allowed on routes when they are converted to OMO. However, some undertakings, notably Waring, which enjoyed great flexibility in the use of vehicles and drivers, have not slackened the running times with the introduction of OMO, and this has caused a greater easing of the staff position than there would have otherwise been.
66. Practice varies widely. In the PTA, for example, once a route has been converted to OMO no crew buses are used on it. In some undertakings crew buses may only be run as duplicates and not as replacements, while in others there is complete flexibility with crew and OMO buses on the same route.
67. In some undertakings OMO drivers will not only do crew driving (at OMO rates of pay) but also perform conducting and certain other non-driving duties.
68. Several industry-wide estimates of savings from OMO have been made. They are all in the range 10–20% of costs. NPBI Report No. 16, para. 73, quoted estimated savings of 15–20%, though others have been less optimistic, e.g. Fishwick (1970) estimated 14.7% and R. M. Brown and Nash (1972) estimated average savings to be 13.7%. Wabe and Coles (1975) estimated savings of about 12% of average cost per mile but argue that these have been reduced over time from 5.9p per mile in 1967 to 3.5p in 1970 (both at 1971 prices, indicating that savings per mile were only 60% of the 1967 value).

over three years without apparent problems. This success resulted from the avoidance of all the cash-handling problems which have proved a stumbling block in many other undertakings, especially in the large conurbations, through fare evasion, unreliability, or pilfering.[69]

Another factor affecting the savings accruing to the undertaking is the nature of the accompanying productivity agreement which determines the flexibility and improved schedule efficiency achieved, and the distribution of savings. The customary formula, which stems from national agreements, is that the savings from OMO should be shared on a 50/50 basis between the undertaking and employees.[70] It is generally management's view that they received far less than half[71] and that they also lose because the estimated savings are generally payable to employees from the date of the agreement, whereas management has to wait until the savings actually accrue.

In general the conclusion must be that in many cases the cost savings accruing to the undertaking have been small. Indeed, were it not for the existence of problems of finance and labour shortage, the attractiveness of OMO to an undertaking would be rather limited.

OMO as an Adjustment to Shortage

The second aim of OMO is the elimination of shortages of labour. In a few cases this involves redundancy amongst conductors, but normally the required reduction in numbers is achieved by slowing down or stopping recruitment. Conductor recruitment also changes in character. In some cases, such as Fishport, all conductors recruited after the decision to introduce OMO are taken on as temporary staff, but a more common change is to increase hiring standards by only taking conductors who are potential drivers. This usually leads to a fall in the proportion of women recruited even in those undertakings where women are permitted to become drivers.[72]

Driver requirements sometimes increase slightly with OMO, because a slowing down in running times means that extra vehicles

---

69. In Fishport all passengers are required to tender the correct fare. No change is given. The public appear to have accepted this system without protest.
70. Whether savings are calculated on a depot or a company basis varies locally.
71. Employees get 50% of the initial savings but there are various premia on top of this which one undertaking, Lambdabus, estimated could give workers as much as 85% of savings. In such cases OMO can hardly be regarded as achieving substantial cost savings.
72. See pp. 85–8 for a further discussion of the effect of OMO on the recruitment of conductors.

are needed if the service frequency is to be maintained. But in several undertakings the number of driver duties was not increased. The effect of OMO on driver quits depends on the strengths of the conflicting pressures of higher strain and higher satisfaction and pay. For LT it seems to be the case that OMO reduces driver wastage both through the effect of increased pay and through the non-pecuniary aspect of the work.[73] However, the experience of several undertakings suggests that the increased strain of OMO driving is reflected in higher absenteeism rather than wastage.

On balance, driver wastage tends to fall and there is also an increasing potential inflow in the form of conductors no longer required.[74] Thus we would expect driver shortages to fall as a result of OMO. A cross-section analysis of LT shows that there is only a small effect. The direct effects of complete OMO would be a reduction in the shortage of 3¼ per cent.[75] This estimate of a modest impact is supported by the experience of other undertakings. Where driver shortages have fallen markedly it has often been attributable to factors other than the direct effects of OMO. In Alphabus, for example, details of which can be found in Appendix B, there was a

---

73. The best regression equation for explaining the quit rate of drivers in LT (based on quarterly data from 1967 I to 1973 II) was:

$$\log Q_D = 5.36 - 3.36 \log AP - 0.559 \log U - 0.079 \log OMO$$
$$(3.14) \quad (-2.68) \qquad (-2.53) \qquad (-2.96)$$
$$R^2 = 0.456$$
$$DW = 1.36$$

where Q_D is the quit rate of drivers, AP is the average scheduled pay of all drivers divided by the monthly index of average earnings (DE *Gazette* (1974), 89), U is the male employment rate in the GLC area, and OMO is the percentage of the total driver establishment which is OMO.

If the AP variable picks up all the variation attributable to changes in pay, then the OMO variable picks up the effect of the non-pecuniary aspects of one-man operation. The AP variable had more explanatory power than a similar variable derived from the average scheduled pay of crew drivers only. For details of this see Deaton (1975). In a similar equation for recruitment, the crew-pay variable had more explanatory power than the all-pay variable. This is what one would expect, since the wages of an OMO driver are only generally known inside the organization, there being no external recruitment of driver/operators.

74. Some undertakings found that OMO attracted more people into driving, from various sources.

75. This result was derived from a comparison of the level of driver shortage, $X(D)$, in each garage in 1968 and 1973 and the proportion of scheduled mileage which was OMO in 1973.

$$X(D73) = 8.93 + 1.04 \ X(D68) - 0.0325 \ OMO. \quad R^2 = 0.667$$
$$(5.96) \quad (10.98) \qquad (-1.54)$$

The indirect effects of OMO on shortage, not included in this estimate, will result from the payment of higher basic rates out of the cost savings.

70

marked fall in driver shortage but this was largely due to the changed pattern of the working week. In the case of conductor shortage the effect of introducing OMO is generally, as expected, much greater than on driver shortage, with marked falls in the establishment figures.

The overall conclusion is that though OMO is a potential cost-saving device which might be attractive at any time, its introduction has been largely a response to problems of labour shortage and declining revenue. However, the cost and labour savings have been considerably less than the PIB had envisaged. The problems, especially in large urban areas, have been more severe than was initially supposed. There have, however, been some highly successful OMO schemes and its introduction has almost certainly alleviated some of the more acute shortages.[76]

6. Productivity

One of the ways in which labour shortages may be reduced is by increased productivity so that the same output can be achieved by using a smaller quantity of labour. The PIB regarded OMO as the chief means of increasing productivity, but it also suggested other areas where there was scope for 'more effective use of manpower'.

Labour productivity is to some extent dependent on the ability of the schedule compiler to arrange duties to coincide as nearly as possible with the guaranteed minimum hours per day and the length of the work week.[77] One measure of schedule efficiency which is adopted by a number of undertakings is the amount of driving time achieved from any given number of hours paid.[78] The aim is to maximize this driving time subject to various constraints embodied in formal or informal agreements on such things as spreadovers, signing on and signing off times, and running times.

Most undertakings in our sample, which used some measure of schedule efficiency as an indicator of performance, felt that there was little scope for any improvement without substantial renegotiation. Schedules were already drawn up in the most efficient manner

76. See, for example, the 1971 *Annual Report* of the NBC, 13.
77. Some undertakings have introduced computer scheduling though in some cases allowances are made for existing custom and practice rules which produce sub-optimal schedules.
78. Driving time as a percentage of hours paid varied across garages in the PTA from 60.3% to 76.8% in the case of crew drivers and from 64.1% to 81.6% in the case of OMO drivers. Other undertakings have often recorded lower percentages.

possible, given the constraints imposed by employees.[79] Hence the main way of increasing efficiency in this sense was by reducing union control over working practices.

The PIB summarized the provincial employers' submission on the 'restrictive practices' which affect duty scheduling thus:

The municipal employers report that it is not infrequent for the men to regard the slowest running times as the norm for all services; to press for excessive stand time; to restrict the length of duties or spells and the number, length and timing of split duties. The companies' list of scheduling restrictions is similar. It includes insistence that the old clocking on and off times should be adhered to despite improved starting of vehicles and modern ticket and paying-in systems, and unwillingness to operate more than a certain number of journeys on particular routes without relief or change-over. A few companies report refusal to accept reductions in the existing scheduled week. (NBPI Report No.16, Appendix D)

The PIB encouraged attempts to eliminate such practices and in most undertakings there have been attempts to secure some relaxation of these various controls through productivity agreements at local level.

The intensity and areas of union control vary considerably between different undertakings, and there is no simple explanation of why some union branches seek to exercise control where others are passive. There is, however, a tendency for the municipal undertakings to experience more union constraints than the company sector. This may reflect an ability on the part of the union to exercise tighter control in the larger depots and in more heavily industrialized areas.[80] On the other hand, NBC subsidiaries have been more ready to negotiate productivity agreements than municipal undertakings.[81] Because of the concentration of large urban depots outside

79. In some cases managements seem merely to assume that a constraint exists. In several undertakings in our sample, for example, it was claimed that unions would be opposed to the use of part-time labour even though its use had never actually been suggested.
80. It is, however, very difficult to generalize in this area. The degree of control and the type of control differ in different parts of the same undertakings, and there may be differences between union attitudes and the rank and file. In LT, for example, there was opposition for a considerable time by the rank and file to women drivers, though the union was in favour.
81. The PIB made a number of strong criticisms of the quality of management in municipal undertakings. Report No. 63, para. 73, for example, argued that 'inadequate management in some parts of the municipal bus industry has led to an accelerating loss of control over actual operation and above all over industrial relations.'

the NBC it is difficult to find evidence to support one hypothesis as against the other.[82]

Productivity bargaining has almost certainly contributed to the reduction of labour shortages in the bus industry, though the provision of bus services has not become any more efficient in a cost-minimizing sense; indeed Wabe and Coles (1975) have produced evidence which shows the reverse to be the case. Moreover, bus undertakings seldom attach the same importance to the elimination of restrictive practices as did the PIB. LT, for instance, did not envisage attempts to increase productivity as having any more than a minor role to play in the reduction of labour shortages.

7. Recruitment

In this section we consider the various ways in which undertakings try to attract more labour, other than by increasing pay or improving working conditions and fringe benefits.[83] The distinction was made in Chapter 2 between two ways in which the inflow of labour might be increased. An undertaking might induce more 'suitable' people to accept jobs or it might recruit people who were previously considered 'unsuitable'. Attracting more 'suitable' people will normally mean extending or intensifying recruitment activity but it could also involve providing more attractive terms of employment.

Recruitment Activity

To a certain extent, wage increases and recruitment advertising must be viewed as complementary adjustment instruments, for without some way of notifying potential recruits of a wage change its impact will be on wastage alone. However, the role of recruitment activity is broader than the mere notification of a change in wages to

82. Two of the more heterogeneous companies, Betabus and Gammabus, both indicated that the union exercised tighter control in the urban depots. However, the mainly urban NBC subsidiary, Townbus, had negotiated a more comprehensive productivity agreement than any undertaking in the NJIC.
83. While many managers expressed the desire to improve the working conditions and the fringe benefits of their employees, these were rarely seen as major instruments for dealing with shortages. However, there were two notable exceptions. In Section 2 we mentioned that high wastage was often attributed to a dislike of shift-working. The corollary of this is that there have been attempts to eliminate shortages by improving the working hours of busmen (see Section 4 and Appendix B). Secondly, assistance with housing has been given both to attract and retain staff (see p. 89 and footnote 85 in this section).

the outside world. Recruitment activity may be intensified or extended as a substitute for a change in wages, and hence it is considered here as a distinct adjustment instrument.

With the exception of Fishport, whose OMO policy had alleviated the shortage, all the undertakings we visited had advertised for staff in the local press, but the effectiveness of this varied a good deal. Most undertakings had used the DE exchanges for recruiting staff but in general the response was poor both in terms of quality and quantity, even during periods of high unemployment and when special campaigns were mounted at exchanges.[84] The outcome of this was a rather casual attitude to the reporting of vacancies — some undertakings had ceased to notify the DE of vacancies while others had a 'standing order'.

Staff shortages had led many undertakings to adopt more expensive methods of recruitment such as national press, cinema, and television advertising, open days, publicity vehicles, and overseas recruitment.[85] One notable exception was the PTA which despite a fairly serious staff shortage relied heavily on informal recruitment channels.[86] This policy stemmed from a prevailing assumption in the PTA that 'everyone knows there are vacancies', and hence the view that widespread advertising for staff would be superfluous.

However, a similar assumption prevailed in LT without it reducing the amount spent on advertising.[87] This is partly accounted for by LT experimenting in persuasive rather than merely informative advertising, but also by the advertising for staff performing an organizational role. The recruitment superintendent exemplified this when he said, 'we have to satisfy people that we are trying to recruit,' indicating that the number of people recruited was only one criterion of successful advertising. This was also the case in some of the smaller undertakings. The general manager at Hamborough said that he had advertised on Saturdays — a poor night to attract job

---

84. Thetabus noted some improvement in response, from a 'new-look' DE exchange.
85. Another expensive recruitment technique was used by Waring which offered council accommodation to new entrants. However, the lack of any guarantee that such entrants would stay with an undertaking and the length of council house waiting lists meant that this instrument was not adopted elsewhere.
86. The reliance on informal recruitment channels does not prevent an undertaking from increasing its recruitment expenditure — several undertakings paid their employees a fee for introducing new staff.
87. This assumption that everyone in London knew about vacancies should not of course restrict attempts to widen the area of recruitment.

searchers — to show the Transport Committee and the public that they were short of staff but trying hard to do something about it.

The lack of data prevented any rigorous test of the hypothesis that recruitment expenditure varied with the level of shortage,[88] though hearsay evidence for LT supported it. The choice of recruitment channel reflected an awareness of relative costs but depended more on folklore about relative effectiveness than any considered assessment of it. Moreover, there was no indication that undertakings weighed up the cost effectiveness of increased recruitment activity against other adjustments such as pay. Though LT's Operational Research Department had estimated the marginal wage cost of drivers, with a view to comparing it with the marginal cost of achieving a similar improvement through increased recruitment activity, there was no evidence that such results had been put into practice.

One device which LT had introduced as an adjustment to shortage was the opening up of recruitment at garage level. Until mid-1973 there were relatively few recruitment centres. Under the new system an applicant can ring an advertised number and be directed to a garage in his locality where he is interviewed by the garage manager. Part of the object of this style of recruitment is to prevent people being put off by having to travel to a recruitment centre, and to convey the impression that bus driving is a local job. However, garage recruitment also plays an organizational role in that it is designed to demonstrate the difficulty of recruitment to garage managers and to increase the incentive for them to reduce wastage. Judging by the accounts of garage managers, this system of local recruitment has met with some success. However, they gave the impression that they were more selective than the officers in the recruitment centres, and hence there may have been an unintended raising of hiring standards.

Part-time and Temporary Employment

Some bus undertakings have succeeded in tapping an additional source of labour through the provision of temporary or part-time employment.

There were two distinct ways in which temporary staff were used. Some undertakings take on students, usually as conductors, during summer vacations to cover the increased demand for staff when the

88. A seven-period time-series regression of advertising expenditure for staff on shortage for Easthampton gave a significant negative relationship, but data were not restricted to platform staff.

holiday allocation is heavy. This will only happen when there is a shortage of conductors and so can be considered as a direct adjustment to shortage. Such an instrument is relatively unconstrained but some managements and union branches dislike temporary staff who are said to lower morale and quality. Temporary staff are also employed in response to a seasonal peak in product demand. Drivers were taken on both by the independent coach operators, and by some of the undertakings operating in seaside resorts to cover summer holiday work. However, this is not strictly an adjustment to a shortage but rather a device to meet predictable demand fluctuations.

The use of part-time platform staff is very much complementary to providing more convenient hours of work for full-time staff. If the weekend can be covered by voluntary overtime and part-time staff, an undertaking only requires its full-time busmen to work from Monday to Friday. However, this adjustment tends to be resisted by the union. It has been introduced only as part of a major productivity agreement.[89] Managements as well as unions display hostility to the idea of part-time platform staff, as they are thought to involve a great deal of administrative effort in checking to see that the law relating to drivers' hours is observed. Also there is a fear that part-timers would not be as disciplined as full-time staff, since any sanctions are necessarily less severe. Moreover, many undertakings feel that they would not be able to attract enough part-time staff to work the rearranged duty systems. This apprehension on the part of management has been offset to some extent by NBC's encouragement of productivity agreements which provide for the employment of part-time staff. Indeed, the only undertakings in our sample which employed part-timers were NBC subsidiaries.

Hiring Standards and Entry Requirements

The hiring standards which an undertaking sets are usually concerned with the job-related attributes of applicants such as their ability to perform the job, their proneness to absenteeism and wastage, and the amount of training they require. However, these attributes are more or less unmeasurable at the time of the selection and so the employer will use a set of selection criteria to indicate the probability of an applicant meeting those hiring standards.

But even changes in selection criteria may be difficult to identify,

---

89. Appendix B on Alphabus outlines one such agreement in detail, and Section 8 outlines LT's use of part-time staff over retirement age.

as we are dealing not only with the formal requirements which are governed by explicit decisions but also with the preference and judgment of those responsible for day-to-day recruitment. Brooks distinguishes between formal and informal selection criteria in LT:

> Considerable emphasis was placed on tests in recruitment, and to that extent the process was a rational one; but there was a large area of subjectivity. Alongside the rationality of selection there coexisted a folklore amongst the recruitment staff: they could 'smell' a good potential busman or railwayman. (1975: 254)

A labour shortage can thus cause changes in selection criteria either through an explicit decision to relax requirements or through pressure on recruitment staff from other parts of the organization, leading to a modification in the informal criteria.

We make an explicit distinction between hiring standards and selection criteria because changes in the two do not always coincide. Where selection criteria express preferences rather than require-ments, a contraction in the supply of labour to the firm may cause a reduction in the average quality of recruits even though the selection criteria remain unchanged. Conversely, selection criteria may be modified as a means of increasing the number of recruits without any adjustment in hiring standards. This usually happens where an employer drops a formal entry requirement, replacing it with a more intensive (and hence more expensive) selection procedure.[90]

The main adverse effect of the undertaking which lowers its hiring standards is a decline in the quality of recruits. Often this merely results in a fall in labour productivity, increased training require-ments, absenteeism, or wastage — all of which can be readily assessed in terms of increased cost. However, in the service sector the quality of recruits may have a direct impact on the quality of the output, which may prove unacceptable to the organization. This feature makes it difficult to present the choice of adjustment instru-ments in terms of a simple cost-minimizing model.

Where selection criteria are adjusted without affecting the quality of recruits, the cost involved results from the increasing resources devoted to selection. Moreover, when an undertaking drops an entry requirement which reflects a bias rather than a genuine proxy for hiring standards, there will be no fall in quality but merely a loss in

---

90. See Doeringer and Piore (1971:102–6) for a rigorous treatment of this form of adjustment.

utility from ending a discriminatory employment policy, or the embarrassment of admitting one had discriminated in the past.[91]

Three main methods can be used to identify changes in selection criteria and hiring standards: one can ask employers when their selection criteria have been changed; one can try to assess whether there have been any changes in the quality of recruits; or one can examine movements in those characteristics of recruits which may reflect changes in selection criteria or hiring standards.

However, changes in the quality and characteristics of recruits may arise from variations in the quality and characteristics of applicants as well as changes in hiring standards and selection criteria. With this reservation in mind we turn to examining the application of these various methods of identification.

1. *Women.* For an industry which was one of the first to implement equal pay for women, some bus undertakings have been surprisingly slow to allow women to drive buses. It is usually the busmen themselves who resist change, but Easthampton's management still refuses to accept women drivers. Even some of those undertakings which do admit women drivers recruit them only from the ranks of conductresses while there is direct entry of male drivers. Undertakings tend not to think of the admission of women as a shortage adjustment but merely as an acknowledgement of growing sexual equality. The reason for this is that management seldom expects many women to apply for driving jobs, so that the effectiveness of the adjustment is small. It does, however, have a demonstration effect of the effort that is made to ease the shortage problem.

Where the recruitment of women was clearly a shortage adjustment was in the case of LT's recruitment of conductresses. Brooks recounts the story:

Although women conductors were employed from the early days of the Second World War this was seen as a temporary expedient for the 'duration of the emergency'; ultimately, the Department would return to its pre-war situation of an all-male operating staff. Some women conductors were discharged in the early post-war years, but it soon became apparent that it was not possible to maintain an all-male staff at existing wages and conditions and the women conductors who had been discharged were invited to return in 1949. (1975: 56–7)

91. By the term 'discrimination' we mean what Chiplin and Sloane call 'pure market discrimination'. This they define as 'any form of unequal treatment between . . . [distinguishable groups of] employees which does not result in cost-minimisation in monetary terms in relation to labour utilization' (1974: 381).

This was a classic example of the use of a temporary adjustment on which the undertaking became heavily dependent and which it found impossible to reverse.

2. *Re-engagement.* Limitations on re-engaging staff normally form part of an undertaking's selection criteria, the aim being to reduce wastage and avoid the unsettling effect of people repeatedly leaving and returning. In some undertakings there is a formal requirement that permits only first-time re-engagements, while in others the recruitment officers scrutinize applicants for re-engagement in greater depth than new applicants. Undertakings with pronounced seasonal fluctuations tended to encourage temporary drivers to return each year at the beginning of the summer season. However, the concern of most *bus* undertakings is to prevent an outflow to the more attractive coach driving during the summer by removing the provision of secure employment in the winter.

There have been a number of adjustments concerning re-engagements. Newcaster responded to a tight market by accepting second-time as well as first-time re-engagements. Easthampton had moved in the reverse direction during the easy market situation of 1970 by henceforth taking only first re-engagements. Here it was felt that they would not wish to relax this requirement if there was a shortage but they acknowledged that they might be forced to do so. Waring was one of the few bus undertakings which would re-engage anyone whose previous service had been satisfactory, saying: 'We could not afford to have a rule of this kind [restricting re-engagement].' LT was one of those undertakings which had no set rules on re-engagements but it was clear from their statistics that the proportion of applicants for re-engagement who were accepted varied directly with the extent of the driver shortage.[92]

3. *Immigrants.* While we came across no cases of colour bars operating in bus undertakings, one undertaking held explicit preferences

92. Data were available on the proportion of re-engagements that were accepted, but were for all grades together. This was regressed on conductor and driver shortfall and requirements (i.e. 4 regressions); the coefficient on conductor shortfall was positive and significant at the 5% level, the coefficient on driver shortfall was positive and almost significant at the 5% level. The coefficient on driver requirements was positive but not significant at the 10% level and that on conductor requirements was negative and not significant. But even where these coefficients were significant, the R^2 was never greater than 0.1. However, this is consistent with a certain level of shortage inducing a non-marginal change in re-engagement policy.

which meant that non-whites were at the back of the queue. The order of preference was whites, West Indians, Indians, and Pakistanis, which reflected a belief that those higher up the queue were more likely to make good busmen. In other undertakings it was clear that the Irish and black immigrant women were unpopular because they were 'poor risks', in that they tended to have high wastage and absenteeism.

The question of race in LT has been the subject of an academic study. Brooks (1975) has made it clear that the original decision to recruit coloured immigrants and even go to the West Indies to do so was a deliberate adjustment to deal with the labour shortage. This instrument was originally constrained by the delegate conference, but resistance after the 1958 strike was negligible.

However, Brooks does point to the continued existence of a racial factor in the informal selection criteria. Following on from his observation of a folklore amongst recruitment staff that they could 'smell' a good busmen, he says:

That they were all ex-operating staff, all white, was probably important in that — intentionally or not — they favoured applicants who were seen to conform closest to the image of the traditional London Transport employee. There was nothing in the data collected during the 'typical week' to indicate deliberate discrimination against coloured applicants, but in some respects the cards were stacked against them.[93]

Data were available on the numbers of West Indians recruited into each grade, enabling one to derive a proportion of that grade's recruits who were West Indians.[94] These proportions were regressed on both the shortfall measure and the requirement measure of staff shortage for the particular grade. For drivers and male conductors the relationship is positive and significant for both measures of shortage. However, on closer examination it became apparent that these correlations were brought about by variations in the racial mix of the labour supply or non-racial changes in selection criteria.[95]

4. *Selection criteria.* A number of undertakings admitted varying their selection criteria with the state of the labour market or

93. (1975: 254). During our study in 1973 we noticed some West Indian recruitment staff.
94. One is not sure how to interpret the classification 'West Indian' — it may be used as a shorthand for a range of ethnic groups. We think it is justifiable to relate this to the proportion of new Commonwealth immigrants in an area.
95. For a detailed discussion of this see Deaton (1976).

with the extent of their own labour shortage. Often such an admission took the positive form of saying that advantage was taken of a mild shortage to raise hiring standards. Others such as Hamborough paid less attention to appearance, presentation, and references when the market was tight.

LT tended to use easily identifiable selection criteria when labour was abundant, and more intensive selection as it became scarce.[96] The PTA and Easthampton relaxed the requirements that recruits must have lived within a specified distance of the garage for a certain length of time. Clement's Coaches had previously insisted on three years' experience as a PSV driver and replaced this with the requirement that entrants should have PSV licences.

In general, however, we came across no case where the undertaking had relaxed formal requirements knowing that the quality of service would fall. The typical attitude was that prevalent in the PTA. Hiring standards were maintained because it was felt by personnel officers that the cost of hiring lower-quality staff (in terms of absenteeism, poor time-keeping, and wastage) outweighed any benefits from reducing the shortage on paper.

5. *Quality.* But, despite the lack of evidence of any serious relaxation in hiring standards, there was a widespread opinion that the quality of busmen had fallen in recent years. Our asking questions about the changes in quality of recruits invariably triggered anecdotes from managers to illustrate how quality had fallen. Older managers talked nostalgically about how busmen used to take a real pride in their appearance while others pointed to long hair. Some of these expressions merely reflected employers' attitudes to our permissive society but it is clear that there are busmen employed today who would not have been tolerated in the high unemployment pre-war era.

To a certain extent the mythology of the traditional busmen has rubbed off on to the union, and hence the narrowness of the conductor/driver differential in the face of the ease of recruiting conductors as compared with drivers has been defended by the union emphasizing 'the selectivity of staff is not what it was . . . let us be in a position to attract some of the best men from the labour market so that there can be built up an experienced and disciplined force of conductors as in days of yore' (Phelps Brown Report, 1964: para. 65).

96. In the terminology adopted in Chapter 5, this represents a change from 'qualifying' selection to 'exploratory' selection. It is unnecessary, however, to make an explicit distinction in this chapter, because the third type — 'rank' selection — is not applied to bus drivers.

The fact remains that bus undertakings are reluctant to lower the quality of their staff or services. Any changes that have taken place have been gradual ones spread over the post-war period.

6. *Queueing and training.* While racial preference has been mentioned in the case of one undertaking, by far the most common preference patterns are for more experienced drivers. Thus in the selection process someone with a PSV licence is at the top of the queue and is followed by those with professional driving experience, car drivers, and those with only provisional licences. As the market tightens, an undertaking will tend to take on people further down the queue. However, this does not imply that the quality of service is reduced because differences in experience tend to be compensated for by increased training.[97] There are limitations on the working of this queue theory which are exemplified in LT where recruitment officers only engage applicants who they believe will stay long enough to justify the training costs. Such a consideration constrains the direct recruitment of provisional-licence holders into driver training because of the fear the undertaking has of being used as a driving school for other employers or private motoring.[98]

There were scarcely any cases of training capacity limiting the number of non-PSV licence holders who could be recruited. Various devices could be used to increase training capacity. OMO or 'type' training can be delayed, the number of trainees on each bus can be increased, extra instructors can be brought in from the inspector and driving grades, and some training schools even borrow buses from the service pool between peak periods. This involves converting a bus for training in the morning and reconverting it for service in the afternoon. The only undertaking which had found itself with a training-capacity constraint was Gammabus which had to halt a special recruitment drive because it had already filled the training school.

Where training length for drivers is increased beyond fifteen days, or if more than two trainees are put on each bus, the RTITB ceases to pay grants to cover training costs. This is a mild disincentive to increasing training capacity or length but it did not appear to have stopped undertakings making these adjustments when faced with a shortage.

97. In this respect the employers of draughtsmen closely reflected the behaviour of employers in the bus industry.
98. LT made this adjustment at the time of writing.

There was no evidence that LT took greater risks[99] in selecting trainees when there was a shortage: there was no significant relationship between the wastage rate during training and the level of shortage. This was true for drivers and conductors and for both measures of shortage.

Conclusions

The variation of recruitment techniques is perhaps the least constrained adjustment that an employer has open to him, and many undertakings readily increased their recruitment expenditure in response to shortage of labour. There was, however, little evidence of any attempt to compare the cost of advertising with the costs of other adjustment instruments. Indeed, quite often job advertising was taken beyond the point where it stopped being cost-effective. Such action is best explained in terms of strong adherence to an output target.

There has been a great reluctance amongst employers in the bus industry to lower hiring standards which might reduce the quality of the services they provide. This attitude has also militated against the widespread use of part-time staff. However, the existence of shortages has led to modifications in those selection criteria which were designed to minimize wastage, absenteeism, and training costs. The realities of the labour market have forced managers to accept staff who do not conform to their image of ideal busmen.

8. Adjustments to Reduce Outflows of Labour

An undertaking has under its control a number of devices which can be used specifically as a means of reducing outflows of labour. It may for instance respond to a labour shortage by reducing its dismissals standards, increasing its maximum age for retirement, charging for training, entering into non-poaching agreements, or discouraging quitters by taking away their chance of re-engagement.

One might expect that an undertaking's policy on dismissals would be relaxed when there was a labour shortage. Indeed, a few of the managers we interviewed believed that their undertakings were less firm on lateness when there was a shortage. However, we found no significant relationship between the dismissal rate and the level of

99. One might suppose that a shortage would induce an undertaking to lower its entry standards for training without lowering the pass standard. Such a move would increase the failure (and hence wastage) rate during training.

shortage for either LT or Easthampton which were the two under-takings where such data were available. To a certain extent the existence of formal dismissals procedures constrained the use of this adjustment. In addition the concern with the quality of the service which was noted in the previous section meant that the benefit from a reduction in the outflow tended to be offset by the cost of retaining unsuitable staff.

An adjustment which does not create the same problems of quality deterioration is the increasing of the retirement age. Several under-takings in our survey had decided to allow staff to remain in service after the age of 65 as an adjustment to shortage. LT, whose policy of considering applications for staff to remain in employment until the age of 70 had been in existence for some time, took the step of encour-aging its older platform staff to continue after the age of 65 by providing part-time employment for them. Other undertakings, in particular the PTA, induced more older staff to stay on by providing a rota of easier duties for them.

Another device designed to discourage wastage was the use of a training bond. In many undertakings a recruit who is trained for driving is required to enter into a bond with the company under which he will pay a certain sum if he leaves before completing a certain length of service. In the undertakings covered, the sum was normally between £12 and £25 and the time ranged from a nominal period of service to a year, though one undertaking charged £50 for someone who was trained from having no car driving licence and left within two years. However, the training bond failed in most cases to deter leavers. A number of managers realized this and were contem-plating an increase in the bond.

The remaining two adjustments which could be employed to lower the quit rate had the additional effect of reducing the number of recruits, and therefore were only viable in particular circumstances. One such adjustment was the adoption of a policy which forbade the re-engagement of anyone who had left the undertaking more than once (or in some cases twice). The aim of such a policy was to dis-courage the cautious leaver who knew there was a safe job to come back to. In particular, it was designed to prevent an annual move to the more lucrative coach-driving jobs at the beginning of the summer and a return to the more secure bus-driving jobs in the winter. However, there is much to be gained in the short-run in the form of increased recruitment by relaxing such re-engagement rules. Our evidence suggested that rule-breaking was much more common than rule-making in times of labour shortage and hence that the crisis reaction was stronger than the rational cost-minimizing strategy.

A similar type of adjustment was the establishment of a non-poaching agreement. This could be expected to reduce both wastage and recruitment. From our survey it appeared that breaking or rescinding a non-poaching agreement was a more common reaction to a labour shortage than the creation of new ones. During the sixties about half of the undertakings had had a non-poaching agreement with at least one other employer in the bus industry, but only one of these remained by the time we interviewed. Several more, though, had been established on the formation of the NBC. Again we see undertakings adopting a policy which means an immediate recruitment gain at the expense of an increase in the outflow of labour.

None of these devices which affect the outflow of labour has had a sizeable impact on a labour shortage. However, their use demonstrates a number of things about the undertaking's reaction to a labour shortage. Firstly, the adjustment which is made sometimes reflects the optimum for the department which controls that instrument rather than the optimum for the undertaking as a whole. Secondly, the concern with quality which was noted in the previous section is apparent here in the reluctance to relax dismissals policy in the face of a shortage.

9. Internal Labour Markets in the Bus Industry

Our primary area of interest in this chapter has been bus drivers, and we have considered conductors only in so far as they affect drivers. In this respect our approach is different from other investigators, notably the PIB, who treated busmen as more or less homogeneous. The relationship between drivers' and conductors' markets carries important implications for the use of OMO as an adjustment instrument. In this section we consider this relationship and examine the effects of a shortage on the operation of the internal labour market. We deal with mobility between grades of platform staff, the deployment of non-platform staff for platform duties, and the transfer of staff between garages.

The Promotion of Conductors to Drivers

In the past, several of our undertakings had not recruited drivers directly but drew mainly on their own conductors. When faced with a driver shortage, the employers' tendency was to open a port of entry to the driver grade. Some undertakings went further and recruited driver/operators directly but this port of entry was opened more in response to increasing OMO than as an adjustment to shortage in its own right. Of the undertakings we visited, only Granchester and Newcaster had no direct entry to the driving grade, but in the case of Newcaster an experienced driver would have only a nominal service as a conductor before being promoted.

One of the assumptions of the PIB's view of OMO was that it would induce more conductors to go forward for driver training. This assumption appeared to be true for LT. There was a significant positive relationship between the level of OMO and the percentage of driver recruits who had been conductors, and the percentage of male conductors becoming drivers.[100]

It was normal for the union to impose a restriction on the direct entry of drivers to ensure that there was always a certain minimum proportion of conductors in driver training. There was, however, pressure from management to keep the proportion of conductors in driver training down when there was a stock shortage and a reasonable supply of direct entrants.

In LT, the number of conductors promoted to driver was small relative to total conductor wastage. The quarterly averages for the period 1966–73 were 1 per cent and 7 per cent respectively of the number of male conductors employed. For the same period only one in six entrants to the driving grade came from the ranks of conductor. It was part of a folklore of the undertaking that the link between drivers' and conductors' markets was closer than this. So, despite its preference for a wider differential between drivers' and conductors' wages, management had consistently given in to the busmen's insistence on flat-rate increases, with adjustment to the relative scarcities being made through changes in hiring standards.[101]

It is normally more difficult to recruit drivers than conductors. Hence one possible adjustment to a driver shortage is to recruit only those conductors who can be considered as potential drivers. A number of undertakings faced with a shortage of drivers insisted that new conductors had at least a car driving licence. However, the state of the labour market, the extent of OMO, and the size of the conductor shortage will also be relevant in setting the hiring standards of conductors.

100. The equations using quarterly data from 1966 I to 1973 II were:

$$CD/\text{Driver Entrants} = 13.8 \quad + \ 0.292 \ OMO. \qquad R^2 = 0.306$$
$$\phantom{CD/\text{Driver Entrants} = } (9.74) \quad (3.51) \qquad\qquad DW = 1.02$$

$$CD/\text{Male Conductors} = \quad 1.07 + \ 0.0177 \ OMO. \qquad R^2 = 0.264$$
$$\phantom{CD/\text{Male Conductors} = } (11.2) \quad (3.17) \qquad\qquad DW = 0.98$$

CD is the number of conductors becoming drivers.

101. In fact the differential between drivers' and conductors' basic rates was increased from 90p to £1.15 in the August 1974 settlement.

Since women only became eligible for bus driving jobs in LT after this study was carried out, we were able to assess the influence of these various factors on the recruitment of conductors by taking the proportion of conductor recruits who were female as an inverse proxy for the extent to which conductors were recruited as potential drivers.

This was done by testing the hypothesis that the female proportion of conductor recruits (*FCR*) varied with the driver shortage, the conductor shortage, the extent of OMO, and the relative states of the male and female labour markets. The expected signs of the regression coefficients were:

Driver shortage	$X(DR)$	−
Conductor shortage	$X(CN)$	+
Male vacancies in GLC areas	VM	+
Female vacancies in GLC areas	VF	−
OMO establishment as a percentage of driver establishment	OMO	−

These expectations are based on the assumption that a driver shortage and OMO will induce an undertaking to concentrate on recruiting males who can be trained for driving, while a conductor shortage offsets this tendency.

In the regressions, *OMO* consistently came out with a significant negative coefficient, whatever other variables were added. The two shortage variables were fairly highly correlated ($r = 0.880$) and often appeared to be picking up each other's variations.[102] The most satisfactory results were found when the conductor shortage variable was omitted:

$$FCR = 19.0 \quad - \quad 0.225X(DR) - \quad 0.000399VF$$
$$ (5.84) \quad (-1.80) \quad\quad\quad (-1.63)$$
$$ + \; 0.000698VM - \quad 0.4490MO. \quad\quad R^2 = 0.830$$
$$ (3.77) \quad\quad\quad (-5.26) \quad\quad\quad DW = 2.08$$

102. When all five variables were used they gave the equation:

$$FCR = 21.8 \quad + \; 0.163\,X(DR) - \quad 0.485\,X(CN) - \quad 0.000478\;VF$$
$$ (6.19) \quad (0.64) \quad\quad\quad (-1.73) \quad\quad\quad (-1.99)$$
$$ + \, 0.000690\;VM - \quad 0.484\;OMO. \quad\quad R^2 = 0.849$$
$$ (3.88) \quad\quad\quad (-5.72) \quad\quad\quad\quad DW = 2.38$$

Here the coefficient on driver shortage was not significant, and that on conductor shortage was negative contrary to expectation. Removing the driver shortage variable still left conductor shortage with a negative sign. Therefore we retained the driver shortage variable and removed the conductor shortage variable.

One can conclude that LT reduces its intake of women conductors as OMO increases and when driver shortage becomes more acute, but does not relax this 'discrimination' in the face of conductor shortage. This statement cannot be made very strongly, however, because of the high correlation between the two shortage variables and the number of 'wrong signs' that appear.

The Use of Non-platform Staff for Platform Duties

The constraints which apply to the use of part-timers are to a certain extent present if management wishes to use inside or clerical staff to carry out platform duties. However, the union constraint is less severe. Although union resistance to the use of part-timers and inside staff tended to occur together, there were a few cases of the union being prepared to accept inside staff but not part-timers. From management's point of view, the administrative problems of dealing with part-timers such as the legal requirement to check that drivers'-hours regulations were observed were not present in using their own employees for platform duties.

About two-thirds of the undertakings used inside staff, though it was rare for employers to train non-platform staff so that they could perform the occasional duty. The size of this adjustment therefore depended on the numbers of non-platform staff who happened to have PSV licences.   ·

Transfer of Staff

For the larger undertakings the existence of more than one garage added a spatial dimension to the internal labour market. The transfer of staff to a garage where shortage is more acute can be seen as an adjustment to shortage, as it makes vacancies on the whole easier to fill. A similar effect can be realized by shifting routes to garages where shortage is less severe.

A few municipal undertakings have an agreement whereby an employee can be required to work from any garage, but this is normally to increase scheduling efficiency and does not cause any significant geographical shift of labour.

Both Alphabus and LT experimented with bussing staff between garages but discontinued the practice because it was too costly. However, there was no evidence to suggest that the cost of bussing was compared with alternative costs of relieving a shortage.

An undertaking is rarely in a position to effect the compulsory transfer of staff, and such management-determined transfer has only been possible where a garage has been closed, reduced in size, or completely converted to OMO.

Changes in the structure of routes must be considered too difficult administratively to be a serious policy-contender. One manager in LT advocated the closing of all garages in central London and moving the starting-points of routes further out. He realized, however, that he could never propose such a radical policy. If nothing else, it would involve an unacceptable fall in scheduling efficiency. Some undertakings had made minor changes along these lines, but it was not a general practice.

The least constrained method of redressing an uneven geographical distribution of labour is by inducing people to transfer. As it is rare for garages within easy commuting distance to have significantly different levels of shortage, effective transfer of staff requires residential change. LT's housing policy attempts to redistribute staff to this end. It has nomination rights for some hundred GLC houses and, to fill the conditions for nomination, staff have to be working in a garage with an acute shortage or be willing to move to one. Redistribution of staff may also be achieved at the recruitment stage. LT found overseas recruitment attractive partly because it believed that immigrants could more readily be placed in the garages with worst shortage. Recruitment policy is sometimes designed to place people in the problem garages but there may be danger in pursuing this policy at the expense of recruitment overall.

Conclusion

We have seen that a closed internal market for platform staff was fairly common in the past, but that shortages have tended to open a port of entry to the driver grade. Indeed, in the present situation one must consider the markets for conductors and drivers separately rather than a market for busmen collectively. However, the importance of the link between conductors' and drivers' markets is shown by the evidence that LT and other undertakings raise the hiring standards of conductors when there is a shortage of drivers.

The use of non-platform staff for platform duties when the undertaking is short of the requisite sort of labour is a fairly common practice because of the convenience and relative cheapness of this form of adjustment, and the fact that it is relatively unconstrained by the union.

The geographical transfer of staff might be an ideal adjustment to an imbalanced shortage over different garages. However, it requires some ingenuity on the part of management to induce its staff to move to the areas where it needs them most.

10. Service Cuts

One of the ways of overcoming a labour shortage is to reduce the desired quantity of labour services by curtailing output. This is a frequent short-run response in manufacturing industry where output plans may not be fulfilled as a result of labour shortages and where there may be longer-term cutbacks in the planned rate of production. In the case of bus undertakings there are severe difficulties in making similar reductions. In a service industry, where there are no inventories to act as a buffer, any cutting of services is felt directly by the public.

However, there are a few minor ways in which output was reduced without affecting scheduled services. First, there have been attempts on the part of some undertakings to persuade other employers in the area to stagger their working hours and so reduce peak-hour demand. This has had some success in Hamborough where a high proportion of office staff now work flexi-time. Second, though the licensing system does not permit the sub-contracting of stage carriage and express services, some undertakings faced with staff shortage have released contract work and curtailed their efforts to secure additional services.[103]

Formal cutting of services is therefore rarely used[104] as a positive adjustment to shortage, but informal cuts in services are frequently used as a residual adjustment. Almost all the undertakings in our sample made unscheduled cuts in services because other adjustments failed to eliminate shortages. This type of service cut is usually done at the discretion of inspectors on duty who make hour-to-hour appraisals of the situation and decide which particular services

103. Townbus proved an interesting exception to this. The general manager was very reluctant to release private hire work because he saw this as an opportunity to improve drivers' job satisfaction. If he heard of someone who was likely to leave because of dissatisfaction with driving as a job, he would book them for a few long-distance coach journeys.
104. There are, however, a few instances of formal service cuts because of shortage. Two of the undertakings in our sample admitted to having done this. In general it is difficult to assess whether services have been reduced because of staff shortage or because they became uneconomic. The two reasons for service cuts may be inter-related since a route with a persistent staff shortage will provide an unreliable service and may lose passengers. A crude attempt was made to test the hypothesis that staff shortages had led to service cuts in LT. The decline in driver establishments between 1968 I and 1972 IV was regressed on driver shortage for 1968 across LT garages. There was a positive association which was not significant at the 10% level.

should be withdrawn,[105] though in some undertakings there are company-wide guidelines as to when services should be cut. LT, for example, has a fleet-level target to cover all services if shortages are less than 9 per cent and for the percentage miles lost to be 9 per cent less than the shortage. In some instances the informal cuts have occurred with such regularity that they have become formalized.[106] Though shortages of platform staff are a cause of many service cuts,[107] it should be stressed that there are other causes of lost mileage, some of which have been far more important in recent years. The results of our survey suggested that, with the exception of LT, fewer miles were lost in 1973 because of platform staff shortage than because of the lack of vehicles and the shortages of spare parts and fitters.[108]

Thus service cuts do occur but the amount of public resentment they cause gives a greatly exaggerated impression of the extent to which they are a response to platform staff shortages. The objective of maintaining output was generally strongly adhered to. This may be because of the context of declining demand for services which means that traffic lost is unlikely to be recovered. Furthermore, there is evidence to suggest that demand for bus services is elastic with respect to the quality of the service, an important element of which is reliability.[109]

However, the strength of adherence to this output objective varied between undertakings. While in our PTA we observed an overriding

105. The criteria used to decide which service should be withdrawn vary though it is generally the practice to reduce the frequency on less heavily used routes. This gives rise to charges of unreliability of services and is frequently blamed as a cause of lost demand for services and the switch to other modes of transport.
106. NBPI Report No. 50, Appendix A, 35, noted that there have been occasions when 'a number of journeys which were habitually not worked due to staff shortage were dropped from the schedules, and this has contributed something to the decline in notional shortage'. More recently LT has avoided extensive cuts on the same service because of the implication that the service is unnecessary.
107. This was acknowledged by the NBC. See their *Annual Report* (1972), 12. In the case of London, driver shortage is a significant explanatory variable for percentage miles lost as the following cross-section result shows:

$$\% \text{ miles lost} = -327.64 + 78.64 \ X(D73) \qquad R^2 = 0.703$$
$$(-2.43) \quad (12.39)$$

where $X(D73)$ is the shortfall from driver establishment in June 1973.
108. A shortage of fully maintained buses is likely to have more of an effect on peak services than on others since these are the ones which require the maximum number of buses.
109. See for instance Thomson and Hunter (1973: 284–5).

concern to provide a public service and the imperative that lost mileage must be avoided at all costs, others such as Lambdabus preferred to cancel services rather than allow any rise in costs. Though all public-sector bus undertakings are set a financial objective as well as being required to run a public service, these formal objectives often conflict. In general, as mentioned earlier, NBC subsidiaries are subject to tighter financial control than those undertakings which are responsible to local authorities. Moreover, local-authority subsidies in the company sector are restricted to specific rural services, while urban-based municipal undertakings may receive a general subsidy from the rates. Hence, there tends to be stronger adherence to the output objective in the municipal sector and amongst PTAs.

11. Conclusions

The bus industry has experienced both declining product demand and shortages of labour in the post-war period. Though the use of establishment figures serves to confuse the measurement of a shortage, there is little doubt that shortages have been felt from time to time, and in some cases they have persisted over long periods.

Section 2 has outlined how the causes to which employers attribute a shortage affect the choice of adjustment instrument. It described the possible adjustment instruments in the bus industry, the extent to which they are inter-related or constrained, and the various objectives which undertakings try to achieve. The subsequent discussion of the instruments themselves has developed this framework and here we draw together a number of strands which help to explain the ultimate choice of adjustment.

A striking feature of the market is the limited role that wage changes play in the process of adjustment to shortages. There are a number of reasons for this. Pay is in general set by negotiations whose areas of jurisdiction are rarely coincident with areas of similar market pressure. Attempts to increase relative pay have either meant breaking away from the national negotiating structure or, in the case of the company sector, concluding some sort of productivity agreement. Moreover, bus undertakings have been wary of granting large pay increases which might result in major fare increases and endanger the already falling demand for bus services. Incomes policies have also constrained the use of pay as an adjustment. Furthermore, there seems to be a widespread management view that unless pay is out of line with comparable groups, particularly semi-skilled occupations in the locality, any shortage must be caused by a non-monetary factor such as a dislike of shiftwork. Thus pay increases have rarely been used aggressively as an adjustment instrument, but when so used they have tended to be large. Pressure builds up for pay increases against these various constraints and when the dam is broken the effect is substantial.

However, the market does respond to shortages through the use of other instruments which affect the pay of busmen. Hours and OMO are the prime examples of this. Indeed, hours have been used as an adjustment in two ways — to get more work done by the existing labour force, and to increase the supply of busmen by increasing average weekly earnings. The variations in hours which we observed were consistent with the predictions of a cost-minimizing model, but it was clear that the simple cost-minimizing model failed to explain several aspects of the way employers adjusted overtime levels.

OMO can be introduced to reduce costs or as an instrument of adjustment to labour shortage. However, we attribute the prevalence of OMO to problem-solving rather than cost-minimizing behaviour. Though the PIB saw OMO as a device to use existing manpower more efficiently, its major role in shortage alleviation has been as a means of increasing the pay of drivers without causing fare increases.

In studying the use or non-use of the various non-wage adjustments, we have revealed some of those factors which influence employers' behaviour. Most undertakings have adopted expensive advertising and recruitment techniques in response to labour shortage, but often as a quasi-political device rather than as a genuine attempt to attract more staff. Indeed, there was no evidence that there was any overt cost-effectiveness comparison between expensive recruitment techniques and other adjustment instruments. Although the NBC's encouragement has led a number of its subsidiaries to employ part-time platform staff, the cost-minimizing model will tend to overpredict the use of this adjustment. Part-time employees are believed to impose a heavy administrative burden, evoke hostility from the union, and reduce the quality of the workforce.

Employers in the bus industry have been reluctant to reduce any hiring standards which might reduce the quality of the service they provide. However, the realities of the labour market have sometimes forced them to accept staff who do not conform to their image of ideal busmen. Thus we have seen an increase in the employment of women, immigrants, re-entrants, and those who do not possess a 'loyalty to the industry'. Where adjustments in hiring standards have played an important role is in adjusting to the shortage of drivers relative to that of conductors. Most undertakings have responded by opening a port of entry to the driver grade, and several have raised the hiring standards of conductors.

There is a reluctance to reduce services which reflects this same concern with the quality of service provided. However, where mileage is regularly lost, the same aim is translated into a desire to stop the situation getting any worse: hence the concern over the flow balance.

We have been faced with the problem of explaining why, in an industry with uniform technology which is predominantly publicly owned, different employers have adopted different responses when faced with the problem of labour shortage. Part of the explanation lies in the emphasis given to the twin objectives of financial viability and the provision of a public service. For, despite an apparent uniformity in objectives, undertakings owned by local authorities have tended to stress the need for a public service whereas NBC subsidiaries have been more concerned with achieving the financial objectives. In addition to this, the constraints within which undertakings must act, whether they stem from local conditions or union action, vary to a considerable extent.

Although we can point to examples of cost-minimizing behaviour in the way bus undertakings respond to labour shortages, it is important to allow for the complexities of the decision-making process when building a cost-minimizing model which is capable of prediction. We have shown that the various constraints which managements face play a crucial role in determining the adjustments made, and these must enter the cost-minimizing model. The model must also handle situations where the objectives which are pursued by managers vary between undertakings. Furthermore, one has to utilize the notion of the undertaking as a complex organization, as opposed to a single rational decision-maker, in order fully to explain the action which is observed.

4
School Teachers

The market for school teachers has many administered features which have a strong influence on the way the adjustment mechanisms work. In this respect it differs from many other labour markets though it is representative of the markets for several public service white-collar groups such as nurses, doctors, and police, who work in industries which, like education, have an output which is extremely difficult to define and measure and where product prices are not charged.

Some of the major characteristics of the teachers' market are outlined in the first section, and then the nature and extent of shortages are discussed in Section 2. This is followed by an analysis of the adjustments which have been used: first in general terms and then in detail in Sections 3–9. Some interpretations and conclusions are given in Section 10.

Our concern in this chapter is with responses which have been made to shortages, though at the time of writing the position in the teachers' market as a whole does not appear to be one of shortage. There is now a surplus, and in this respect the situation differs markedly from the rest of the post-war period when the problem was one of teacher shortages. It is still true that in some localities, and in some subject groups, difficulties occur in attracting sufficient teachers to meet demand, but overall this is not the case. Newly trained teachers are finding it harder to obtain jobs, at least in their preferred localities, and some teacher unemployment has emerged. The DES has drastically reduced the rate of growth of training places and there has been some closure and merger of training colleges.

The teacher unemployment and the college cutbacks are in fact on a limited scale but the contrast with the earlier period of shortage is sharp. What is interesting is the way the shortages were transformed into a surplus. This has largely been due to the responses made to shortages though there have been exogenous factors such as the fall in the birth rate. However, since we are primarily interested in responses to shortage, this chapter will concentrate on the post-war period up to the early 1970s.

1. The Main Characteristics of the Teachers' Market

Teachers form one of the largest identifiable groups in the highly qualified labour force but the homogeneity of the group is often exaggerated. There is in fact a wide range of academic qualifications, with at one extreme teachers having good honours degrees and post-graduate qualifications, and at the other teachers who have completed a two-year course of training which they entered on the basis of Ordinary Level passes in the General Certificate of Education. This spread of educational attainments is probably greater than for other professions and leads to a variety of reference groups, aspirations, and transfer earnings. Moreover, there is a high proportion of women in teaching,[1] and this affects teacher supply and mobility. The re-entry pool becomes important and gives rise to a cycle of training, employment, wastage, and re-entry.

A number of sub-markets can be distinguished on the basis of a lack of substitutability between certain teachers, and differing relationships with the wider labour market, but a general view of the market is taken here and the discussion focuses on the national level.

The organization of the education industry is complex. There are many different levels at which decisions concerning adjustments to excess supply or demand are made: the DES, the LEAs, the school, and the individual teacher. Decision-makers at these different levels may be concerned with different things. This is consistent with a monopsony model where national wage negotiators set wages at a level which still leaves LEAs with shortages.

Responsibility for the provision of education lies at local level with the LEAs, though they operate within a framework set at national level and much of their spending is mandatory with considerable centralization of financial control. Teachers are hired and employed by LEAs but their pay is set nationally and, though teacher training colleges are run at local level, the scale of training facilities is set nationally, and the forecasting of teacher

---

1. In 1970 about 60% of the stock of teachers was female. In primary schools the proportion was 74% and in the secondary schools it was 41%.

'requirements' is in national terms. Many of the day-to-day decisions about the employment of teachers — such as the extent to which the part-time teachers will be used and the deployment of staff within schools — are taken locally, but most of the major adjustments are initiated at a national level. Furthermore, most of the administered features of the market are set nationally.

Education is a growth industry. Education expenditure by central and local government authorities increased from about 3 per cent of GNP in 1951 to about 6.5 per cent in 1972, and there has been a marked growth in the number of teachers and pupils. The stock of teachers in service has increased at a faster pace than the working population as a whole. In 1970 there were 327,000 teachers in maintained schools, half in primary schools and half in secondary schools. This contrasts sharply with the position in 1950 when the proportions were about two-thirds and one-third respectively. Most of the growth has thus been in secondary schools, especially in the late 1950s when the immediate post-war population bulge was passing through the secondary schools. The number of pupils also grew rapidly — by 41 per cent between 1950 and 1970. In 1970 about 62 per cent of pupils were in primary schools and 38 per cent in secondary schools.

This rapid expansion in the number of pupils and teachers has been accompanied by a continual pressure for improvements in the quality of service provided. Thus quantitative and qualitative advance have been major features of post-war education history.

The definition of the teachers' market, for the present purposes, is school teachers in state-maintained primary and secondary schools. The exclusion of teachers in further and higher education sectors is justifiable on the grounds that they are paid on separate salary scales with different negotiating machinery, they belong to different unions, and their work is usually of a different character requiring different qualifications. There is, of course, no hard-and-fast line to be drawn in the nature of the work especially between colleges of further education and the upper forms of secondary schools, but the mobility of teachers between these two is limited. A more important group of teachers excluded are those outside the schools maintained by the state. (In 1970 about 82 per cent of the teachers were in maintained schools.) Information is, however, difficult to obtain on some aspects of the private sector and since the machinery for determining salaries, the minimum certification requirements, the desired teacher–pupil ratio, and other features of the public sector differ from those of the private sector, attention will be confined to teachers in maintained schools.

2. The Shortage of Teachers

In Chapter 2 a distinction was drawn between 'establishments' based on formal norms and 'demand' based on working norms. The situation in the case of the teachers' market is complicated by the fact that there are, as already noted, different levels at which decisions concerning the use of various adjustment instruments are made. At national level, for example, decisions are made about the extent of any expansion of training college facilities; at LEA level, decisions are made about the extent to which part-time teachers will be used; and at school level 'a head master, for instance, determines how his staff are deployed and whether he is prepared to accept over-sized classes among younger children in order to widen the range of options available in the sixth form' (DES, 1970:11). In this section the distinction will be made between the national level where shortages can be measured in terms of the shortfall from 'requirements', and LEA level where the shortage can most appropriately be measured as the shortfall from 'demand'. These two concepts of 'requirements' and 'demand' will now be examined.

'Requirements'

Teacher 'requirements' are based on the desired level of output, which in this context can be regarded as the number of pupils and the desired labour–output ratio. The number of pupils depends on the size of the school-age population and the proportion in school, and is therefore set largely by the government. The designation of a particular teacher–pupil ratio rests on the assumption that there should be some maximum class size and that teaching in classes larger than this size represents a less-than-ideal quality of education. This ideal standard is based on educational tenets and is set by the government.[2] It is apparent that this definition of 'requirements' is independent of salary levels and technological possibilities. It is entirely administered.

The use of a specified teacher–pupil ratio is not entirely satisfactory. The idea of what is a 'teacher' and a 'class' have undergone change over time. There is now an increasing number of specialists being involved in education such as text-book writers, producers of schools broadcasts, and specialist advisers who would

---

2. It is often assumed that smaller classes are 'better', though there is considerable doubt as to whether, at least over wide ranges, smaller classes do have much influence on students' achievements. See Cumming (1971) for a review of the evidence.

at one time simply have been teachers,[3] and in recent years there has been considerable flexibility introduced into the notion of the traditional teacher group. Children tend to be organized in groups of different sizes throughout the day, depending on the activity. In these circumstances it is questionable whether the teacher–pupil ratio means anything at all in practice. A given ratio can be consistent with various patterns in the distribution of classes by size and need not therefore indicate precisely how many classes are 'oversize'.[4]

However, despite a recognition of the problems of finding a suitable measure of staffing objectives, the teacher–pupil ratio has always been used as a convenient yardstick for assessing the overall position, and for virtually the whole of the post-war period staffing objectives have been represented by a fixed teacher–pupil ratio.[5]

Teacher 'requirements' are thus equal to the number of pupils times the desired teacher–pupil ratio, which is based on desired class size.

'Demand'

The 'requirements' figure is based on ideal staffing standards. It is a long-term target which is calculated at the aggregate level, whereas hiring takes place at local level and it is the LEAs which set the working norms. It is at this local level that the concept of 'demand' becomes appropriate. This takes account of financial and other constraints which do not affect the 'requirements' figure.

The 'demand' for teachers is the number of teachers which an LEA seeks to hire in any period. There are variations between LEAs in

3. See Vaizey (1969).
4. For a fuller discussion of the inadequacies of the teacher–pupil ratio as a measure of staffing standards see Thomas (1973a). Officially, the shortfall from the desired staffing standard has been measured in terms of the number of 'oversize' classes. Towards the end of the 1960s it was increasingly recognized that schools were pursuing a number of objectives in the deployment of teachers, such as broader choice of curricula and smaller classes for backward pupils, in addition to attempting to reduce the average size of class. See for example *Statistics of Education*, IV (1967), 77–8, *Report on Education*, No. 51, 2, OECD (1971:241). This led to the formulation of staffing objectives specified in looser terms, in Circular 16/69, para. 6, which recognized the need to give more emphasis to variations rather than pay homage to a single desired class size.
5. In December 1968 the DES stated that specified teacher–pupil ratios would 'remain the basis accepted by the Secretary of State for determining the current national target number of teachers' (*Report on Education*, No. 51), and they have been used subsequently in the DES (1972) White Paper, and in *Reports on Education*, No. 78, on the supply of teachers, July 1973.

how 'demand' in any year is set but it is usually on the following basis:

$$D_t = r_{t-1}P_t + A$$

where D_t is the current 'demand', $r_{t-1}P_t$ is the number of pupils multiplied by the *prevailing* (not the ideal) teacher–pupil ratio,[6] and A is an improvement factor.[7] This improvement factor represents the desire to improve staffing standards and is a quite different cause of increase in the 'demand' for teachers from the growth in the number of pupils. An increase in pupils is automatically taken care of by the expression $r_{t-1} P_t$. The size of improvement in staffing standards in any year, A, depends on two factors. The first is the budget constraint and this has operated throughout the post-war period. The second is the availability of complementary inputs, especially the lack of accommodation which became a pressing problem in the late 1960s. Some LEAs claimed that they would have hired more teachers if they had anywhere to put them.[8]

The 'demand' as defined here thus represents the number of teachers which an LEA is actually trying to recruit. However, it may not be set entirely independently of the anticipated supply situation since the size of the improvement factor may be modified if supply difficulties are expected.

The Measure of Shortage

Shortages can be measured as the shortfall from either 'requirements' or demand. This is shown, in a stylized manner, in Figure 4.1, for an LEA which is considered to be relatively attractive to teachers. The 'requirements', D^*, are shown as rising over time because of the growth in the size of the school population, assuming no change in the formal norms on desired staffing standards. These staffing standards are set nationally, although the figure relates to an LEA. Demand, D, is increasing at a faster rate than D^* because of

6. In practice a set of teacher–pupil ratios for different groups of pupils is used.
7. Some LEAs add an allowance for contingencies, for distributional aspects, and for anticipated wastage over the year, so that a 'demand' figure for the beginning of the year is set slightly above the intended average 'demand' over the year.
8. 'In the overwhelming majority of LEAs, shortage of accommodation was seen as the chief externally produced cause of over large classes' *Reports on Education*, No. 70 (1971). This is obviously closely linked to the financial constraints. Some of the teachers' unions, in particular the NUT, have been so concerned by this constraint that they have sought information on costs and problems of various types of temporary classrooms and have pressed some LEAs to erect more of these.

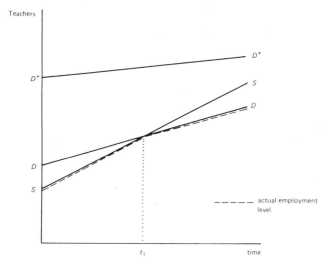

FIGURE 4.1. 'REQUIREMENTS' AND DEMAND FOR TEACHERS

the desire to improve on the previous position and approach the ideal standards embodied in D^*.

The supply of teachers, S, is shown as increasing over time. This is due to some natural growth in the number of potential teachers and to the efforts to increase the supply. The number of new vacancies which the LEA has will be $D-S$.[9] After time t_1 there are no unfilled vacancies since the LEA can meet all its current recruitment desires. The employment level is of course still below D^* and in this sense there is a shortage.[10]

Some LEAs are undoubtedly in this position though some are still in the position as shown to the left of t_1 in Figure 4.1, and are unable to meet current demand, D. The way the shortages are distributed between different LEAs is of considerable interest but lies outside our immediate scope since we are focusing attention on the national

9. There will also be vacancies to cover the replacement of teachers moving from one school to another within the LEA, and replacement of teachers leaving the LEA's service.

10. The gap would have to be covered by residual adjustments if it is assumed that S represents the supply after the various positive adjustments on the demand side. It is argued later that this is usually the case.

level. The measure of shortage which will be used in the following discussion is the shortfall from 'requirements'. This is the measure with which the national decision-makers are concerned and to which many of the responses at national level are made.[11]

Over the period 1951–70, the shortages calculated in this manner[12] fell considerably, though most of the reduction came in the 1960s. The total shortage, as a percentage of 'requirements', fell from 19.3 per cent in 1951 to 7.7 per cent in 1970. In the case of primary schools,[13] 'requirements' grew rapidly up to 1955, then remained steady for a couple of years before falling until 1962 when a rapid growth again occurred. During the early 1950s the supply grew but did not keep pace with the growth in demand and hence the shortage grew. Thereafter the number of teachers was prevented from falling by much, at a time when 'requirements' were falling quite markedly, and the shortage narrowed considerably. The upsurge of 'requirements' in the 1960s was well matched by faster growth in supply, and the shortage continued to be eliminated, but at a much slower pace.

The position in secondary schools reveals a simpler pattern. In the early 1950s up to 1954, 'requirements' were steady whilst supply

11. Since there was virtually no unemployment amongst teachers, the supply of teachers can be taken as the same as the number of teachers employed nationally.
12. Calculations can be made of the size of the teacher shortage, using 'requirements' less supply as the measure. The 'requirements' are calculated on the basis of the estimated teacher–pupil ratios which would eliminate classes of over 40 pupils in maintained primary schools and over 30 in maintained secondary schools. There have been several estimates of the appropriate teacher–pupil ratios for eliminating oversize classes. Those prepared by the Robbins Committee have been used here, namely 0.038:1 for primary schools and 0.064:1 for secondary schools. Supply figures are the number of teachers employed and they include both full-time and part-time teachers. Part-time teachers are measured in terms of full-time equivalents.
13. The calculations are actually based on the position for junior classes and senior classes. These roughly correspond to primary and secondary schools respectively. Junior classes comprise all classes in primary schools and classes in all-age schools consisting entirely or almost entirely of pupils aged under 11. Senior classes are the remaining classes in all-age schools and all classes in secondary schools. All-age schools had virtually disappeared by the end of the period as the following figures show:

All-age schools	1950	1968
Number	6,357	32
Pupils	945,902	7,288

SOURCE: *Statistics of Education*, I (1968), 10.
The correspondence of junior and senior classes with primary and secondary schools has thus become almost perfect.

increased, thereby causing a slight reduction in the shortage. The rapid growth in 'requirements' in the later 1950s was not accompanied by an equivalent growth in supply and the shortage grew larger. During the 1960s the 'requirements' again remained steady, and supply continued to grow causing considerable reduction in the shortage. The most acute shortage in primary schools preceded that for secondary schools, reflecting the passing through the school system of the population bulge of the immediate post-war years. As the bulge left the school system in the 1960s (at a time when there was rapid expansion in further and higher education) the shortage of teachers for primary and secondary schools together diminished.

The picture described here is confirmed by the paths traced by other closely allied measures of shortage such as movements in the average size of classes, the percentage of classes with more than the desired number of pupils, and the number of pupils per teacher.

The Supply of Teachers

The discussion so far has referred to supply in general terms but it is important to identify the various components. It is useful to think of the available stock of teachers in any period as being composed of the previous stock plus the inflow, minus the outflow.

The flows are small in relation to the size of the stock, and any substantial change in the stock will be a lengthy process since this requires large changes in the flows. For example, for *all* teachers, the initial impact of a 10 per cent increase in new entrants, which would involve a major expansion of the training facilities, would be a 1 per cent increase in the stock of teachers.[14] Similarly, large increases in the flow of re-entrants or a fall in the gross wastage rate would produce only minor changes in the stock.[15]

Table 4.1 shows the accumulated flows over the period 1963–70. During this time the gross wastage was relatively large especially for females. Indeed it was greater than the flow of new entrants, and so any increase in the stock of female teachers has depended on re-entrants. The re-entry pool has thus been of crucial importance: Table 4.1 shows that the flow of re-entrants was almost half the size

14. These figures are based on the size of the stocks and flows in 1970. The figures relate to a single time period only, but they do show that any increase in supply is only likely to occur over several periods.

15. Wastage includes 'transfers out', i.e. teachers moving from maintained primary and secondary schools to other parts of the education system. Re-entrants includes 'transfers in', i.e. teachers coming into the state sector from other parts of the system.

TABLE 4.1
COMPONENTS OF TEACHER SUPPLY 1963–1970[a]

		Female	Male	Total
1.	Full-time stock in service 1963	155,710	114,780	270,490
2.	New entrants	122,450	57,894	180,344
3.	Re-entrants	59,002	14,849	73,851
4.	Wastage	149,899	52,371	202,270
5.	Full-time stock in service 1970 (1 + 2 + 3 − 4)	187,263	135,152	322,415
5a.	Actual full-time stock 1970	(189,952)	(136,120)	(326,072)
6.	Increase in full-time stock 1963–70 (5 − 1)	31,553	20,372	51,925
7.	Increase in part-time stock 1963–70			10,077
8.	Increase in total stock 1963–70			62,002

NOTE:

a. A number of points should be noted about this table. The figures are culled from different volumes of *Statistics of Education* and, because of slight discrepancies in the figures presented there, the actual figures of the stock for 1970 (5a) differ slightly from the calculated figure (5). 1963 was the first year for which a breakdown in this detail was possible, though some less detailed calculations would have been possible back to 1958. However, the main purpose of the figures here is only to indicate the relative importance of the components of supply, and the time covered is not crucial. The figures relate to March each year for the full-timers and February for the part-timers.

of the flow of new entrants. The importance of the different inflows and outflows has, however, varied and in the late 1960s there was an important change. The total number of female leavers was held steady whilst the flow of new entrants increased, so that by 1970 it actually exceeded the gross outflow. This resulted in a rapid enlargement of the annual increase in the stock of women teachers.

In the case of males the flow of re-entrants is much less important for increasing the stock. Unlike females, for the whole of the period shown in Table 4.1 the flow of new entrants exceeded the flow of leavers. Taking all teachers together, however, the position was one of wastage exceeding new entrants, which made it necessary to rely on other sources of supply.

3. The Adjustment Instruments

We have defined teacher shortage as 'requirements' minus supply. This can be expressed as follows:

$$X_t = r^*P_t - [T_{t-1} + cG_{t-1} - (w - e)T_{t-1}]$$

where X is the shortage, r^* the desired teacher–pupil ratio, P the number of pupils, T the stock of teachers, G the output of newly trained teachers, c the proportion of G which enters the teaching force, w the wastage rate, and e the flow of re-entrants expressed as a proportion of the previous stock. Alterations in any of these operands will produce variations in the shortage.

It should be noted, however, that the 'requirements' for and the supply of teachers are determined by several factors apart from the adjustment made by the DES or the LEAs. Supply in any period will depend on exogenous factors such as the state of the labour market in similar occupations as well as the relative salaries paid and the hiring standards imposed. 'Requirements' will be set not only on the basis of desired staffing standards, which in turn will be affected by the way education is provided,[16] but also on the basis of the number of pupils, which depends on many factors beyond the control of the education administrators.

Table 4.2 shows the major instruments which have been used in England and Wales. The table relates to the national level and thus does not include responses which affect the distributional aspects of shortage. It may, for example, be possible to transfer teachers within the education system from sub-sectors with low shortages to sub-sectors with high shortages. One other important response which is not shown, since it affects the whole nature of the adjustment process, is information acquisition. Resources may be devoted to acquiring an understanding of the way the system works and the effects of various policy decisions, over and above that instrument shown as search activity. It is an attempt to enhance the effectiveness of the selection of adjustment instruments.

Table 4.2 shows the different instruments which have been used to reduce teacher shortage. Generally speaking, those instruments designed to raise the inflows of labour have been used in preference to other operands. Attempts to reduce 'requirements' have not been

16. The average size and geographical distribution of schools will affect the number of teachers 'required' to give the desired staffing standards in terms of the number of oversize classes.

105

used as a positive adjustment, since the formal norms on the quantity of schooling provided are strongly adhered to. The norms are also generally adhered to in the case of the number of hours worked per employee which means that overtime is hardly used as a means of adjusting to shortages. What is more surprising is that the large wastage flow has not been a major target. The importance of the gross outflow has certainly been recognized[17] but there has been a tendency to regard it as inevitable[18] and intractable because of the variety of causes. The DES report on teacher turnover, for example, concluded that 'it does not seem possible to identify particular causes so important that their remedy would provide a solution. Remedies, like the causes of the malaise, must take many forms.'[19] Much more attention has been paid to attempts to reduce *net* wastage by encouraging re-entrants. Thus most efforts to reduce shortage have been by using instruments to affect various inflows.

As a generalization it is true to say that the positive instruments affect mainly the supply-side operands, the inflows and outflows, whereas the residual ones affect the demand-side, though we must qualify this assertion slightly in so far as 'requirements' may not be independent of supply. 'Requirements' are primarily set on the basis of the number of pupils but the number of pupils may be affected by the supply of teachers. This probably applies more especially to the number of pupils in particular subject groups (swings to or from

17. Two major reports on the supply of teachers, the NACTST *7th Report*, para. 12, and the *9th Report*, para. 38, both referred to wastage as 'the heart of the supply problem'. The Plowden Report (1967: 493) referred to a 'catastrophic exodus', and Boyle who was Minister of Education from 1963 to 1964 referred to the 'Paschendaele Policy of marching young girls into the classroom as fast as the training colleges can turn them out, while — almost equally quickly — their immediate predecessors marry and leave'.

18. The DES has used a number of studies by Kelsall and his associates (1963), (1968), (1970) to argue that wastage of teachers is not any higher than for broadly comparable professions and in the case of graduates it has an outstandingly low wastage rate.

19. *Reports on Education*, No. 79 (May 1974). There have, however, been some instruments directed at reducing outflows but these have been relatively minor. For example, apart from pay there have been some efforts to make the job more attractive through the provision of various kinds of helpers to perform uncongenial non-teaching tasks like meals supervision, and the decision to make teacher training compulsory for all university graduates who become teachers in the hope that trained graduates would experience higher job satisfaction if they had more specific preparation. There have also been some occasional attempts to persuade teachers to stay beyond the minimum retiring age. (In 1970 about 17 per cent of all leavers were in the over-60 age-group. Almost all of these would be retirements.)

TABLE 4.2
INSTRUMENTS USED TO REDUCE TEACHER SHORTAGES

Instrument	Operand	Intensity of Use
Positive Adjustments		
Reduce desired staffing standards, e.g. by higher 'productivity', substituting non-teaching labour	r *	Nil (Proposed)[a]
Reduce length of schooling	P	Nil (Proposed)[b]
Later retirement	w	Slight
More appropriate training	w	Slight
Ancillary staff	w	Some
Increase pay[c]	w, c, e	Some
Increase fringe benefits, e.g. pensions, housing assistance	w, c, e	Some
Change structure of hours Part-time employment	w, e	Heavy
Reduce hiring standards Use of dilutees	G, c, e	Some
Reduce college entry standards	G	Some
Provide extra training facilities	G	Heavy
More intensive use of existing training facilities	G	Slight
Accelerated training	G	Some
Increase inducements to train, e.g. more facilities for part-time students	G	Slight
Search activity	c, e	Some
Residual Adjustments		
Reduce actual staffing standards		Heavy
Reduce hours per pupil		Slight

NOTES:
a. See Section 8.
b. See Section 9.
c. This involves consideration of both levels and structure.

certain subject groups depend on the number and quality of teachers in those subjects), but more generally it may affect the numbers staying beyond the compulsory years of attendance.

Two other points emerge from Table 4.2. The first is that the use of particular adjustment instruments may well have consequences apart from the influence on some operand. For instance, a decision to lower hiring standards may have the intended effect of increasing supply, but it may also have the side-effect of reducing the quality of education. This latter effect can be regarded as a cost which would be taken into account in the choice of instruments. The second point is that a distinction can be drawn between those instruments which are direct attempts to influence certain flows, such as more intensive search activity to increase the flows of new entrants and re-entrants, and those instruments which are deferments of improvements which would otherwise have taken place, such as the decisions to delay the raising of the school-leaving age[20] and the decision to postpone the introduction of a graduate training requirement for maths and science teachers.[21]

One of the major factors in the choice of instruments is the set of constraints which impinge upon the decision-makers.[22] These constraints will act in different ways: some will affect the timing of response,[23] some the nature of the response, and some both. They will also vary in which adjustment instruments they affect. The budget, for instance, may act as a constraint on raising relative pay but not on redesigning the job, whereas the reverse might be true in the case of unions acting as a constraint. Some constraints will limit the range of values of possible adjustments and they will vary in the time over which they operate.

One of the most important constraints is the set of administered rules. The long-term overall education policy provides a framework of administered rules which constitute a set of formal norms governing many aspects of the provision of education. In the final analysis, of course, everything can be altered including these norms but we can draw a distinction between the long-term policy decisions and the operational decisions. There is no hard-and-fast line between these two, and indeed some adjustment instruments may change from time to time. At one time they may be a matter of cabinet-level policy, at another it may be within the discretion of the DES. The distinction can be thought of partly in terms of the level of decision-making and partly in terms of the political opportunity cost of the decisions. The higher this opportunity cost the less likely it is that a particular decision will be within the discretion of low-level decision-makers.

20. See Section 9.
21. See Section 7.
22. This approach has also been found useful elsewhere, e.g. Freeman (1971:29), in discussing decision-making in universities writes, 'in the absence of knowledge of the weights placed by university decision makers on diverse objectives it is best to focus on the impact of the major constraints . . . on the decision process.'
23. The shortage itself may act as a constraint on the timing of certain desired reforms. For example, it was only after the passing of the first population bulge that some countries were able to extend the period of teacher training. See OECD (1971: 203).

There are many examples of administered rules: the principal ones relate to the length and timing of schooling, the 'quality' of education, and the labour–output ratio. Since the length of compulsory schooling is fixed, it means that eliminating the shortage of teachers by reducing 'requirements', say by raising the starting age or lowering the leaving age or the number of hours in school,[24] is not generally permissible. Rules governing the times at which children shall be schooled also inhibit some types of action. For example, all children are required to be in school at the same time, and there is thus no possibility of shift systems, and 'overtime' working is severely restricted. (There is, however, a kind of 'overtime', which occurs on a very limited scale, in the form of reducing the number of 'free' periods which teachers have in particular schools where shortages are acute.) Other rules relate to the 'quality' of education, as expressed in a concern over minimum certification require-ments,[25] which introduce a constraint on the ability to vary hiring standards. There is also specification of a desired class size and a desire for some fixed ratio of teachers to pupils,[26] which virtually rules out capital substitution as an adjustment instrument. A further administered rule which inhibits the use of pay as an instrument for eliminating shortages of particular types of teacher is the existence of a common salary scale for all types of teacher.

24. Vaizey (1963:234) suggested raising the school entry age from 5 to 6½ (with a firm commitment to raise the school-leaving age from 15 to 16½ so that no child would have less than 10 years' schooling).
25. The DES aims to provide 'the highest possible standards of education according to child's age, aptitude and ability' (1970). The quality of education is, however, very difficult to measure because of the problems in identifying the objectives of education, and assigning some sort of priority to them. Several indicators of quality have been suggested, such as pupils' performance in reading tests or examination results, employers' assessments of school leavers, social adjustment indicators such as juvenile delinquency rates etc., but there is considerable dis-agreement on the reliability and validity of these measures; see Woodhall and Blaug (1968). An alternative to measuring the quality of *output* directly, would be to look at *inputs*. If more inputs or better-quality inputs (more efficiency units) were used to produce a given output, then, assuming there were no decrease in the efficiency with which they were used, one might suppose that this would lead to better-quality output. In the case of education, if there were more and 'better' teachers for the same number of pupils, this would represent an increase in the quality of education being received. Unfortunately, improved quality, in this latter sense of looking at the input side, does not necessarily correspond with improved quality as measured by examination performance etc., but it is nevertheless easier and more convenient to look at minimum hiring standards than output quality.
26. Freeman (1971:29) makes the important point that 'adoption of a fixed ratio goal to guide decisions may be rational in the context of a non-profit institution whose output is difficult to measure.'

The rules play an important role in the understanding of adjustments and, though there is clearly some variation in the extent to which they are adhered to, they are fairly rigid in the short run. The question of what determines these particular rules, which vary from one country to another, is relevant to the choice of particular adjustment instruments though it lies outside the scope of this study.

Closely allied to the idea of administered rules are the political constraints existing on some types of adjustment because the decision-makers lack the power to pursue certain courses of action. The notion of power raises many problems of definition, and there seems to be little agreement between various political and organizational theorists on what is meant. For the present purpose use will be made of the term 'political opportunity cost' since this has been used in the literature.[27]

The resource constraint operates despite the continual pressure to expand the education budget. The education sector is in competition with other claimants on public funds, and the way the budget constraint operates introduces some reliance on incremental or marginal behaviour. Discussions on the size of the Support Grant which involves consultation between the Secretary of State and the local authority associations take into account the current level of service provision (and expected variations in costs), the probable fluctuation in the demand for services, and the improvements on the existing level which are needed. At LEA level, the education committee's estimates to the local authority finance committee are based on a similar pattern of considering some percentage 'improvement' on existing levels of service rather than presenting estimates of the cost of providing the service at ideal standards.

A different type of constraint is that imposed by unions. Certain types of adjustment may be prevented because of union ability to control the production methods and working conditions. The unions' antipathy to any substantial capital substitution,[28] the resistance to dilution, and bans on 'overtime'[29] and the refusal to

---

27. See Schultze (1968).
28. As it happens, in this case they reinforce the administered rules.
29. The NAS in some areas has refused to mark homework outside the normal 9–4 school hours. The NUT and NAS have sometimes also imposed a ban on covering for nonexistent staff or those ill for more than three days. This has been one cause of part-time schooling especially in London. These, however, are more in the nature of short-term industrial actions designed to reinforce wage claims rather than being long-term controls on the work relationship.

cover absentees, are examples of this. In general, however, unions have exerted little or no control over the supply of teachers.

Technological constraints have not figured prominently in the process of selecting adjustment instruments. They set only very broad limits to the adjustment process — for example, by preventing adjustments to labour shortages via inventory changes.

Two other constraints which have limited the use of certain instruments are government policies on employment and pay, in particular incomes policies which have almost certainly had some short-run effect on teachers' pay (as argued in Section 6), and the state of the labour markets for similar occupations which will, via their effects on supply and earnings, influence the choice of adjustment.

Constraints by themselves do not provide an explanation of the choice of instruments, and cost-minimizing behaviour, as outlined in Chapter 2, will serve as a useful postulate if modified to incorporate the costs of acquiring information and to allow for the fact that decision-makers in a bureaucratic organization are likely to be governed by habit to some extent. It is also necessary to modify the assumption of cost-minimizing behaviour to allow for an objective function which in the case of education gives considerable weight to the quantity and quality of education.

On the basis of these contentions some order of priorities in the choice of instruments can be suggested. The first adjustments are likely to be the residual ones such as allowing the teacher–pupil ratio to fall. These incur no costs[30] and in that respect are desirable though there may be a conflict with other education objectives relating to quantity and quality. The second group of instruments to be used consists of those which can be quickly implemented and those which are cheap. Altering the job characteristics, increasing the utilization of training facilities, and increasing search costs are examples. In the third place will come those instruments which are costly or long-term such as pay increases and expanding the training facilities.[31]

4. The Flow of New Teachers

The major response to teacher shortage has been to increase the number of trainees. Generally speaking, there has not been any

30. Though, if the quality of education is thought to suffer by having teacher–pupil ratios below the long-term formal norm, this can be regarded as a cost.
31. Conflicts may arise between those measures which are primarily short-run and those which are primarily long-run. See, for example, Vaizey (1963: 236).

difficulty in filling training college places in post-war years. There has been a queue of applicants with the minimum formal entry qualifications, and it has been more a question of taking those most highly placed in the queue rather than leaving places unfilled.

Where there is no excess training capacity the number of trainees can usually be increased only with a time-lag, because of the need for new building and recruitment of extra college staff. However, some short-term increase may be achieved if makeshift facilities and undesirably low college staff–student ratios are accepted while permanent facilities are brought into use. These are temporary adjustments, as defined in Chapter 2, since they involve no alteration of the working norms. One other temporary adjustment is to have an accelerated training programme for a limited period. The Emergency Teacher Training Scheme[32] in the immediate post-war years was such an adjustment and it showed that in the face of exceptionally severe shortages the norms governing entry standards to training courses and the length of training were not adhered to. There was no change in the norms but there was a conscious acceptance for a limited period of sub-normal standards. The Emergency Scheme was therefore, as its name suggests, a temporary adjustment designed to produce a short-term increase in the flow of newly trained teachers.

This temporary measure was, however, unusual, and most of the responses have been attempts to secure a permanent increase in the flow of trainees. One of the principal determinants of this flow of trainees is the physical capacity of the training sector.[33] This involves

32. There was a marked growth in the demand for teachers both to provide for the growth of the school population (there was a rise in the birth rate just after the war and the school-leaving age was raised from 14 to 15 in 1947) and to reduce class size. The 1944 Education Act and the end of the war had brought a new determination to improve standards of educational provision. The supply was inadequate to meet these demands partly because many of the men who might have gone to teacher training college a few years previously had been on active military service. A crash training programme was therefore launched. The essential feature of the Emergency Scheme was the provision of one-year intensive courses, for those over the age of 21 who had been on some form of national service during the war, leading to qualified teacher status, 'approval being based on the satisfactory completion of the course and a careful assessment by the college staff, and not on any formal external examination' (DES, *Annual Report*, 1947:41). The scheme reached its peak with 55 colleges providing 13,414 training places in 1947. Thereafter there was a gradual rundown and all the emergency colleges were phased out by 1951. Over the life of the scheme 35,000 teachers received training through the emergency colleges.
33. It is possible to increase output of the teacher training institutions by accepting a reduction in the staff–student ratio in colleges, or by improving the utilization of

consideration of the building programme as a long-term response to shortages. The time-lags involved are complex[34] but, despite the difficulties of unravelling the timing, it is apparent that periods of teacher shortage and heavy spending on teacher training go together. This can be seen from Table 4.3.

TABLE 4.3
TEACHER SHORTAGES AND CAPITAL EXPENDITURE

	Average Level of Shortage (% shortfall from 'requirements')			Annual % Increase in Capital Expenditure	
	Primary	Secondary	Total	Teacher Training	All Education
1960–65	8.50	20.09	14.74	41.8	12.9
1965–70	5.41	13.48	9.52	−0.3	5.6
1960–70	6.94	16.86	12.19	18.9	9.2

SOURCE: *Statistics of Education*, IV (1969), Introduction.

In the late 1960s the rate of increase in capital expenditure on education as a whole was roughly half that in the early 1960s, but expenditure on teacher training actually declined. This was associated with more modest reductions in the size of the shortage, as shown in the first three columns of the table, and this suggests either that there is a critical level of shortages in percentage terms, above which the authorities react very strongly and below which they are relatively unconcerned, or that perhaps other methods of alleviating shortages were tried during the second period.

---

existing college resources through more intensive use of existing accommodation and arrangements such as having some students out of college on teaching practice in the schools when others are in college. All these have been tried, but they have led only to minor changes in flows.

34. In the light of the government's declared policy on the provision of places, its forecasts of 'requirements', and the financial allocations, 'individual universities and colleges then determine their own development and take account of such factors as the possibility of expanding old buildings, the possibility of constructing new buildings, the availability of teachers and the demand for places. The influence of these factors will depend upon the times at which decisions have been taken in the past. For example, while it may take one year to adapt existing buildings to new uses, it may take five years to erect and bring into commission a new building, i.e. one factor may depend upon a decision taken a year ago whereas another will depend upon decisions taken five years ago' (Armitage *et al.*, 1969:61).

Table 4.3 must obviously be treated with considerable caution since the periods are very broad and arbitrarily defined, but there can be little doubt that the general picture is accurate. Over the early 1950s the net increase in the number of teachers was just under 7,000 per annum, but it fell in 1957 to 4,400,[35] just at a time when the NACTST was forecasting substantial increases in teacher 'requirements'. The situation resulting from this combination of a deteriorating supply position and increasing demand was exacerbated by the need to provide for the impending lengthening of the teacher training course. The result was the authorization of a major expansion in the training colleges.

This expansion programme was remarkably bunched.[36] Some bunching is to be expected because of the accelerator relationship in investment behaviour, but it was so pronounced that it seems likely that other forces were also at work. A strong possibility is the existence of some threshold of shortage levels which when crossed leads to a massive once-for-all response, rather than there being a smooth continuous process of marginal adjustments. Although the decision-makers did appear to make use of the forecasts of teacher 'requirements', *impending* shortages did not seem to be particularly influential in decisions on the building programme. Rather, it was existing shortages, or those of the immediate past, which seemed to determine the timing. Perhaps it is impossible to overcome the political constraints and achieve an expansion without some existing proof that there is a need.[37]

---

35. This was due to an increase in the number of married women leaving and also to an increase in age retirements in 1957 because many teachers had deferred retirements in 1956 in order to gain the benefit of the new Burnham award and the Teachers Superannuation Act. See DES, *Annual Report* (1957: 791).
36. The value of building work (major projects) approved for the training of teachers averaged £1.13m. per annum over the period 1948–58. It was never more than £1.6m. In 1959 it increased to £2.3m. and then leapt dramatically to £14.7m. in 1960. It fell to £8.3m. the following year and then declined steadily to £2.8m. in 1970.
37. A positive relationship was found between changes in building expenditure on training colleges and changes in previous shortages of secondary school teachers, as the following regression, taking first differences, shows.

$$\Delta Y_t = 0.335 + 0.876 \; \Delta X_{t-1} \qquad R^2 = 0.290$$
$$(0.319) \quad (2.394) \qquad\qquad DW = 2.428$$

where Y_t = total approved value of the major educational building projects for the training of teachers in year t, as a percentage of all approved educational buildings in year t; X_{t-1} = the absolute shortage of teachers in secondary schools in the *preceding year* (in thousands); t values are shown in brackets. The period covered is 1954–69.

114

The discussion so far has been in terms of changes in the major building works. Three further points deserve mention. First, as a matter of short-term expedience, some attempts were made to extend the life of existing facilities.[38] Second, there has been a move away from the provision of residential college places, presumably in order to reduce the costs per student of the extra building required to expand supply.[39] Third, there was an effort to increase potential sources of supply, by making special arrangements for older men and women such as the provision of day-training colleges and accepting those with suitable educational backgrounds for shortened courses of training of one or two years.[40]

So far as the actual number of students in training is concerned, there was a pause in expansion after the crash programme of the immediate post-war years. However, the persistent shortages throughout the 1950s of over 50,000 teachers led to efforts to increase the flow of new teachers by taking more trainees. There was a sharp jump after 1956, but the training lags[41] meant that it was not

38. In the early 1960s it was estimated that facilities for about 1,500 students were being kept in temporary use, i.e. beyond the time when they were scheduled to be given up when replaced by expansion; see DES, *Annual Report* (1962: 53).

39. The following figures show the move away from residential places.

	% Resident in College	% Resident in Approved Lodgings	% Day Students
1957–8	88.5		11.5
1962–3	66.7	17.1	15.2
1969–70	39.8	22.1	38.1

SOURCE: Calculated from *Statistics of Education*.

40. See *Reports on Education*, No. 7 (January 1964).

41. Most teachers are trained in colleges of education. In the year 1969–70, 70.6% of men and 87.0% of women students completing initial training were in colleges of education where the length of the training course is three years, compared with one year in a university department of education. This means that the training lag tends to be large and, given the relative sizes of the stocks and flows shown earlier, rapid changes in the stock of teachers in service are unlikely to result from expanding training facilities. It is interesting to note that in recent years there has been a rise in the number of mixed colleges of education, which has increased the likelihood of marriages between teachers. In view of the relatively low earning power of male teachers compared with other members of the highly qualified labour force, there is perhaps a greater chance of the women teachers who are married to male teachers continuing to seek employment in order to maintain a standard of living similar to that enjoyed by those in the teachers' reference group. Mixed colleges may therefore increase the supply of teachers. Such an adjustment is not listed as a possibility in Chapter 2, since increasing the participation of married women via the income as opposed to the substitution effect is seldom possible.

until 1959 that the total shortage of teachers began to decline. After the 1957–8 spurt in admissions to training courses, there was little further expansion until the physical capacity of the training colleges was increased at the end of the 1950s. When the new buildings were brought into use this allowed a major expansion in the number of students admitted to training. The number of students admitted to colleges doubled between 1960 and 1967.

This increase in students helped to bring about a reduction in the level of shortage, which, given the competing claims on the budget, removed the need to maintain the rate of expansion of the early 1960s. In the late 1960s the number of students admitted to colleges levelled off.

The question of what is the appropriate level of intake of trainee teachers has been the subject of much debate. It is generally possible to cut back the intake of trainees fairly quickly but there are lags involved in adjusting the flow of newly trained teachers downwards because of the numbers already in training. A surplus of teachers could result from a failure to reduce the trainee intake *before* the target stock of teachers in service is reached. The DES White Paper (1972) forecast that 510,000 teachers would be needed by 1981, to secure a 10 per cent improvement on the 1971 staffing standards for the more numerous and relatively older pupils forecast for 1981, and to provide for an expansion of nursery education and for the replacement of teachers to be released to in-service and induction training. On plausible values of rates of wastage and re-entry, there is likely to be a surplus of teachers before the end of the decade and it would therefore be appropriate to start cutting back on the intake of teachers now in order to achieve a gradual reduction in numbers. Given the desire for graduates this would alter the balance between different sources of recruitment and less non-degree college of education trainees would be required.

Cutbacks in the number of college of education places have in fact been implemented recently, though this is partly due to financial stringency. Opposition to this policy has come from those who dispute the acceptability of the standards of education embodied in the target requirements figure. They argue that far more staff are needed in order to provide extra teachers for dealing with special groups such as socially disadvantaged, 'problem', and retarded children.

One development in the early 1960s which had a pronounced effect on the number of student teachers was the decision to lengthen the training course in colleges of education from two to three years. The nature of the supply equation is such that we expect two consequences of such a decision, namely a permanent increase in the number of teachers in training and a temporary suspension in the flow of new teachers. The increase in the number of students in training is self-evident. The temporary suspension arises because students who would normally leave colleges stay on to complete the additional training prescribed. Both expected consequences occurred. The effect on the total stock of teachers was to produce a dip in the year in which one age cohort failed to enter, and then a gradual return to the former trend.[42]

It was noted earlier that there had been some attempts to tap a wider pool of potential student teachers by providing 'day-training colleges'. This, however, was only on a small scale and there was little serious effort to increase potential inflows to training, for instance by providing part-time training,[43] or by offering limited training for those interested in short-service commissions.[44]

Most of the efforts to influence supply have been directed at the overall shortage of teachers, and it is on these that our discussion has concentrated. However, the government has to some extent been concerned with the distributional aspects of shortages and has made some attempts to control them. The most important of these attempts was the use of the quota system.

The extent of the shortage of teachers varies between LEAs because of differences in their ability to recruit teachers, depending on the number of teachers the LEA itself is able to produce and the relative attractiveness of the physical and educational environment. It is, for example, more difficult to attract teachers to slum schools with a large proportion of immigrant children than to schools which have a middle-class white intake and are in physically attractive areas. The existence of a uniform salary scale has prevented exclusive reliance on salary differentials to redistribute the stock of teachers and, since the same regulations governing class size apply to all authorities,[45] there have been attempts to impose a rationing

42. The model predicts that there is a gradual convergence on the previous stock position rather than an immediate return when the inflow of newly trained teachers to the stock was resumed, because a complete age-group has been permanently removed from the stock of teachers.

43. There had been some small-scale use of part-time training in England and Wales but it has been much more extensively used elsewhere, e.g. Yugoslavia. See OECD (1971: 285).

44. This was suggested by a minority of the Plowden Committee: Plowden Report (1967: 494).

45. On educational grounds the argument is sometimes put forward that 'disadvantaged' children, such as those in EPAs, require a higher ratio of teachers to pupils. In fact the formal norm is the same in all cases.

system in order to give 'badly placed' LEAs a larger proportionate share of any increase in the stock of teachers.

Such rationing devices were first used, for limited groups of teachers, in 1948 when a maximum establishment for women was fixed for each LEA. The arrangement initially applied to all women but later certain categories, such as married women returning, were exempted. In 1956 the scheme was discontinued and LEAs were free to make as many appointments as they wished, though the 'well-placed' authorities were asked to exercise restraint and to make the maximum use of married women teachers and of teachers over pensionable age. This arrangement became formalized later in the year when each LEA was given a quota expressed in terms of the *total* number of teachers who should be employed. The scheme was therefore much broader than the earlier one which had related only to women, and the better-off authorities were asked to refrain from improving their staffing standards and in some cases to accept a worsening of these standards. The movement towards more equal staffing ratios was deliberately gradual and by 1964 the gap between the staffing standards of the best-placed and the worst-placed authorities was about half of what it was at the beginning of the scheme. By 1968 the quota represented a similar staffing standard for all authorities. It should be stressed that the scheme applies only to LEAs and is therefore not capable of solving particular local difficulties *within* LEAs. Nor does the scheme cover part-time teachers and it has sometime been argued that this may have led LEAs to offer only part-time posts to teachers who would be willing to serve full-time. This does not, however, appear to have been the case in practice.

It is difficult to judge the extent to which the quota system achieved its purpose as a rationing device in the absence of price differentials. In some cases it seems merely to have held back the better-placed authorities from making further improvements in their staffing standards, without alleviating the problem of the worse-placed authorities.[46] In general, however, the system seems to have

---

46. One LEA, for example, has claimed that it was prevented by the quota system from making improvements in its staffing standards. In one year, when the scheme was in its infancy, this particular authority was well above its quota and therefore took nobody from the teacher training colleges in that year. In the following year it got virtually no applicants from the colleges, as newly qualified teachers had apparently been deterred by the failure to take anybody on the previous year. This led to a severe temporary shortage of teachers.

achieved some success since the original purpose of the quota[47] has now been replaced by an aim which is just the opposite.

The system is now more of a device for making sure that authorities take up their share of teachers to improve staffing standards, and some authorities have to be written to in order to persuade them to take up their quota. Thus, instead of the quota allocation being a maximum it is now a minimum. This turn-about reflects the diminished shortage of teachers as a whole.

5. Re-Entrants and Part-Timers

There have been many attempts to boost the flow of re-entrants to teaching, the most important being the efforts to make provision for part-timers.

The greatest potential source of re-entrants is married women,[48] and in 1961 a campaign was launched to attract more women back into teaching. The timing of this campaign was prompted not only by the fact that the flow of leavers had been increasing gently (and there were associated increases in future school population), but also by the so-called 'year of intermission' which was imminent as a result of the lengthening of the training course in colleges of education. The campaign received heavy publicity. It included personal letters to teachers not in service, house-to-house canvasses, exhibitions, and many other methods.[49] There was also encouragement given to LEAs to increase their recruitment of married women returners under the quota system, with the object of persuading all authorities to use 'immobile' teachers as far as possible and thereby limit their calls on 'mobile' teachers.[50]

Perhaps a more important development was the attempt to change the nature of the job to make it more attractive to potential

47. The Annual Circular from the DES stating quotas was replaced in 1971 by an Annual Letter from the Minister.
48. Over 80% of those who return to teaching are women: see Table 4.1, line 3. The use of married women re-entrants has sometimes been regarded as a qualitative deterioration in the teaching force, and hence characterized as a short-term expedient and not a long-term solution. Armitage (1970:47) for example, has argued that 'they generate undesirable properties in the teaching force in its age and subject composition and in its career prospects.'
49. The number of married women who returned to teaching, either full-time or part-time, increased from 4,600 in 1961 to 7,200 in 1965, and this must have been due in part to the campaign. See OECD (1971: 297-8). 'The best recruiting agents were the teachers themselves' (DES, *Annual Report*, 1961:11).
50. Circular 17/60, 29 December 1960.

returners. The DES commissioned a survey amongst women teachers not in service, which identified a number of changes in the job which would encourage married women to return.[51] As a result of the survey some changes were made, in particular the provision of part-time posts.

The growth in the number of part-time posts was directly encouraged in a circular from the DES in 1965.[52] There were also changes such as bringing conditions of service, especially on matters such as tenure and sick leave, into line with those for full-time teachers. From May 1968 the pay of part-timers became nationally regulated and proportional to full-time salaries, and from December 1967 the service of certain part-time teachers became pensionable.

These developments were almost certainly important in encouraging the greater use of part-timers but it must be emphasized that this adjustment was already being used. There had been a growing trend in the use of such teachers since the later 1950s. The growth in the use of part-timers is positively related to the level of teacher shortage. However, there are some surprisingly long time-lags, of two or three years, which suggest that the business of deciding to tap this source of supply and eventually procuring the teachers is a protracted process.[53] This may be due in part to the fact that the recog-

51. See Kelsall (1963), especially Tables 25 and 26.
52. 'The Secretary of State asks all authorities to deal with this problem with a sense of urgency and to share his determination that this powerful source of supply be tapped to the full' (Circular 6/65, 6). The authorities were asked to adopt as their minimum aim the prevailing national average of 5% (in terms of full-time equivalent) of total teaching staff. Those already achieving this were asked to try for 10%.
53. When the percentage rate of change of the number of part-time teachers was regressed on the level of shortage as measured by the percentage shortfall from 'requirements' the following results were obtained.

	Constant	$X(PRI)_{-3}$	$X(SEC)_{-2}$	$X(TOT)_{-3}$	R^2	DW	Period
			Independent Variables				
RI)	−11.168 (−1.404)	+3.212 (+4.295)			0.626	2.257	1958−70
EC)	−5.322 (0.643)		+0.957 (+2.408)		0.326	1.877	1957−70
OT)	−15.164 (−1.722)			+2.055 (+3.741)	0.600	2.187	1958−70

NOTES:
t values are given in brackets.
(*PRI*) (*SEC*) and (*TOT*) refer to primary, secondary, and total.

nition of a need for such teachers during a school year would not be built into teachers' estimated establishment figure until the following year and then there might be delays in recruiting them.

The attitude of the unions to the use of part-time teachers was largely neutral. They neither enthusiastically welcomed nor effectively imposed any constraints on the use of such teachers.[54] On cost grounds, part-timers may be slightly more expensive than full-timers (because of the fixed costs of employment) but their employment probably represents a cost-minimizing strategy for replacing them by full-timers could only be done by incurring extra costs through raising salaries and training expenditure. Part-timers represent a more flexible element in the teaching force.[55] This was dramatically demonstrated in Coventry in 1969 when, following the 1968 cuts in government spending, 193 part-time teachers were dismissed as an economy measure.

6. Pay

Pay changes are one of the more obvious possible adjustment instruments, the assumption being that increases in pay will increase the supply of teachers by raising the flow of the new entrants plus re-entrants or by reducing wastage. The relationship between pay changes and shortage level can be examined at the level of the market for all teachers and at a disaggregated level where consideration is given to the structure of teachers' salaries and the differences in pay within teaching.

The appropriate measure of pay is 'relative pay'. Though there is no single reference group for teachers, it is convenient to work with a single index of relative pay, and this is done by taking pay relative to all manual or non-manual workers. Nevertheless, it should be remembered that it may be comparisons with *particular* occupations which are important in the minds of teachers, rather than com-

---

On a cross-subject basis it does not seem to be the case that part-timers are used to a greater extent in those subjects where shortages are greatest, though the evidence on this is very slender.

54. The NAS, for example, whilst having no formal policy against part-timers except where full-timers are unemployed, thought part-timers represented a deterioration in teaching standards because they do not contribute to the full life of school and were rarely involved in extra-curricular activities.

55. There is sometimes a preference for the use of part-time teachers where there are a large number of small schools. See Pratt *et al.* (1973: 33).

parison with some general group.[56] Generally speaking the position of women teachers in the female pay structure is more favourable than that for men teachers in the male salary structure. This may be due to the fact that women have enjoyed equal pay in teaching since 1961. One important factor which may be taken account of by those considering entering teaching is the dispersion of salaries. On the whole there is little dispersion in teachers' salaries compared with that of other white-collar groups.[57] This is due to the existence of a formal salary scale.

The main interest here, however, is with the changes in the relative pay of teachers over time, rather than the static picture. In calculating an index of the relative pay of teachers, the most appropriate group with which to compare pay might be thought to be some white-collar group such as 'Administrative, Technical, and Clerical' workers, though from a bargaining point of view it is clear that their position relative to manual workers has been of concern to teachers. In fact, indexes of teachers' pay relative to other white-collar workers and relative to manual workers have moved in an almost identical manner. In the post-war period up to 1963 there was a general increase in relative pay but these gains were lost during the later 1960s and the position of teachers in the pay structure in 1970 was about the same as a decade earlier. The movement of real pay confirms the fact that the principal advances in teachers' pay were made in 1956–7 and 1962–3, with increases in money pay over the last half of the 1960s producing no gains in real pay.

56. In making pay comparisons, allowance should be made for the fact that the structure of salary scales will be affected by such factors as changes in the age and sex structure of the groups concerned. During the early 1960s the proportion of younger teachers fell sharply in the case of females, when the lengthening of the training course from two to three years drastically, though temporarily, reduced the number of new entrants into teaching. In the later 1960s the growth in the proportion of younger teachers was restored. This change in age structure is what one would expect to observe in a rapidly expanding profession where the major port of entry is people entering employment for the first time. This information on age structure means that some of the rise in relative salaries in the early 1960s, discussed later, may have been attributable to the higher proportion of older workers and some of the subsequent fall in the relative salaries due to the fall in this proportion. Apart from the age structure, it would also be desirable to take account of net advantages in different jobs, when making pay comparisons. It is sometimes alleged that teachers enjoy substantial benefits, especially in the form of long holidays, though an Economist Intelligence Unit Report (1970) which compared fringe benefits in teaching and other professions concluded that, although teachers may enjoy some slight advantage, the gap is small.
57. This can be seen from the data on distribution of earnings by occupation shown in the *New Earnings Survey*.

It is not possible to understand the movements in teachers' pay without taking account of institutional factors. There has been a highly formalized negotiating structure and a high level of union membership, and incomes policies appear to have been a significant restraining influence on teachers' pay.[58] Given this background we might suppose that teachers' pay was mainly determined by institutional pressures without much reference to the state of the market, in which case we would not expect to pick up a relationship between pay changes and shortage levels, as initially envisaged on the assumption that pay was a major adjustment instrument.

It is, however, clear from the history of negotiations that there has been an almost total failure of the negotiating machinery (the Burnham Committee) throughout the 1960s,[59] and it would be premature to dismiss the link between pay and shortages without a closer inspection of whether pay has been used as an adjustment instrument.

We postulate that the rate of change of the relative salaries of school teachers, $\dot{S}$, is positively related to the level of the shortage of teachers, X, and the rate of change of teachers' union density, $\dot{D}$. The latter variable is incorporated as a crude proxy for union push-fulness.[60]

The following regressions, for 1962–70, show the expected positive sign for the coefficients on the shortage variable both significant at the 5 per cent level:

$$\dot{S}(PRI)_t = -15.267 + 1.283 \ X(TOT)_t + 0.740 \ \dot{D}_t \qquad R^2 = 0.522$$
$$\phantom{\dot{S}(PRI)_t =} (-2.276) \quad (2.170) \qquad\qquad (1.207) \qquad\quad DW = 2.250$$

$$\dot{S}(SEC)_t = -17.207 + 0.987 \ X(SEC)_{t-1} + 0.635 \ \dot{D}_t \qquad R^2 = 0.566$$
$$\phantom{\dot{S}(SEC)_t =} (-2.624) \quad (2.577) \qquad\qquad (1.079) \qquad\quad DW = 2.497$$

where $\dot{S}$ is the rate of change of an index of teachers' average salaries relative to the salaries of 'Administrative, Technical, and Clerical'

58. The history of post-war settlements has been traced elsewhere. See Thomas (1973b).
59. Many of the settlements in the 1970s were also arbitration awards. Various reasons have been put forward to explain the failure of Burnham. The Treasury, which is the ultimate paymaster, is not represented on the management side, yet the DES is. However, according to the AEC, its presence only hampers managerial flexibility, since the management panel has to make a concordat with the government. The most important cause of Burnham failure however, is the uneven composition of the union representation. Out of 28 seats on the Teachers' Panel the NUT holds 16 and the other 12 are shared between seven unions.
60. For a discussion of its justification, limitations, and measurement, see Thomas (1973b).

workers; X is the shortage of teachers measured as the percentage shortfall from 'requirements', and $\dot{D}$ is the rate of change in union density.

In the case of primary school teachers' salaries the *total* shortage of teachers performed better than the *primary* shortage. This is perhaps an indication that the *secondary* school teachers' shortage, which has been more severe over the period under consideration, is the principal determinant of salary scales which apply uniformly to both primary and secondary schools. In the case of secondary school teachers' salaries it was clear that the secondary school teachers' shortage is significant, especially when lagged one period as shown in the second equation. Similar results were obtained when salaries of all teachers and salaries of female teachers were used as dependent variables. In the case of males the expected positive sign appeared but it was insignificant.

These results offer some confirmation of the view that relative pay changes respond to the size of the shortage at the level of the teachers' market as a whole.

The union variable always has the expected positive sign but is generally not significantly different from zero.[61] This poor performance in the regression analysis does not, however, necessarily mean that unions do not influence the rate of change of teachers' relative pay since an undeniably crude measure of 'pushfulness' has been used. An analysis of individual settlements suggests that the union probably was important in particular cases. The 1970 award, for example, would very likely not have been achieved without union activity, which was manifest on that occasion by striking, rather than recruiting fervour.

Perhaps more important is the influence of incomes policies, which have almost certainly affected the size of some of the teachers' pay awards, and this may account to some extent for the decline in relative pay of teachers since the early 1960s, and for the lack of advance in real pay from 1965 to 1970. This period of declining relative pay coincides with the decline in the shortage of teachers, which was picked up in the regression analysis. A part of this decline in pay may, however, have been due to the fact that over the 1960s teachers were more willing to submit to the constraints of incomes policy than were other groups.[62] This does not contradict the argu-

61. When the union variable was omitted from the equations, the size and significance of the shortage variable remained unchanged, though the R^2 was reduced.
62. The reasons why teachers have tended to accept incomes-policy constraints, and why they have eschewed militant action until recently, lie outside the scope of this study.

ment that union 'pushfulness' has been important. Indeed, it supports the poor performance in the regressions of the union variable. The influence of incomes policy would tend to strengthen the observed relationship between pay changes and shortage levels. This possibility of the regression coefficients picking up some of the influence of incomes policy means that the conclusion that pay has been used as an adjustment must not be argued too strongly though there is no reason to doubt its general validity.

The discussion so far has been concerned with the level of teachers' salaries as a whole. The structure of salaries is also important. On a cross-subject basis there is some evidence of teachers who are most scarce getting higher pay.[63] Though there are no formal primary–secondary differentials built into the salary scales,[64] we would expect secondary school teachers' salaries to be higher in view of the greater shortage (the shortage of secondary school teachers was more than three times that of primary school teachers in 1970).[65] When age–earnings profiles for different types of teacher (male, female, graduate, non-graduate) in primary and secondary schools are compared there is a clear differential in favour of secondary schools for every group except non-graduate males.[66] Over the period 1961–70 the primary–secondary average earnings differential tended to widen in favour of secondary schools though it did not appear to be systematically related to changes in the relative shortages of primary and secondary school teachers.

It is clear that there are some pronounced differences in the intensity of teacher shortage between different LEAs, and one would expect corresponding geographical variations in pay if this is used as an adjustment instrument. Unfortunately there is a lack of data on regional variations in teachers' earnings, and this expectation can

63. See Thomas (1973b). The data are for broadly defined groups and must be treated cautiously. Lack of data prevents consideration of the movement of subject differentials over time.
64. There are special allowances for some types of school, e.g. schools of special difficulty (which are designated on the basis of such criteria as the social and economic status of the parents of children at the school, the absence of amenities, the proportion of children in the school who have serious linguistic difficulties, etc.) and special schools (which cater for children who are blind, deaf, ESN, etc.).
65. The salary and career structure also gives a built-in bias, via the promotional system, in favour of the secondary sector.
66. Non-graduate males fare better in primary schools because there are so few male graduates in primary schools that they have high chances of getting headships. In secondary schools the competition from graduates is severe and most higher-scale posts go to graduates.

not therefore be confirmed. One of the areas of greatest staffing diffi-culty is London,[67] where there is a formal differential in the shape of the London allowance. The size of this allowance has been the subject of much discontent, and there have been several strikes in recent years on this issue.[68] The Pay Board (1974b) made a two-tier recommendation that the allowance should be increased from £118 to £400 in inner London and £200 in outer London, and this produced a divided reaction from different teachers' unions and management representatives. If the allowance for the whole of London averaged £250 this would represent about a 9–10 per cent bonus over teachers' earnings in the rest of the country. It is difficult, however, to view the teachers' London allowance as a device for raising relative pay — it is rather a means of equalizing real pay between London and elsewhere.

Recently an intensified effort was made to pay more to those schools experiencing staffing difficulties arising from the unusually demanding nature of the job: schools in areas of social deprivation were often those where staff were under the greatest stress and where there is a rapid turnover. In May 1974 the government authorized an increase of about £10 million per annum in the pay of teachers in such schools.[69]

In conclusion to this section we can say that a positive relationship over time was found between the rate of change of teachers' relative salaries and the level of shortage, thus providing support for the view that pay changes are used as an adjustment instrument, though the results were not very strong and other factors were shown to be relevant in determining teachers' pay. At a disaggregated level the ranking of salaries by subject group and by primary and secondary schools shows that higher salaries are paid where the shortage was

67. The difficulties of London schools have been widely discussed. The problem is not strictly one of shortage in terms of numbers but rather a shortage of experienced teachers. London attracts, apparently independently of salary considerations, a much higher proportion of new entrants than any other region (see Turnbull and Zabalza, 1974) but gross turnover rates, i.e. including deaths and retirements, were nearly half as much again as the national average. See *Reports on Education*, No. 79. There is some evidence that young inexperienced teachers are more prone to be absent, thus aggravating the problem.
68. Some of them have been in defiance of majority wishes of NUT membership in London.
69. Since 1973 each LEA can designate individual schools as facing special difficulties and allow a 20% increase in the number of teachers receiving payments for posts of special responsibility. Many such schools have been designated by the ILEA. Previously the EPA scheme, which was introduced in 1968, covered only 600 schools in the whole of England and Wales.

126

most acute, though the fact that there are still differences in the intensity of shortages within teaching shows that the constraints of uniform salary scales for all teachers have prevented the use of complete flexibility in salary adjustments.

7. The Quality of Teachers

One of the adjustments which may take place in response to shortages is a reduction in the quality of the teaching force. The decision-makers are interested in the quality of the whole stock but this changes only through variations in the quality of the flows, assuming there is no substantial in-service training.[70] Most attention is given to the quality of entrants rather than leavers since this is where conscious policy decisions can most easily be brought into effect.[71] There have, however, been some measures which have been designed to reduce the wastage of high-quality teachers. For example, in introducing the graduate training requirements it was claimed that this would offer a more adequate preparation for teaching and thus reduce wastage.

In general, we expect that the quality of entrants to teaching and to courses of training will fall in response to shortages, other things being equal. Before examining the evidence, two points need to be discussed. The first is that throughout the period under consideration there have been continual pressures to raise hiring standards. This upward pressure has been a constant factor though it has sometimes appeared as a sharp jump where it has been formalized in terms of specific qualifications, as in the case of the decision to lengthen the course of training in colleges of education from two to three years and the recent introduction of a graduate training requirement. Other general pressures which may well affect the quality of teachers are the extent to which formal education qualifications remain

---

70. In-service training for most of the post-war period has been on a small scale and uncoordinated. In 1970 about £5½m. was spent on in-service training compared with an annual expenditure of about £80m. on initial training. There may be nominal changes in the stock quality if there is regrading, e.g. the decision to confer 'qualified teacher status' on former uncertificated teachers with long service, but such upgrading does not eliminate a shortage. The Open University has provided an opportunity for many serving teachers to study part-time for a degree, and this increases the quality of the stock of teachers in service.
71. Bibby (1970) has shown how the average quality of the stock changes if there are different wastage rates for 'good' and 'bad' teachers.

constant over time[72] and the general growth of the higher education sector.

The second point is that there is no direct objective measure of the quality of teachers since teaching ability is very difficult to define. This difficulty stems from the fact that the output of the education industry is ill-defined. In practice various characteristics of the stock of teachers, such as the length of service, the proportion of males, or the proportion of mature entrants, are used as indicators of quality but all these have obvious limitations as measures of quality.[73] The characteristic which is most widely used as a proxy for quality is formal educational qualifications of teachers. The drawbacks of this are widely recognized but educational achievements nevertheless remain the most commonly accepted and least ambiguous indicator of quality.

There are two levels of decision-making which affect the quality of teachers. The first is the decision to accept applicants for training and this concerns the training colleges and university departments of education, and the second is the hiring of applicants for teaching posts which concerns a different set of decision-makers. (For many occupations there is just one decision to accept applicants for training and employment.) The hiring-for-employment decision will be dealt with first.

The minimum formal requirements are that teachers must achieve 'qualified teacher status'. There has been no lowering of formal requirements in response to shortage. On the contrary, they have been raised by lengthening the training course in colleges of education and by introducing a graduate training requirement.[74] And the appointment of certain categories of unqualified teacher was stopped in 1968. The timing of these rises in standard was governed to a large extent by the size of the shortage.

72. For example, if A-level or degree standards have risen there may be an (un-measured) increase in the quality of teachers even though the proportion with such qualifications remains the same.
73. Ideally quality would be measured by a weighted index of various teacher characteristics but there is no consensus on what weights should be used. Toder (1972) uses such an index in his study of teachers in Massachusetts. He includes mean educational attainment, mean years of experience, the percentage of males, etc.
74. It is interesting to note that the introduction of the training requirement for maths and science teachers has been postponed. These are teachers for which there is the greatest shortage and this fact clearly illustrates the way in which improvements are sacrificed as a response to shortage. The decision to postpone training for these groups has caused a strong reaction from many groups involved in teaching, on the basis of the wastage argument mentioned earlier.

The Quality of Teachers

Virtually all teachers meet the 'qualified status' requirements,[75] and it is more useful therefore to look at educational achievements over and above the minimum formal requirements. So far as the proportion of graduates in the stock, and more especially in the inflow, were concerned it was expected that the rate of change of these would be negatively related to the levels of shortage. However, no such link was apparent. In the years of intense shortage in the 1950s the proportion of graduates in the stock actually rose, which implied an even more rapid rise in the proportion of graduates in the inflow. This was contrary to expectations and shows how strong was the pressure to employ graduates despite the high level of shortage during this period.[76] During the 1960s the proportion of graduates in the inflow did fall but rose again after 1968. During the 1960s the expected correspondence with the level of shortage is closer.

A much clearer relationship between changes in teachers' characteristics and shortage levels was found when the proportion of graduates with teacher training was examined. When shortages were greatest LEAs appeared more ready to employ untrained graduates.[77] It seems therefore as if LEAs were anxious to try to

75. Throughout the 1950s and 1960s it was generally the case that less than 2% of all teachers were unqualified. The proportion rose to about 2.4% in the mid-1960s when greater numbers of unqualified teachers were accepted as a small and temporary response to cope with the year of intermission when the output of training colleges fell. After 1968 the proportion fell to about 0.1% in 1970.
76. Other factors are almost certainly influential. The rise in graduate unemployment probably accounts for the post-1968 rise in the proportion of graduates. See Thomas (1975) and Zabalza (1974b) for a discussion of the role of salaries and unemployment in determining the proportion of graduates going into teaching.
77. This can be seen from the following regression results, for the period 1955–70.

Dependent Variable	Constant	X(SEC)	R^2	DW
$\dot{H}$ (Female)	2.026 (1.766)	−0.149 (−2.588)	0.324	1.940
$\dot{H}$ (Male)	0.922 (0.954)	−0.075 (−1.545)	0.146	2.541
$\dot{H}$ (Total)	1.348 (1.527)	−1.037 (−2.345)	0.282	2.098

NOTES:
t values are given in brackets.
X (SEC) is the percentage of shortfall from 'requirements' of secondary school teachers.
H is the rate of change of the proportion of the stock of graduate teachers who are trained (*continued on next page*).

129

preserve the proportion of graduates employed but did not particularly care whether they had had a course of teacher training. On
the cross-subject basis there is evidence that teachers with the highest
academic qualifications are found in those subjects where shortages
were least.[78]

The other point at which teacher characteristics may be changed is
entry to courses of initial training. Observed entry standards, as
measured by the proportion of entrants having one or more A-level,
have not fallen though this is largely due to the increasing tendency
for pupils to stay on at school beyond the minimum leaving age, and
when allowance is made for this the college entry standards are
found to have fallen.[79]

On the whole, then, the evidence does not suggest that reductions
in the quality of teachers, brought about by being less demanding in
the characteristics required, have been a major adjustment. This is
partly due to the offsetting pressure to raise the quality of teachers in
pursuit of the goal of qualitative improvements in education.

8. The Substitution of Other Factors and the Employment of Non-Teaching Labour

One of the possible responses to the shortage of teachers is to substitute other factors of production. There is little evidence on the

---

The negative sign on shortages is found in all cases, though it is weaker in the case
of males where the coefficient is only significant at the 10% level on a one tail test.
The secondary school shortage, as reported above, seemed slightly more relevant
than the total shortage (indicated by higher t values and R^2). This is not
surprising in view of the heavy concentration of graduates in secondary schools.
When lagged versions of the shortage variable were tried, the results were weaker
which suggests that the willingness to accept untrained graduates is a response to
the current shortage positions.

78. A weak statistical association between the proportion of graduates with 'good
honours' degrees and the extent of shortage was found on a cross-subject basis,
though there are severe problems in matching data from different sources. The
anecdotal evidence in this area is, however, very convincing. For example, see the
Royal Society survey (1969) for reports on the poor-quality maths and science
teachers who have had to be accepted as a result of shortages of these teachers.

79. Entry standards depend on the number of applicants per place. The number of
applicants will depend on the number of school-leavers aged 17 and over, the
relative attractiveness of teaching, and the state of the labour market. There have,
in post-war years, been more applicants than places and the rationing of places has
generally been on the basis of performance in public examinations. The growth in
the number of places provided which was discussed in Section 4 has been matched
by the number of applicants and this has enabled entry standards to be preserved.

nature of the production function in education but some substitution of non-teaching inputs for teachers would almost certainly
be possible[80] since the process is technologically primitive at present
with 'simple materials, walls, workers and overseers' (L. C. Taylor,
1971:36). There have been several changes in teaching methods over
the years, and televisions, tape-recorders, and teaching machines
have been used on a limited scale. But some of the changes such as
'team teaching' have been purely organizational, and much more
capital substitution would seem possible. There is, however, disagree-
ment among educationalists on whether this would represent a
deterioration in the quality of education, and the norms of a fixed
pupil–teacher ratio act as a powerful constraint.

There is evidence of a decline in teacher intensity in education[81]
but there is little basis for supposing that this represents factor substitution in response to shortage. It is rather part of a secular trend in
which the whole schooling process has become more resource-
intensive. As part of the long-term qualitative improvement in education more inputs of all kinds are now being used per child. The rate
of growth of non-teaching inputs has, however, been faster than that
of teachers so we have observed a rise in the teacher–pupil ratio
accompanied by a fall in the ratio of teachers to other inputs.

Thus there has been no substitution of other factors as an adjustment, though there was an attempt at dilution in the face of staffing
difficulties. In 1962 the then Minister of Education suggested that
girls with about 12–15 weeks' training could be used to work under
qualified teachers, and that girls with a longer period of training, but
less than the full three-year period, might take a short-service commission, and if they later returned to teaching they could complete

80. Vaizey *et al.* (1972:192) argue that the elasticity of substitution, between teachers
and other inputs, 'appears to be approximately unity since despite a price increase
of over 100% between 1955 and 1967 in labour inputs, compared with an increase
of less than 50% in the price of non-labour inputs, the relative share of teachers in
total costs was approximately constant'.
81. Analysis of expenditure on teachers' salaries as a proportion of all expenditure
shows that in *current* price terms salaries have accounted for a roughly constant
proportion of current expenditure, about 70% in primary schools and 65% in
secondary schools, over the period 1950–70. However, *current* price figures do not
show how the volume of resources used has changed, and examination of
expenditure on education and the component items in *constant* price terms
suggests that there has been a decline in teacher intensity in post-war years. In
constant price terms teachers' salaries as a proportion of total current expenditure
fell from 69% in 1950 to 60% in 1965 in secondary schools and from 73% to 62%
over the same period in primary schools. These calculations are based on Vaizey
and Sheehan (1968: Appendix B). Later figures on a per pupil basis have been
produced by Vaizey *et al.* (1972), which show the trend continuing to 1967.

their training. These suggestions did not actually refer to substitute teachers but it was clear from the context that it was a proposal for dilution in the face of a shortage of fully qualified teachers.

This formal proposal came at a time when there was already use of temporary teachers and auxiliaries for teaching duties[82] and it received hostile reception from the unions,[83] with the result that formal dilution proposals were abandoned and alternative strategy pursued. The use of ancillary workers was encouraged and these were welcomed by the NUT and the NAS,[84] who felt that the use of such 'helpers' would reduce the time and energy spent on non-teaching tasks and allow scarce teaching skills to be more fully utilized. There is no way of tracing, in detail, the link between the introduction of ancillaries and shortages since figures are only available for 1965 (when about 86,000 full-time or part-time helpers were employed) (AEC, 1966). This strategy represents an increase in the net advantages of the job through the removal of what teachers often regard as disagreeable chores.

9. Reducing 'Requirements'

In many labour markets, shortages are frequently met by reducing the rate of output. This is sometimes a conscious decision to reduce production activity but more often it is a residual adjustment which takes the form of a desired output plan not being achieved. In the case of schools the number of pupils, and hence the teacher 'requirements', can be reduced either by reducing the period of compulsory schooling or by reducing the length of the school day or year.

The minimum period of compulsory schooling is statutorily laid down. It would be possible to reduce this, for example, by raising the starting age from 5 to 6 years, but this would require changing a formal norm which has been regarded almost as an article of faith by education administrators. Most of the pressure in post-war years has in fact been to increase the length of compulsory schooling and this

82. Some reports indicate heavy reliance on such teachers by some authorities. For example, Chapman (1965: 6) alleged that 'at Luton about a quarter of the teachers are temporaries.' He also claimed that in some places, 'when a teacher is ill, or no teacher can be found, untrained girls of 17 may be looking after a class.'
83. See NAS (1967) for an account of this opposition.
84. They made the proviso that teachers' salaries should not be affected. In some areas graded posts had been given to teachers undertaking non-teaching duties such as milk distribution, and these duties would no longer be done by teachers. See NAS (1965:14).

has been achieved by raising the leaving age, by taking in 'rising fives'[85] and by encouraging more children to stay beyond the minimum school-leaving age. In each case, however, the rate of implementation of these desires to increase the period of schooling seems to have been affected by the extent of the shortage of teachers.

The extent to which 'rising fives' can be taken is conditioned by the availability of staff, and in periods of staff shortage young children are not admitted or are taken only on a part-time basis. A more striking example is the length of time it took for the raising of the school-leaving age to become a reality. The 1944 Education Act had stated the objective of having a school-leaving age of 16 (it was then only 14) but after raising it to 15 in 1947 nothing further was done during the whole of the 1950s when the shortages of teachers were most intense. It was not until 1959, the year that the shortage of teachers began to decrease, that the first detailed recommendation appeared.[86] By 1964 it was quite clear that this decline in the shortage level was a permanent and large reduction,[87] and the decision was taken by the DES to raise the leaving age to 16 in 1971. Preparations began but towards the end of the 1960s the budgetary constraint was suddenly tightened,[88] and in 1968 the implementation was postponed from 1971 to 1972–3. The fact that it took so long to bring in this change — 28 years since the objective was publicly stated as desirable and 13 years since the first practical proposals — was very largely governed by the shortage position.

The second way of altering the quantity of schooling provided is by varying the length of the school day and year. Although there have been very minor changes in the length of the school year, there has never been any major alteration in the three-term structure, nor any attempt to have children attending on a rota basis. The norms here are rigid, as are those governing the hours of attendance during the day, so that shift-working and overtime tend to be ruled out.

85. These are children whose fifth birthday is due to fall in the academic year. Strictly there is no statutory obligation to take them until they are 5 years old.
86. See Crowther Report (1959). These proposals were supported by the Newsom Report (1963).
87. Between 1959 and 1964 the shortage of teachers fell by almost 16,000. Over the period 1951–9 the shortfall from 'requirements' had never been less than 18.7% and it averaged 19.4%. After 1959 it fell in successive years to 17.6%, 16.6%, and 14.9% and by 1964 it had reached 13.6%.
88. In January 1968 public expenditure cuts were announced as part of a strategy to take advantage of devaluation and divert resources to exports. The deferment of the raising of the school-leaving age was designed principally to reduce the school building programme.

More recently, however, there has been some use of part-time education in inner-city schools where teacher shortages are relatively acute.[89]

Thus it is quite clear that largely because of the constraints of administered rules the use of output reduction has scarcely been used as an adjustment, though the teacher shortage has probably affected the timing of the implementation of measures to extend the period of schooling.

Apart from altering the number of pupils, the 'requirements' may be reduced by reducing the staffing standards. Once again, however, the formal norms governing the desired teacher–pupil ratio have been so strong that this has not been used as a positive adjustment.[90] Nevertheless it has been an important residual adjustment, and variations in the actual ratio have been directly related to movements in the level of teacher shortage.

The conclusion to be drawn from this discussion is that there has been little positive attempt to reduce teacher 'requirements' either by output reduction or changes in staffing standards or changes in the distribution of teachers. There may, however, be substantial changes in the quality of output as a consequence of shortages. Unfortunately there is only impressionistic evidence on this question, often provided by interested parties, but there are many reports of poor quality of education resulting from teacher shortages. One of the less obvious ways in which shortages affect the quality of teaching is in slowing down or preventing the introduction of new teaching methods or curricula. Innovation of this kind usually involves additional hours of preparation by teachers, who, when burdened with the strain of large classes and the need to use their 'free' periods to cover for other teachers, find their time and energy dissipated.[91] In

89. In the last six months of 1973 and early part of 1974 there were numerous newspaper headlines and accounts of part-time education especially in London. The prominence given by the press to this phenomenon greatly exaggerates the extent to which this adjustment has been used nationally, though locally and in the short term it may be important, e.g. a *Guardian* report (13 May 1974) claimed that about 100 London schools were having to send children home.

90. Although there has been no formal alteration in the desired ratio, there have been some changes in the way the staffing objectives have been expressed which have allowed more flexibility in the size of any individual class. This is merely a recognition of the fact that teaching methods over the last decade have changed considerably and that children are now taught in groups of varying size thoughout the day.

91. The proposal to reform the school examination system put forward by the Schools Council in the late 1960s met a hostile reception from the Royal Society which simply argued that any reform was impossible because of the shortage of maths and science teachers.

134

more serious shortage situations, not only may improvements be delayed but the structure of courses itself may become affected.[92]

10. Conclusions

The principal adjustments which have been used in the teachers' market are summarized in Figure 4.2 which shows their timing in relation to the shortage. The general question which arises in connection with this figure is to explain why, at given times, particular instruments have been used rather than others.

Three particular features of Figure 4.2 require comment. First, it is clear that only a few of the possible instruments have been used. Second, the positive adjustments have mainly been in the form of attempts to influence supply-side rather than demand-side operands. Third, for the first half of the 20-year period covered there was a reliance on residual adjustments which meant that the shortage persisted at a high level.

Experience in other countries shows that there are many possible forms of response which have not been used in England and Wales. Explicit salary differentials for teachers in different subject groups have been used in Ireland and Denmark. Non-salary financial inducements to potential teachers have been used in Kenya which gives 'free' training to teachers, but not to other higher education students. In Switzerland, accelerated training programmes have been used extensively. Brazil has made it compulsory for all women in higher education to undertake teacher training. Dilution, in the form of creating special 'shortage' posts which may be filled by people who do not fully meet the usual minimum requirements for qualified teacher status has been used by Sweden. Overtime working for teachers has been used frequently in many European countries. It would be easy to add to this list but sufficient examples have been provided to make the point.

The use of such a restricted range of instruments in England and Wales can partly be explained in terms of cost-minimizing behaviour but only so long as full recognition is given to the particular constraints which operate. The resource constraint has always been

---

92. L. C. Taylor wrote the following account of some of the consequences of an acute shortage situation in one school. 'Last year the younger boys had physics but the physicist had moved to another school and a retired chemist is the only possible replacement; for physics on the timetable read chemistry. A school develops strange specialities for brief periods' (1971: 35).

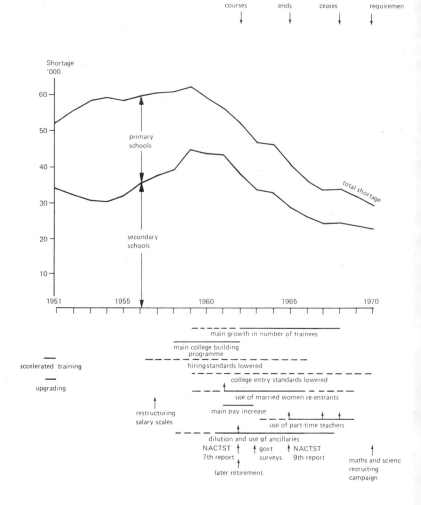

FIGURE 4.2. SHORTAGES OF TEACHERS AND THE
ADJUSTMENTS USED

NOTE: It should be noted that this figure records only the principal adjustments which have been used. There are some others such as the provision by some LEAs of crèche facilities to enable mothers with young children to teach, and small-scale

present in post-war years despite the continuous rise in real expenditure on education, but of more interest is the set of administered rules. These are a mixture of financial considerations, 'ideal targets' for output and labour–output ratios, and these norms which are often based on educational and other non-economic criteria determine the 'requirements' and the adjustments used.

The second point concerned the reliance on adjustments which affect supply rather than demand. There has been virtually no attempt, at least formally, to reduce 'requirements'. To explain this we must consider the goals of the education decision-makers and the weights attached to them.

It was argued in Section 1 that the whole history of school education in the post-war period has been one of expansion and improvement and that it is essential to see adjustments against this background. It was assumed that there was a preference for quantity over quality in the desire for general advance and this seems to be borne out by the facts. The authorities were initially concerned with getting the 'right' number of teachers, and only when the shortage lessened was attention directed to the quality of teachers. Thus most of the earlier adjustments which occurred when shortages were greatest, such as the provision of additional training college places between 1958 and 1962, were not at all concerned with the subject specialism of teachers. Later on, when the shortages eased, attempts were made to recruit specific types of teacher. For example, in the late 1960s, when the overall shortage was only about half of what it was during the main college building era, there was the campaign to attract maths and science teachers specifically. And it was not until the later 1960s that LEAs began to consider, when recruiting, the age and sex as well as subject balance within schools. In terms of the characteristics of individual teachers too, it was only at the end of the 1960s that employment of teachers not of 'qualified status' was stopped

---

efforts to use teacher training colleges more intensively by keeping college buildings in service beyond their scheduled life, but these have been comparatively minor measures. The dates shown in the figure are only rough approximations in the cases where the instrument is shown as operating over several years. In some cases, particular adjustments were used before receiving formal encouragement from the DES and it is often impossible to identify a specific starting-point. The use of part-timers is an example of a case where it is difficult to pin down a starting-date. The unbroken lines, showing when instruments were used, indicate the most intensive use of the instruments. Broken lines indicate less intensive use (or lack of information on the intensity of use).

and a graduate training requirement introduced. One major adjustment, which could be considered an exception to this general picture of qualitative considerations always following quantitative ones, is the lengthening of teacher training courses in colleges of education from two to three years, which came into effect as early as 1962 when the teacher shortage was still about 15 per cent of 'requirements'. This was, however, *after* the peak in post-war shortage figures and after many years of pressure for this measure, especially from the unions. On balance, it is reasonable to accept the view that priority has been given to quantity over quality in expanding the teaching force.

The concern with the quality and quantity of education partly explains why positive adjustments have mainly been attempts to influence the supply-side operands. Any formal reduction in 'requirements' would be incompatible with the pursuit of improvements in the quality and quantity of education provided, whereas most supply-side adjustments are entirely compatible with these goals. This is obviously the case with permanent adjustments such as the provision of more training college places or the growth in the use of part-timers. It is less true of temporary supply-side adjustments such as reduction in hiring standards, since this can be regarded as a fall in the quality of the education provided. However, given the ranking of quantity and quality goals, this is preferable to reducing teacher 'requirements', whether this be in the form of reducing the number of pupils or the amount of schooling given to each pupil. This preference for supply-side adjustment in the form of reduced hiring standards was recognized by the Plowden Committee when they noted that *'to avoid keeping children out of school,* authorities with insufficient qualified staff employ unqualified temporary and occasional teachers to take charge of a class.'[93]

The positive supply-side adjustments were not, however, sufficient to eliminate the shortage, and residual adjustments were necessary. The third point mentioned earlier was that shortages persisted because of this reliance on residual adjustments in the 1950s. These were clearly not effective in reducing the size of the shortage, which did not begin to fall until the positive adjustments were used on a larger scale in the 1960s.

Cost-minimizing behaviour provides some explanation for this pattern of adjustments since the residual adjustments, incurring no direct costs, are in one sense the cheapest. However, they do involve costs, in the form of failure to reach the desired quality of output. We

93. Plowden Report (1967: para. 926); our italics.

have shown that the quality of output has been given less weight as a goal than the quantity, and this therefore helps to explain why residual adjustments were so common in the earlier period. It also shows again that the cost-minimizing hypothesis is only meaningful when the objective function is specified.

Cost-minimizing behaviour is, however, only a part of the story and some of the explanation for the heavy use of residual adjustments in the 1950s, and the consequent persistence of shortages, lies with the fact that in the early post-war years there was no decision-making machinery capable of implementing large-scale positive adjustments. During the period 1955–65, there was a great expansion of the DES and a growing centralization of its power.[94] Its place in the cabinet became established and its efforts to provide and appraise information on the state of the teachers' market and other aspects of education improved dramatically in the late 1950s.[95] This growth in the stature of the DES and its improved control coincided with the increasing propensity to eliminate shortages.

The structure of the decision-making machinery is in fact of interest in a more general way than just accounting for the late emergence of positive adjustments. The split between the LEAs and the DES has been noted. The former are responsible for the provision of education and the employment of teachers, yet many of the decisions are taken at national level and involve the DES: for example, the terms and conditions, and the scale, of employment and the principal forms of adjustment. A different structure of decision-making could produce different adjustments. If, for example, each LEA were free to adjust in whatever way it wished, then a variety of responses may occur depending on local circumstances. As it is, the superimposition of national standards and policies produces a degree of uniformity in the type of adjustment used.

This survey of adjustments in the teachers' market has shown, as with other occupations in this study, that there are several operands

---

94. See Vaizey and Sheehan (1968:20) for an account of the improvement in the political standing of education and the statistical services, though Vaizey writing as late as 1967 noted that 'it is greatly to be doubted whether the role of the Department as the central planning body for a vast field of public expenditure has yet been fully reflected in the calibre of the senior officials.'

95. The principal attempts to improve its knowledge of the labour market for teachers and the extent of the shortage began in the early 1960s (one aspect of which was the publication of more detailed statistics than previously). However, despite the various forecasting exercises, it has generally been true to say that adjustments rarely tried to anticipate shortage. They have been responses to existing shortages.

and a wide range of instruments which can be used to affect them. Numerous forms of adjustment are therefore observed.

The cost-minimizing hypothesis requires filling out by explicit consideration of constraints and objectives if it is to provide a suitable basis for explaining the choice of adjustments in the teachers' market. When this is done, it offers some predictions relating to the mix and sequence of instruments used which are broadly confirmed. There are, however, other factors, most notably the nature of the decision-making machinery, which must be taken into account.

5
Draughtsmen

While this study is concerned mainly with labour shortages, the market for draughtsmen is one which has exhibited both shortages and surpluses in recent years. Moreover, the job of a draughtsman is less well defined than the job of a bus driver or a school teacher. For these reasons we begin by describing the draughtsman's job and recent trends in the market, before considering the adjustments which have been made to imbalances of labour. The first section deals with the question of what constitutes the boundary of this occupation, and outlines some of the characteristics of the market which are apparent from published data. Section 2 discusses the nature of shortages and surpluses in this market, and subsequent sections deal with a number of adjustment instruments in turn. Section 7 deals with redundancy and labour surplus, and Section 8 draws some conclusions.

The evidence on which this chapter is based is drawn from interviews with managers and trade union representatives in ten engineering plants. Each plant has been given a pseudonym but brief descriptions of its products and labour-market situation are given when the firm is first mentioned.

1. Introduction

Draughtsmen and their Market
In selecting occupations for this study we were influenced by two main considerations: the occupations were to be easily identifiable as occupations, and have markets with dissimilar characteristics. In line with the second consideration we have two occupations with mainly public employers and one with mainly private employers,

two with atomistic decision-making and one with central decision-making, two white-collar and one blue-collar. But in selecting draughtsmen we have a further difference. Whereas bus drivers' and school teachers' markets have fairly clear boundaries, the boundary of the draughtsmen's market is somewhat confused. But paradoxically the confused boundary exists without jeopardizing our first consideration to select easily identifiable occupations.[1]

The employees of a drawing office whose job it is to produce detailed drawings from a rough outline are certainly draughtsmen. This is beyond dispute. However, there is a grey area of the technical labour force whose members are sometimes considered to be draughtsmen. Some people are content to call all engineering technicians 'draughtsmen', while others use the term to denote those engaged in producing detailed drawings.

However, many technicians outside the drawing office see themselves as engineers rather than draughtsmen regardless of whether their output resembles a conventional engineering drawing or not. Instead of identifying an occupation by its organizational role or by some superficial characteristic of its output, these technicians distinguish between the draughtsman, who is given a specific task to perform, and the engineer, who is allocated an area of responsibility.[2]

Moreover, within drawing offices the distinction is sometimes made between designers and draughtsmen. Since all but the most junior draughtsmen will be involved in design as well as detailing, this distinction tends to be arbitrary and is not drawn consistently across firms.

Before the war the situation was much simpler. An engineer was someone of high status who developed an overall view of a project, with a number of draughtsmen under him. These draughtsmen carried out designing and detailing, planned the production, and ordered materials. Since then, two trends have been instrumental in changing this job structure. The introduction of war-time dilutees,

1. B. C. Roberts *et al.* comment on this. 'Draughtsmen differed from other groups of technicians in that they had a strong sense of belonging to [an] occupation . . . This is not altogether surprising, since draughtsmen tend to be employed in groups in the drawing office, isolated from other groups in the plant, and this has naturally led to a feeling of identity' (1972:126).
2. Neither is there a clear distinction between technicians and other occupational groups such as clerical workers, craftsmen, and technologists. Most definitions of a technician treat this occupational group as a residual (see p. 144). For a wider discussion of the definition of a technician see B. C. Roberts *et al.* (1972: Chapter 2).

who merely detailed, devalued the status of the draughtsmen to the extent that the term 'designer' has been brought in to restore the former prestige of the job. Alongside this has been a growing specialization in the technical field. This has brought into existence a wide range of technicians whose work is related to draughtsmanship but who are not called draughtsmen. There has been a corresponding shrinkage in the range of the draughtsman's job.[3] In addition to this there are a number of specialisms within the current use of the term draughtsman (e.g. engineering, electrical, and architectural). Hence the 'solution' to the paradox. The proliferation of meanings attached to the term 'draughtsman' arises from changes in status and the degree of specialization, and the lag in the linguistic response to them. Nowadays the job title of 'draughtsman' tends to denote those engaged on the single identifiable activity of drawing but excludes those technicians with similar training who would consequently be included in the same labour market. When the title was a less accurate description of the job, it was, however, a better delineation of the market.

Changes in job titles and job content have been reflected in the policies of the union. In so far as one can classify unions, TASS is an open craft union.[4] For some time it was reluctant to recruit outside the drawing office but the growing range of technical jobs threatening to usurp some of the draughtsman's functions forced it to change its policy even to the extent of changing its name twice.[5]

3. Cooley spells this out: 'The function of the design draughtsmen is becoming more and more fragmented and specialised. The draughtsman in the '30s was the centre of the design activity. He would design the component, draw it, stress it, select the materials for it, write the test specifications for it, liaise with the customer and usually liaise with the work-shop floor for production. Towards the end of the '30s, and certainly during the War, all of these functions were broken down into discernible separate jobs. The calculations were carried out by stressmen, the materials selected by metallurgists, the form of lubrication determined by tribologists, the draughtsmen did the drawing, production engineering was carried out by methods and planning engineers, and customer liaison by specialist customer liaison engineers' (1972: 77–8).
4. See Turner (1962) for a discussion of trade union classification.
5. The Association of Engineering and Shipbuilding Draughtsmen was formed in 1913. In 1961 its name was changed to the Draughtsmen's and Allied Technicians' Association. In 1970 it amalgamated with the AEF becoming the Technical and Supervisory Section of the AUEW. One drawing office manager claimed that the break-up of the old draughting jobs was partly due to firms trying to take people out of the TASS procedure by changing their job title. Our study did not indicate that such moves initiated a change in job title, but rather that firms may try to take advantage of a re-organization to cut some tasks out of the TASS area.

143

The evolution of a complex job structure has important implications for the operation of the market. The manipulation of the job structure becomes a potential adjustment instrument, and job titles become artefacts of the market rather than boundaries of it. The spread of union membership over a variety of jobs has to a certain extent constrained the use of wages as an adjustment device. Since the coverage of TASS agreements extends further than the drawing office, a firm is less likely to adjust to a shortage of draughtsmen by raising wage rates.

What is a Draughtsman?

The definition of a draughtsman varies, as we have seen, with the role of the person doing the defining. The researcher must choose his own definition from amongst a number of possibilities. The appropriate definition will depend on the problem being studied, and because this investigation of the labour market for draughtsmen tackles a set of problems, a variety of definitions will have to be employed in the course of it.

In official statistics, the category 'draughtsmen' is defined for us, though there is some variation in the way in which managements categorize employees when making their official returns. Broadly speaking, the draughtsman category includes those designated draughtsmen together with drawing checkers, stressmen, loftsmen, and technical illustrators. But for questions concerning the change in the draughtsman's job it is necessary to look at that group of employees who are now performing work done wholly or partly by those designated draughtsmen in the past.

On questions of pay, the appropriate delineation is that group which is covered by TASS in negotiations. This may be more or less coincidental with the official definition of a technician: 'Draughtsman or other person carrying out functions of a grade intermediate between scientists and technologists on the one hand and skilled craftsmen and operators on the other.'[6]

When dealing with questions of labour shortage, we must recognize the heterogeneity of the occupation. The organizational distinction between product draughtsmen and jig-and-tool draughtsmen reflects different skills, and though it is acknowledged that tool draughtsmen could well adapt themselves to product design the

6. This is the form of words used by the EITB (1969). It is similar to the definition in the DE's instructions to employers for completing its questionnaires.

reverse is less true. Typically an engineering firm distinguishes between mechanical and electrical draughtsmen, but specialization within the aircraft industry goes further than this. Aircraft firms tend to have drawing offices which specialize in avionics, aerodynamics, lofting, and stress work, and make distinctions within offices between hydraulic, systems, and structural draughtsmen.[7] Opinions differ as to the ease with which draughtsmen can move from one type of work to another but the most fundamental cleavage is between draughtsmen performing intricate work and those involved with greater tolerances. There exists, therefore, a pattern of sub-markets with norms of acceptable mobility. As we shall see in Section 6 these norms are sometimes adjusted in the face of a labour shortage.

Employment of Draughtsmen

This study of the market for draughtsmen will concentrate on the decisions made at the level of the firm. It is, however, useful to examine some of the trends which are apparent from occupational statistics. The decline in the numbers of draughtsmen employed is considered here and the steep increase in draughtsmen's unemployment in the early 1970s is dealt with in Appendix C.

While bus drivers and school teachers are employed almost exclusively in one industry, draughtsmen are employed in almost all industries. Our concern, however, is primarily with draughtsmen in the engineering industry though the official statistics which are quoted will refer to all draughtsmen.

An important feature of the draughtsmen's market is that draughtsmen constitute a small proportion of the labour force in any one industry. In the 1966 Census of Population, draughtsmen as a percentage of all employees were highest in the engineering and electrical goods industry with the figure of 3 per cent.[8] Bus drivers constitute 32 per cent of the labour force in transport and school teachers 54 per cent of the educational labour force.

In the first half of this century the number of draughtsmen has increased very rapidly compared with the total economically active population. This rapid growth petered out in the last decade as shown in Table 5.1. At the same time the number of other technicians has grown, which leads one to suspect that the trends of

---

7. For a description of these various specialisms see DE (1972: 231–8).
8. This is the SIC order with the highest percentage of draughtsmen. At the MLH level 5% of aircraft employees and 9% of employees in Scientific Services are draughtsmen.

TABLE 5.1
AVERAGE ANNUAL GROWTH RATES FOR VARIOUS
OCCUPATIONS
(Males and females: Great Britain)

	Draughtsmen	Scientists and Engineers	Total Occupied/ Economically Active[a]
1921–31	5.3	4.0	1.4
1931–51	4.0	5.0	0.3
1951–61	3.4	7.3	0.6
1961–66	−1.1	5.0	0.8
1966–71	−0.6	2.9	0.1

SOURCES: 1921 occupational figure from Bain (1970:13). Other figures from *Census of Population.*
NOTE: a. There is a slight change in coverage of the total occupied/ economically active series between 1951 and 1961. See *British Labour Statistics: Historical Abstract,* Table 104.

specialization and job re-titling described above were largely responsible.[9]

The effect of these trends on the employment data for draughtsmen is impossible to estimate, but we can get an indication of the size of the effect from what at first sight seemed a minor change in job title. In 1962, one firm re-titled their architectural draughtsmen and plant layout draughtsmen 'Factory Planning Engineers'. By 1966 there were 78 employees working for the plant who would be classified as draughtsmen under the Census, but there were also 28 employees who were classified as engineers who, without this change

9. This can be seen from changes in the employment of draughtsmen and technicians in engineering from the 'Occupations of Employees in Manufacturing Industries/Engineering' in the DE *Gazette.* The survey covers firms employing more than 10 people in 1958 orders VI–IX in May each year. These figures are for males and females.

	Draughtsmen	Other Technicians
1966	92,670	106,920
1967	88,270	118,720
1968	89,980	129,420
1969	86,130	134,060
1970	86,840	147,490
1971	80,960	152,190
1972	75,250	145,620

in job title, would be classified as draughtsmen. If this plant had been typical of the whole country, correcting for the effect of a change in job title would have given an annual growth rate of 5.2 per cent in the number of draughtsmen between 1961 and 1966 rather than a decline of 1.0 per cent per annum. This illustrates the sensitivity of official statistics to changes in job title.

A decline in the recorded number of draughtsmen will also occur when the scope of the drawing office is reduced. In most plants visited, at least one drawing office function had been transferred to a department of its own in the previous decade. This trend has been so widespread that almost any draughtsman or engineer over the age of forty will tell one about the 'break-up of the old draughtsman's job'. These job changes can be attributed mainly to the increasing complexity of the design and development function.[10]

Other possible explanations for this decline in the number of draughtsmen were examined. We tested for the effects of changes in industrial composition but the result suggested that in the absence of any such changes the fall in the number of draughtsmen between 1961 and 1966 would have been even greater.[11]

It is sometimes suggested that the adoption of CAD techniques has been responsible for a reduction in demand for draughtsmen. But the application of this type of equipment is limited mainly to electronics, mapping, and vehicle body design, whereas the decline in the number of draughtsmen has been more widespread than in just

---

10. In the midst of these changes in job titles and job structure, official occupational definitions become confused and hence the reliability of published data is questionable. The DE's 'Occupations of Employees in Manufacturing Industries' is based on annual returns by companies. The DE gives the employer a choice of categories (viz. draughtsmen, other technicians, and scientists and technologists). The classification of jobs into occupations is made by the firms themselves and in practice there is a good deal of variation in the way this is done. In some firms the draughtsman category was merely those who were called draughtsmen, or the technical staff in the drawing office. In other firms the category covered planners and laboratory assistants as well as design staff. The increasing use of the title 'designer', adds to the confusion. Designers were sometimes classified as 'draughtsmen', sometimes as 'other technicians' and occasionally as 'scientists and technologists'. Because of these inconsistencies we would recommend any investigator working with such data to group together the categories of 'draughtsmen' and 'other technicians', even though this may involve the loss of one degree of freedom. The Census of Population leaves the individual to state his job title which can be classified more specifically but the effects of the changes described will be seen here as well.

11. The actual ratio of male draughtsmen to total employment fell from 1.027% in 1961 to 0.978% in 1966. The average of the 1961 industrial ratios weighted by the 1966 industrial composition of employment was 1.058%.

these industries. However, in those firms visited which used CAD it was evident that there was a wide range of technicians outside the drawing office who were involved in the design process. It seems that computerized techniques merely reinforce the substitution of other technicians for draughtsmen.

The forces which have brought changes in job title and job structure form the major part of the explanation for the fall in the number of draughtsmen, but the question remains whether any pattern can be found in this quasi-substitution of other technicians for draughtsmen.

It was noticeable in the course of this study that in the smaller companies draughtsmen tended to be performing a wider range of tasks than in the larger companies. The drawing office in smaller companies often covers planning and production engineering. The EITB report (1970) on technicians confirms that there is a higher ratio of other technicians to draughtsmen in the larger firms, as Table 5.2 shows. This being the case, it seemed possible that the growth in establishment size might explain the quasi-substitution of other technicians for draughtsmen. But in fact this accounted for very little, if any, of the change in job structure. Between the 1958 and 1963 Censuses of Production the distribution of employment by establishment size remained fairly constant in the Engineering and Electrical Goods Order, and between 1963 and 1968 there was a fall in employment in the large establishments (1,000 employees and over) relative to smaller ones. The increase in establishment size in vehicles 'explains' a growth in the number of other technicians of 0.7 per cent and a decline in the number of draughtsmen of 1.8 per cent between 1958 and 1963. However, between 1963 and 1968, these changes in employment predict a rise in the proportion of draughts-

TABLE 5.2
PERCENTAGE DISTRIBUTION OF DRAUGHTSMEN
AND OTHERS BY SIZE OF ESTABLISHMENT
(May 1969, industries covered by EITB, males and females)

Employees	Draughtsmen	Other Technicians	All Employees
100–249	17.9	9.8	14.0
250–499	15.9	12.3	14.5
500–999	20.9	14.4	17.9
1,000 or more	45.3	63.5	53.6

SOURCE: EITB (1970: Tables 3 and 4).

men to other technicians.[12] One must conclude that, although the break-up of the draughtsman's job is more marked in large establishments, the degree of specialization is not simply a function of the size of establishments.

Summary

A number of problems arise in delineating the boundary of the draughtsmen's market. The coverage of the term 'draughtsman' has changed in the post-war period, and consequently there is no clear-cut distinction between draughtsmen and engineers. The scope of the drawing office has narrowed and, in response to this, the catchment area of the union has been extended. There being no consistent definition of a draughtsman, the precise group of jobs we will deal with in this chapter will vary according to the problem under consideration.

A number of features of the market are apparent from published data. Unlike school teachers and bus drivers, draughtsmen are not concentrated in one industry nor do they form a substantial section of the workforce in any industry. We have observed a decline in the absolute number of draughtsmen in the last decade which has been coincident with a rise in the number of 'other technicians'. Our analysis leads us to believe that this is due to the changes in the draughtsman's job which have been described. Though these changes are more marked in larger establishments, the growth in the size of establishment does not account for much of this change.

2. Shortage and Surplus

Two of the features of the draughtsmen's market are important in the formulation of a framework within which to consider shortages and surpluses. First, there is competition on the buyers' side of the market; in most localities there will be a number of firms who wish to employ draughtsmen. Second, the time and cost required to train a draughtsman are sufficient to identify draughtsmen in terms of their skill and not just through the nature of the job they are performing or have recently performed. Thus a firm when recruiting maybe seen as entering the market for draughtsmen. This can be contrasted with the firm which requires semi-skilled or unskilled labour

12. The effect of changes in the size of establishments was isolated by calculating the numbers of draughtsmen and other technicians that there would have been if the ratios of draughtsmen to all employees, and other technicians to all employees, had been constant at the 1969 levels for each range of establishment size.

entering *the* labour market. In this chapter, therefore, we will consider market shortages and surpluses of draughtsmen in addition to firms' imbalance. This is a contrast to the teachers' market where we dealt with a monopsonist, and the bus industry which was characterized by near-monopsony and relatively low-skilled operators.

We distinguish between a firm's adjustment to an internal shortage and its response to a market shortage, but the two phenomena are related. The state of the external market will affect the firm's ability to alleviate a manpower shortage, and the total number of vacancies in the market will be the sum of vacancies in individual firms. A market shortage does not imply that all firms in the market experience a shortage, but it does mean that the 'typical' firm experiences a shortage.

This distinction between external and internal imbalances is even more important when considering surpluses. Whereas firms' shortages add up to the market vacancy figure,[13] firms' internal surpluses — hoarded labour — have no necessary connection with the total unemployment level. Again, there are two distinct stimuli acting upon decision-makers: an excess of labour inside the firm and an excess of unemployed workers over vacancies in the market.

Strictly speaking, the state of the external market is not of direct concern to an employer. His concern is with the effect the external market has on his recruitment and quit rates. When considering the action of the decision-maker rather than the operation of the market, it is best to distinguish between the stock and the flow stimuli rather than the internal and external balances.

So far we have referred loosely to the firm's demand for draughtsmen without adequately defining 'demand'. Conventionally, 'demand for labour' means the number of men a firm wishes to employ at a given wage rate. However, by attributing goals, desires, and behaviour to the collective entity of a firm, one is in danger of ignoring the possible internal conflict between departments and individuals. Quite often, for example, the employing department and the financial department of a firm have different ideas of what amount of labour is required. This is akin to the distinction made in Chapter 2 (and developed in the bus drivers' and teachers' chapters) between establishments and demand. In the case of draughtsmen, however, the distinction is important not so much because of the extent of a shortage, but rather in the creation of a redundancy

---

13. Where a firm reports vacancies which allow for expected quits and expected changes in demand, as Holt and David (1966) predict, the vacancy figure is not identical to the shortage of labour.

situation or where the employment department, which defines a shortage, is overruled by the financial sector which prohibits the recruitment of more staff.

Conflict over the level of requirements is more likely to arise in the case of indirect labour, such as draughtsmen, which is classified under the financial category of overheads. Whereas the demand for bus drivers and teachers is directly derived from an externally defined demand, there is no simple measure of the output of draughtsmen, still less is there a straightforward way of assessing the demand for their services. What can be said is that the demand for their services fluctuates a good deal. Fluctuations can take the form of long-run changes in demand, caused by the introduction or cancellation of projects, or temporary peaks in the workload.

When these three factors, the distinction between stock and flow imbalances, inter-departmental conflict, and ill-defined but fluctuating demand, are considered, it becomes apparent that there is a variety of situations which can loosely be described as shortages (or surpluses). Some of these concern only a limited section of an organization, while others are acknowledged as common problems. Because the way in which the problem is defined carries implications for the type of adjustment which might be deployed, it is appropriate to examine the possible adjustments to a series of problems rather than to a number of objective stimuli. Here shortages alone are considered, with the question of surpluses being taken up again in Section 7.

The most straightforward problem is the stock shortage of labour which is recognized by the whole organization. Any of the adjustments listed in Chapter 2 could be used as devices to overcome such a shortage. Thus the firm may try to lower the quit rate, increase the numbers hired, or reduce the numbers of draughtsmen required. Alternatively it may refrain from taking positive action and merely allow the output of the drawing office to fall below the desired level. Where a stock shortage is commonly acknowledged, inter-departmental conflict is limited to the appropriateness of particular adjustments.

However, in a number of the firms we visited, only the department employing draughtsmen defined the situation as being one of labour shortage. While the department argued that it needed more staff in order to perform the task required of it, the financial section of the organization refused to sanction the recruitment of extra staff. In some cases this went so far as to prohibit the replacement of staff who left. Here the employing department can only use those adjustments under its own control. It will try to avoid further deterioration in the number of staff, but the main response must be to reduce (if only as a temporary measure) the number of staff required. Hence, the department may increase overtime working, delay less urgent work, increase productivity, call upon the resources of other departments or, if permitted, sub-contract work outside the firm. The choice of adjustment is governed by the capacity for absorbing work in these various areas, and tends to be jointly determined by management and union at office level.

The use of a temporary adjustment disguises rather than alleviates a stock shortage and thus merely changes the focus of attention for the employer. Where such an adjustment is made in response to a shortage which was expected to be temporary, the firm will simply wait for the market or the product demand to return to normal. However, if the problem is more permanent, a temporary adjustment is seen as a deviation from the norm, and may provide a stimulus to further action. Thus resistance to the temporary measure may precipitate a further adjustment without any apparent change in the manpower situation. Alternatively, the temporary adjustment may reduce the urgency of the problem. Either the temporary adjustment becomes more acceptable through familiarity, or the problem created by the adjustment is less acute than the problem of the original shortage. Hence, working norms may be adapted to the prevailing circumstances, so that the temporary adjustment becomes fossilized as a permanent one.

We now turn to examine problems which arise out of flow imbalances. Recruitment difficulty is largely a problem for the personnel department at least until it creates a stock shortage, and the personnel department controls a limited number of adjustment instruments. While it may be free to vary recruitment activity and selection procedure, demand-side adjustments are inappropriate and the salary structure is usually outside its control. It may be able to adjust the salaries of recruits and to vary hiring standards, though this depends on its relationship with other parts of the organization. Where the personnel department is supported by other departments in its attempts to combat recruitment difficulties, its range of adjustment instruments will be extended.

Wastage of staff may be a problem either because it is costly[14] or simply because it threatens to develop into a stock shortage. There are, however, only a few adjustments appropriate for dealing with the problem of high wastage. They fall into three types: increasing

14. The replacement of voluntary leavers usually involves some recruitment cost. However, when the firm loses high-quality staff with enterprise-specific skills, the cost of wastage is increased because of the need to train replacements.

pay, improving conditions of work, and provision of better promotion opportunities. These are rarely employed in response to a wastage problem unless they are seen as attacking the cause of the problem. Thus, pay is unlikely to be increased in response to high wastage unless the employer believes that high wastage results from low relative pay. In the absence of a specific cause being attributed to wastage, the firm will allow the situation to develop into a stock shortage before any action is taken.

Drawing office managers often have to face the problem of a temporary peak in the workload which cannot be met with the existing work patterns and the incumbent labour force. Because the problem is defined as a temporary one, a number of adjustments are inadmissible. The number of permanent staff cannot be increased, and irreversible adjustments such as capital substitution are inappropriate. The problem is akin to a stock shortage which is felt by the departmental manager but unacknowledged by the financial departments. The range of adjustments is the same, and the choice again depends on the capacity available and is normally made jointly by the departmental manager and the union office committee. However, there are some factors absent in the case of a temporary peak which may affect the choice. The departmental manager and office committee are not involved in a political game with the financial sector. Hence, there is no attempt to coerce the financial sector into allowing the recruitment of more staff. Indeed, the departmental manager is more free to spend money on sub-contracting, and the office committee is more likely to accept the need for temporary measures. Furthermore, the departmental manager is less concerned with wastage because he is allowed to replace staff. These factors may mean that a different response is made to the same market situation because of the absence of a financial constraint.

Long-term changes in demand for draughtsmen can create another type of problem, the large projected shortage. Such a problem arises typically from a decision to take on a large project such as the development of a new aircraft. Many of the possible adjustments will be ruled out as having insufficient impact on the problem. To overcome the problem before it develops into a serious stock shortage will require a major recruitment strategy or a programme of capital substitution. One of the firms in our study which was faced with a projected shortage embarked on a programme of CAD (see Section 5) while others used a combination of training programmes, recruitment drives, and pay to attract staff. Often, however, the shortage was allowed to develop before positive action was taken.

This discussion of the various manifestations of shortages has illustrated the importance of several factors in the selection of adjustment instruments. It is argued that the relationship between departments in an organization and their different aims, powers, and responsibilities will modify the influence of the overall organization goals in the decision-making process. The way a problem is perceived and the cause attributed to it will restrict the range of instruments applicable to its correction. Moreover, the degree of urgency associated with the shortage and its expected duration both affect the choice of instrument. However, though these factors limit the range of adjustments, they do not necessarily determine the choice. Various attributes of the instruments themselves are important: the firm's experience of the instrument, constraints imposed upon it by unions and technology, and the extent to which it has to be used as a complement of other instruments.

Before we turn to examining various adjustment instruments in detail, it is necessary to consider briefly the notion of adjustments as actions. So far we have looked at the various courses of action which might be taken by a firm in response to a perceived problem. But this is only one side of the response to imbalance. Shortages and surpluses may have effects on the market other than those arising from the conscious action which is taken to remedy imbalances. For example, the state of the market will influence pay negotiations, perhaps through relative bargaining power, regardless of any conscious attempt to use pay to eliminate a shortage. The quality of recruits may also reflect the state of the market even when no deliberate action is taken to alter hiring standards. The effects of the market as well as action to remedy problems are therefore considered in the following sections on individual instruments.

3. Pay

In this section we examine from the evidence of our case studies the use of pay as an instrument to a labour shortage, the effects of constraints on its use, and the influence of the external market.

The form of the salary payment system commonly used in large engineering firms acts as a major constraint on the use of pay increases as a direct adjustment to a shortage of labour. In most of the plants visited, there was a job-grading system which institutionalized pay comparisons between departments or specialisms. In

AES,[15] for instance, TASS was the only recognized staff union and whatever salary increase it negotiated set the rates for the rest of the staff who were linked to technicians through the job-grading system. But, even where TASS negotiated separately from the other staff unions, a job-grading system would still prevent a sectional pay increase as an adjustment to shortage because of the link with other TASS members.

The job evaluation system introduced in AFP[16] represented the opposite extreme to that in AES. It had been devised so as to provide flexibility in salary adjustments. Jobs were divided into market groups with each market group representing a cluster of jobs for which roughly similar levels of skill, training, and education were required and between which employees could move fairly readily by extending or adapting their skills. Thus in the technical areas, design and jig-and-tool draughtsmen formed one market group, methods and factory-planning engineers another. In theory, the firm might adjust to a shortage of draughtsmen by increasing the salary levels in the design market group leaving other salary levels in the technical area unaffected. But in practice, flat-rate increases had been negotiated for all TASS members and any proposal for a sectional increase was heavily resisted.

The constraints imposed by the salary determination process meant that a pay increase for shortage adjustment had either to be embodied in the general negotiated increase or else achieved through discreet manipulation of the pay structure. This latter form of adjustment was employed in a number of ways. Autocar[17] at one point was threatened with a high outflow of technicians to another car firm and responded quickly by paying them a merit increase to bring salaries up to a comparable level with the other company. However, AES was prevented from using a device such as this because employees had to fall into a predetermined structure of merit payment. In a few

15. Aero Electrical Systems Ltd (AES) manufactures a range of specialized electronic equipment including computer systems for aircraft and ships and its own CAD system. Its market is both for government contracts and commercial use. The company is privately owned with plants in both the United Kingdom and North America. The plant visited was the centre of the Scottish operation which covers about one-third of the company's total employment.
16. Associated Farm Products (AFP) is a multi-national company which manufactures tractors and other agricultural implements. There are a number of plants in Britain but design is concentrated in one establishment situated in a predominantly engineering area.
17. Autocar is part of a large multi-national motor-car manufacturer, situated in a predominantly engineering area.

firms an additional grade of designer[18] had been created so that more draughtsmen could reach the level of section leader than was required by the supervisory needs of the office. An alternative to this is regrading within a given structure. When AFP was suffering from a high quit rate, a number of draughtsmen were promoted to senior draughtsmen. The average age of those promoted was 30 as against the norm for promotion at 34. At CFE[19] there had been a number of 'special exercises' which involved a similar process of regrading. Here our informant stressed the care that had to be taken in such exercises lest perceived differentials were upset. Where such an adjustment does not provoke a reaction it proves quite attractive to the firm. It is considerably cheaper than a straight salary increase because it is selective and aimed at those people who are most likely to leave the firm. However, this type of adjustment can only be directed towards lowering the quit rate and hence must be classed as a response to a difficult flow position rather than to a stock shortage. Where there is a wastage problem which is attributed to pay, the selective pay increase is an obvious adjustment to make.

The major part of this study was conducted during a period of compulsory incomes policy. This imposed a severe constraint on any attempt to increase relative pay but the severity of the incomes-policy constraint can be over-emphasized. One plant which was experiencing a net outflow of technical staff could only pay an increase of £2.40 under the prevailing policy (the Phase Two £1 + 4 per cent formula), but there was a merit scheme which enabled a total increase of £4.60 despite the fact that merit payments had not been paid in the past. A neighbouring plant in the same group was not experiencing the same labour-supply problems, and merit payments were not made. A North-American-owned plant was able to pay a 9 per cent increase during Phase Two, which had been held back under the freeze, on the grounds that this increase had been agreed by the North American management before November 1972. One might suppose that, *ceteris paribus*, the greater the level of shortage or net outflow of labour, the greater is management's ingenuity in interpreting a pay code. But this would neglect the

---

18. This adjustment should be distinguished from the use of the job title 'designer' to make the job more attractive to potential recruits.
19. Civil Flight Enterprises (CFE) is the aircraft division of a large consortium whose other main division makes guided weapons. The plant in which the design and development section is situated is in the same town as the guided weapons establishment, and to a certain extent the two divisions of the consortium are in competition for labour. All work done by CFE is on government contracts, the main one being the Atlas project.

union's role in persuading management to look more carefully for loop-holes. In a third plant there was again a shortage of technical labour, but, in the opinion of the TASS chairman, management could have alleviated the shortage by adjusting the salaries of new recruits. Thus the breach of Phase Two was not essential for management in the absence of action by the union. This opinion was confirmed by management's behaviour during the negotiations. The final settlement clearly exceeded Phase Two,[20] but this was not arrived at originally by straight management/union collusion. Indeed, management claimed it had submitted the package to the Pay Board and had it rejected. The union put pressure on management by playing on a number of factors; emphasizing the shortage, pointing to their control of overtime, and arguing that the product market was such that management would require a lot of co-operation from its technical staff. Management returned to the Pay Board which then approved the settlement. Here we have an example of shortage affecting the extent of a pay increase which cannot simply be seen as the outcome of a managerial decision about how to adjust to a labour shortage. In this case the union's role was active in that the shortage was used to press for a positive course of action, rather than passively constraining the use of an adjustment which it opposed.

Incomes policy and the activities of the union are the most important constraints on pay, but it should be noted that there are others. Fixed-price contracts act as a severe disincentive to increase pay, while the local Engineering Employers' Association or firms competing for labour may discourage 'aggressive' pay policies. However, the latter constraint was not seen as being relevant to the period in which our study was conducted.

There was a tendency amongst firms in this study to act as price takers in the technician's market. This occurred in two main ways: firms tried to negotiate salary increases which aligned the mid-point of the salary range for a particular grade with the average market salary; and there was a tendency to relate the pay of new entrants to the salary that they had been receiving in their previous employment.

Aligning the salary scales with the market rates meant management fighting off the favourite comparisons made by TASS which

20. The strict application of the £1 +4% formula implied an average weekly increase of £2.75, but the actual settlement guaranteed a weekly increase of £3.50, some members getting an increase of £600 per annum. This was achieved by upgrading some staff and paying merit increases to the rest. The agreement also provided for automatic progression through grades, whereas previously promotion had been on the basis of merit.

were, particularly in the Midlands, with toolmakers and car firms. It also meant collecting information about local salary levels. Some firms, however, were prepared to deviate systematically from the market rate. Helico,[21] on the one hand, had reckoned on being somewhat below the salary levels paid in its region's larger towns because local housing was cheaper and the environment more pleasant. AFP, on the other hand, aimed at being slightly above the market rate because they were on the outskirts of a town. Autocar paid a salary rate to their industry-specific designers which was in line with the car industry. This had the effect of making them a high payer in the market for detail draughtsmen.

In a number of plants the actual salary structures deviated from the ideals conceived by management because TASS has succeeded in negotiating across the board flat-rate increases in pay. This had the effect of compressing the salary structure, those in the higher grade being paid less than equivalent people outside. In some firms management was able to compensate for this by paying differential merit payments but in others TASS would not agree to this.

A policy of accepting the market rate by recruiting people at the salary level to which they had been accustomed was often constrained by the rules of the payment system. For instance, in Carbits[22] external entrants could not be offered salaries above the mid-point on the salary scale. This sometimes prevented the firm from paying the market rate. There was a similar rule in Autocar but it could be broken to ease recruitment problems. United Missiles's[23] policy on the salaries of recruits was rather devious. Apart from negotiated cost-of-living increases, salaries were under the unilateral control of the drawing office manager. He tended to set entry salaries by the salary paid to the entrant previously, but sometimes when recruitment was difficult he would pay a 'honeymoon' salary in order to attract someone and then let it fall back to the market rate by

---

21. Helico differed from all the other plants studied in that it was the only large employer of draughtsmen within its local labour market, and this had an important influence on its employment policy. The company aimed to keep a stable labour force, as job security was considered to be an important element in attracting and retaining labour both in the firm and the locality.
22. The tool drawing office of Carbits Ltd acted as a service department for plants in the company which made a range of electrical goods. Car accessories formed an important part of the firm's demand. The rate of product development was governed largely by the firm rather than the orders obtained, but sometimes fashion as interpreted by car manufacturers would influence this.
23. UM's plant in the Home Counties designs a range of military equipment, and builds and tests the prototypes. The production side is at the company's northern plant.

delaying any salary increase to him. This was one of the 'advantages' of rapid inflation.

The evidence of our case studies has suggested that the use of pay increases as an adjustment to shortage has been constrained both by incomes policy and by negotiating arrangements which militate against sectional pay increases. However, these constraints have not been prohibitive but have merely affected the nature of the pay adjustment. The continued importance of the external market has been demonstrated both by the firm acting to some extent as a price taker, and also in the way constraints have forced the firm to react to wastage and recruitment problems rather than to the extent of the stock shortage.

4. Sub-Contracting and Overtime

The required number of draughtsmen in an individual establishment will tend to fluctuate a good deal. Where a company has a number of establishments working on different products it may be able to meet this problem by shifting work or draughtsmen between them. However, this is not always possible. Some companies are too small to require draughtsmen continuously, and even in large companies the design requirements will be increased considerably when big projects are taken on. This has led to the growth of a sub-contract sector which at its peak in 1969 was employing 10 per cent of the country's draughtsmen.[24] Sub-contracting has become an important instrument which, like overtime, can increase the output of drawings without addition to the amount of capital or labour employed

Contract Drawing Offices

The history of contract drawing offices can be traced back to the late 1930s when the car industry in the UK and the US required substantial numbers of draughtsmen for infrequent re-tooling on a new model. The high post-war demand for draughtsmen stimulated a growth of contract drawing in areas other than just tooling. Many large companies started using sub-contractors in the late 1940s and early 1950s, particularly the aircraft firms. Concern was expressed by the union (then AESD) in the mid-1950s both at the growing use of sub-contractors and the numbers of freelance draughtsmen.[25] Between 1961 and 1966 the growth of the industry was fairly rapid.

24. See Smedley (1969).
25. See Mortimer (1960: 340–41).

Contract drawing offices can conveniently be divided into three groups. The first includes companies without their own drawing office which merely loan labour to firms. These tend not to specialize but are ready to service all grades and all industries. Some companies in this category may be no more than agents supplying self-employed draughtsmen to a firm — others will be employers. Where there are self-employed draughtsmen, the agency will find the work and then offer it to the self-employed draughtsmen, taking a percentage cut of the salary. There are advantages on both sides. The agency does not have the usual employment costs; the self-employed draughtsmen can claim expenses against tax. Companies in the second group have their own drawing offices and will hire labour to firms or take drawing work in their own office. The choice of where the sub-contract draughtsmen work will depend on a number of factors: the client's policy, security and space considerations, the state of the sub-contract market, and the attitude of the chief draughtsman.[26] These companies tend to specialize in one sector. The third group of companies take work into their own office and do not hire out draughtsmen. These are normally jig-and-tool specialists, and may undertake some manufacturing work. Eighty per cent of the members of FEDC are in the second group, the remainder being in the third group.[27]

Manufacturing Firms' Use of Sub-Contracting

Only one of the ten firms studied had not sub-contracted draughting work at one time or another. Six others had only used sub-contracting as a short-run adjustment. GMT,[28] for instance,

26. The experiences of the CFE Engineering Manager were typical. There are advantages and disadvantages with having sub-contractors inside the office. A man in the office is part of the team, his job can be monitored better, and mistakes are corrected quicker. On the other hand sub-contractors inside the office create dissatisfaction amongst the firm's draughtsmen. His experience made him prefer to have the sub-contract draughtsmen outside the office with a liaison man provided by the sub-contractor. In a buoyant market the sub-contractor can dictate terms. One contract office manager said it was more advantageous for him to take work into his own office, because then payment was on the basis of an agreed estimate, and if the work was done faster the difference was pure profit.
27. FEDC companies supply no self-employed draughtsmen. In the 1971 Census of Population there were 5,100 self-employed draughtsmen out of a total of 166,200 draughtsmen (1% Sample, Table 14).
28. General Machine Tools is a subsidiary company of a large general engineering concern, and it is situated in part of the country where engineering is the predominant employer. Despite its name it produces a specific range of machine tools mostly to perform grinding operations.

sometimes did specialist tooling jobs for other manufacturing firms which meant sub-contracting the bulk of the detailing work because its own drawing office could not cope with the extra work involved. A drawing office can in some cases double its output through the use of sub-contracting, the upper limit stemming from the administrative capacity for keeping in contact with the sub-contract office. However, such extensive use of sub-contracting is rare. More typical was Carbits whose maximum usage was the equivalent to the drawing office staff working three hours overtime a week for a period of six months.[29]

Autocar and London Planemakers,[30] however, did make regular use of sub-contracting. LP said they 'find it useful to have a small float of about twenty contract draughtsmen — partly because they will do low level work which the full-time design draughtsmen would object to'. Autocar's policy was to employ very few jig-and-tool draughtsmen and to sub-contract most of the work. Neither of these was an example of the use of sub-contracting to alleviate a long-term shortage, but any shortage which did arise would simply be met by further sub-contracting.

CFE was the only company which used sub-contracting extensively as a long-run shortage adjustment. This, however, was not deliberate. The engineering manager had a rule of thumb for dealing with an excess workload: if it was to last less than six months — work overtime, if it was over six months but less than two years — sub-contracting, and if the excess would last longer than two years, permanent staff should be recruited. However, this ideal could not always be observed. The capacity for overtime working was limited and, we were told, 'there are times when one can't get permanent staff.' This inability to find sufficient permanent staff (at prevailing wages) had meant that throughout the late 1960s more than a quarter of the work in the product development area was done by sub-contractors. Moreover, some of the individuals supplied by the sub-contractors had during their long sojourn with CFE (one had been working there for eight years) acquired skills which became indispensable to the firm.

This quantitative and qualitative dependence on sub-contractors suggests that the temporary adjustment had become fossilized into a

29. One contract office manager reported that quite a lot of his orders were received on a Friday to start on the following Monday. This suggests that sub-contracting is being used as an adjustment in the last resort.
30. London Planemakers (LP) is one of the establishments of a large aircraft group. The plant is situated in suburban London and design is concentrated there.

permanent one. Had it remained a temporary adjustment with the actual state of affairs diverging from the working norm, the engagement of sub-contractors would have acted as a stimulus to management, independently of any union pressure, to make some permanent adjustment. In reality, permanent staff were only substituted for sub-contractors in response to an *external* stimulus — the increasing unemployment amongst draughtsmen during 1970.[31]

Where firms had to choose between sub-contracting and overtime, the relative costs of the two adjustment instruments played a minor role in the choice. Only one manager had an immediate answer to the question of which adjustment was cheaper. In most cases the choice was made with reference to the size of the problem and the staff's readiness to work overtime or accept sub-contractors, and depended heavily on the drawing office manager's own opinion of the work of contract offices.

Managerial attitudes to contract offices varied a good deal. The CFE manager who had used them extensively was impressed by the quality of the draughtsmen supplied. Several other firms entrusted them with detailing only, in order to save their own draughtsmen for more intensive design work. However, managers were less anxious about the quality of sub-contractors than about their effect on the social environment in the drawing office. The reaction of staff to sub-contractors may mould managerial attitudes, but the essential relationship between management and staff on this issue is one of collective bargaining.

The use of sub-contracting is often formally constrained by the union through a collective agreement. It is TASS policy to eliminate the self-employed draughtsmen and to control the sub-contractor who employs draughtsmen. When a contract office fulfils certain conditions,[32] it can be approved by TASS.[33] Many firms have agree-

31. It has been stated earlier that the distinction between temporary and permanent adjustments is not clear cut. In the case of CFE, the action taken by the firm suggests that the engagement of sub-contractors became a permanent adjustment with the use of sub-contracting accepted as a working norm. However, at least one important individual, the engineering manager, did not fully adhere to the norm. He continued to pay lip service to the 'rule of thumb' for adjusting to peak work loads and was inclined to measure the labour shortage by the number of sub-contractors in use. Both attitudes imply that it was the norm to have no sub-contracting.

32. These conditions are no self-employed personnel, 100% membership, a check-off, agreed pay and conditions, an ability to accommodate a substantial proportion of staff on the company's premises, and an undertaking to support any industrial action in firms for whom it is working.

33. FEDC was formed in 1955 as a trade association for 'Engineering Design

ments with TASS to use only those contract offices which have been approved. Indeed, for offices in the engineering industry, TASS approval is virtually a precondition for survival.

However, custom and practice and the constraints imposed by office committees go further than merely restricting the firm's use of sub-contracting to approved offices. Sub-contracting is rarely tolerated in a redundancy situation and quite often a ban on sub-contracting is imposed during periods of unemployment both to safeguard the jobs of employed draughtsmen and to encourage firms to recruit.[34] In general, there is considerable hostility towards sub-contractors, particularly those inside the offices, because, in the words of one office representative, 'they don't know any of our procedures, they get paid more than we do and we've got to show them what to do'.

Doeringer and Piore (1971) point out that there is a secondary way in which sub-contracting is used as an adjustment instrument. An employer may wish to screen potential recruits more intensively and so reduce his dependence on formal selection criteria. Screening the employees of the sub-contractor is a way of doing this. Of course this is only possible with those sub-contractors who work in the firm's own drawing office. So, given the union attitudes described above, such an adjustment is more heavily constrained than the straightforward use of sub-contracting. Only one firm admitted that it used sub-contracting as a screening device. Others had recruited men from its sub-contractors, but did not sub-contract with this motive in mind. In CFE there was an unwritten agreement not to poach labour from sub-contractors but occasionally someone became indispensable and they would ask the sub-contractors if they could employ him permanently. FEDC reported that the practice of screening through sub-contracting was quite common, but that the sub-

Consultants' aiming partly to improve the image of contract drawing offices. In 1969 it represented 20% of the sub-contract industry. In recent years it has taken on the role of an employers' association, negotiating basic rates and conditions. FEDC has supported the TASS campaign to eliminate freelance draughtsmen and negotiates with TASS over their approval agreements.

34. This stance has been criticized by some managements and FEDC as being against the interests of TASS members. The FEDC chairman maintained that draughtsmen in contract drawing offices were being treated as second-class members. The engineering manager at CFE was concerned to avoid a further redundancy by taking on sub-contractors whilst net wastage exceeded desired rundown in the labour force. Recruitment at that point, he said, would lead to redundancy later in the year, but TASS insisted on no sub-contracting following the last redundancy.

contractor would usually have a non-poaching agreement or charge an introductory fee of 6 per cent of the draughtsman's salary.

Overtime

All the plants visited had used overtime to deal with short-run peaks in the workload. The extent of its use varied: in CFE, draughtsmen had worked on average ten hours' overtime per week in 1969–70, whilst in AES the level of overtime working was negligible. With the redundancies and the onset of heavy unemployment amongst draughtsmen since 1970, overtime had been banned by the TASS members in the majority of the plants. Hardware[35] had taken the ban as an opportunity to cut overtime out completely since it had been used in the late 1960s as a 'device to increase pay rather than to get more work done'. These overtime bans had been relaxed by the middle of 1973, but in some cases overtime was still severely controlled by TASS. The form of control was either to make management argue a case for overtime in each situation, or only to work overtime when there was evidence that steps were being taken to recruit permanent staff.

The Effect of Sub-contracting on the Draughtsmen's Market

The existence of a sub-contract sector enables a greater geographical matching of supply and demand for draughting skills. To a certain extent the high mobility of aircraft draughtsmen in the immediate post-war period has been replaced by sub-contracting. Moreover, there has been a trend towards an international contract drawing market. Some British contract offices serve only foreign firms, and most do some foreign work. Foreign outlets became increasingly important with the slump in British demand for draughting in the early 1970s.

A hypothesis worth examining is that the sub-contract sector provides a means of paying the marginal worker more than the average, so increasing supply at relatively low cost. The prevailing belief throughout the occupation was that contract offices paid more than manufacturing firms,[36] but this was not borne out in the TASS

35. Hardware Ltd makes computers and some of the CAD equipment that is used in the company's own drawing office. There was a fairly steady growth in the product market during the 1960s though there were cutbacks in the early 1970s.
36. This belief was supported by citations of relative earnings (e.g. a sub-contract employee getting £2,650 at 24 against a £1,750 norm). This was in January 1973 when the average salary for sub-contractors aged 24 was £1,678 according to TASS salary. A number of firms experienced tough competition for labour from contract offices in periods of labour shortage. GMT pointed to contract offices as being the major area attracting their voluntary leavers. UM which had a policy of setting salaries according to a man's previous salary found this 'impossible in the case of men from contract offices'.

salary surveys for January 1972 and 1973.[37] There are, however, a number of possible explanations of why this evidence does not confirm what is believed. Firstly, there is more overtime available in contract offices. Secondly, some sorts of contract work provide an opportunity to enhance one's earnings through illicit claiming of travelling expenses. Thirdly, though contract offices have traditionally been high payers, the declining demand for sub-contractors' services has caused a decline in relative salaries. Given the existing data, one is not able to test any of these explanations in a rigorous manner. It is evident, however, that during periods of shortage there are draughtsmen who drift into contract offices, and it would be strange if this were not for a financial advantage. Entrants to the contract offices are, in the main, trained draughtsmen in their early twenties.[38] The pace of work is hectic and the job insecure, so at about the age of 35 most sub-contract draughtsmen seek the security and relative comfort of a manufacturing firm. If contract offices do not keep the marginal worker in draughtsmanship by paying him more, they certainly seem to increase his productivity.

A third effect of the sub-contract sector is that of lowering total demand through the reduction in the need for labour hoarding in manufacturing firms' drawing offices. Both a TASS divisional organizer and the FEDC chairman thought that contract offices ran more efficiently, in terms of output per unit of time paid for, than most manufacturing firms' drawing offices. A corollary of this is that a contract drawing office is unable to hoard much labour when demand falls. This might account for some of the severe unemployment that has been seen amongst draughtsmen in recent years.

The State of the Sub-contract Sector

The small manufacturing companies which redesign occasionally are not the staple diet of the sub-contract sector. It is more economical for a contract drawing office to work on big projects to gain economies of scale and acquire a permanent relationship with their clients. Although to a certain extent contract offices rely on one section being up when another is down, the fate of the sector is very much tied up with the large aircraft projects. The cancellation of

37. The salary surveys before 1972 do not give the contract offices as a separate industry. In 1972 and 1973 the average salaries for each age-group (21 to 29 separately, 30 and over, and section leader) were higher in the country as a whole than in contract offices. For 1973 (and for most age-groups in 1972) the average salaries in contract offices were higher than in electronics and mechanical engineering but not those in aerospace and motor vehicles.
38. Some of the larger offices do train their own draughtsmen particularly when there is a shortage of labour.

TSR2 in 1965 caused a minor slump but the sector subsequently picked up with Concorde and the Rolls-Royce RB211. At their peak these two projects employed about 3,000 sub-contract draughtsmen. In 1969 and 1970 the contract offices themselves were experiencing difficulty in getting labour and turnover of staff was high. In early 1971, Rolls-Royce crashed and the British Aircraft Corporation reduced the amount of sub-contracting on Concorde. These fluctuations in demand have affected the number of offices as well as the level of employment. FEDC estimated that in 1969 there were between 1,500 and 2,000 contract drawing offices employing 25,000 draughtsmen. By 1972 both the number of offices and the number of employees had fallen by half.[39] Draughtsmen in contract offices are thus considerably more insecure than those in manufacturing firms.

Conclusion

The major use of sub-contracting and overtime in draughtsmanship has been to overcome temporary peaks in the workload or temporary labour shortages, and this is entirely consistent with a cost-minimizing strategy. Yet we see examples of sub-contracting being used persistently which indicate that a temporary adjustment can become fossilized into a permanent one. However, one of the most important elements in the choice of whether to use sub-contractors is the attitude of the firm's own draughtsmen. TASS members have shown a reluctance to accept sub-contracting, particularly where self-employed draughtsmen are involved or when unemployment is high.

The sub-contract sector can be seen as a device which, in the short-run at least, increases labour supply by paying the marginal workers more than the average. Sub-contracting can act as a form of geographical mobility, and it may reduce the need for firms to hoard draughtsmen in the anticipation of shortages. In short, the existence of a sub-contract sector brings about a closer relationship between the employment of draughtsmen and the demand for their services.

---

39. The nearest published employment figures are the numbers of draughtsmen employed in Professional and Scientific Services.

1961	16,590
1966	21,280
1971	20,220

These figures will include draughtsmen who are not in the contract drawing industry such as those employed by architects.

5. Capital Substitution

CAD as an Adjustment Instrument

The scope for capital substitution in an occupational market clearly depends on the nature of the job. In many occupations capital substitution is not possible. Until fairly recently, draughtsmanship[40] was one of these but with the advent of the computer and some of its sophisticated appendages this is no longer the case. In the first instance the computer is used as a mathematical tool so that some of the more routine tasks of the draughtsman such as calculation are speeded up. At a more developed stage, where machines are run by computer tapes and detailed drawings are unnecessary, the draughtsmen working from a rough drawing will use a device (called a 'reader') which can record co-ordinates and note that lines or curves have to go through them. This has been termed non-creative computer-aided design (CAD). The computer can also be used at the creative design stage but this is largely a thing of the future.[41]

The essence of capital substitution in the drawing or design office is twofold. First, it enables draughtsmen to spend more time on creative thinking and less on routine work.[42] Second, the communication of engineering design, conventionally done by means of detailed drawings, is achieved through the passage of what is largely numerical information.[43] Where NC machinery is in use, the system enables the draughtsman, working from a rough drawing, to input precise information which is translated by the computer into a tape to drive an NC machine. A typical application of the system is seen in

40. Devices such as calculating machines and photostating machines, however, saved labour before the introduction of the computer.
41. The use of the computer in creative design involves the designer working with a graphical display on a cathode ray tube. This allows the designer to call up information and design outlines as well as to test a series of possibilities in a very short time. Bell reports 'it is generally felt that a considerable amount of development work has still to be done before a large scale flexible system is paying its way' (1972:16). This being the case, the use of the cathode ray tube is not important in our consideration of adjustment instruments.
42. Estimates of the breakdown of engineers' work into activities vary, but the National Engineering Laboratory have made an estimate, quoted by Eastwood (1970), which is claimed to be borne out by general experience in the industry: 'A designer may spend 50% of his time searching for, collecting and assessing design information, 25% giving and receiving instructions, and only the remaining 25% in direct design work.' This shows that there is considerable scope for increasing the design content of an employee's work through introducing computer aids. Whether the 75% non-intensive work is necessary to a man's wellbeing and efficiency remains to be seen.
43. For a more extensive description of CAD, see Cooley (1972).

the manufacture of printed circuits. A circuit can be printed from a film produced by the computer, and the electrical components are fitted into holes bored by an NC machine.

As CAD facilitates the substitution of capital for labour, it can be considered as a possible adjustment instrument for the firm facing a labour shortage. Indeed, in two of the firms visited, the lack of available technical labour had been an important factor in the decision to introduce CAD.

At AES, the projected workload in the mid-1960s threatened to create severe shortages if no remedial action was taken. The firm was experiencing holdups at the design stage. The more drawings that went into the machine shops, the more there were that came back for modification. In the initial design stage, where the basic ideas of design are worked out, the workload was predictable, but in the modification stage the workload increased rapidly, becoming almost exponential.

The potential shortage was averted partly by the loss of a major government contract, but also through the introduction of CAD. For AES, CAD was seen as a device to reduce lead time,[44] but, as the company itself developed the system, it was also a commercial venture.

Although one must attribute an important role to shortage in spurring on this development, the introduction of CAD was by no means a simple adjustment to shortage. If anything it was a long-run adjustment to a potential shortage. One might explain a desire to reduce lead time in terms of shortage adjustment but there is a danger, in doing so, that the explanation would miss the important factors which determined the decision. No one at AES said that there were significant savings in labour costs, but the alternative ways of achieving the same amount of design work and the same reduction in lead time would have been very expensive in terms of labour costs.

At Hardware Ltd we saw a better example of CAD being used as an adjustment to shortage. There the new machines were brought in when there was a shortage of draughtsmen and to some extent because of it. All the economic aspects of the alternative systems were examined: capital cost, labour cost, lead time; and the state of the labour market was an important consideration.

In other firms CAD had been dismissed as a possible adjustment instrument either because it was not technically feasible or because it was unsuited to the type of shortage the firm faced. Helico, for

44. Lead time is defined as the time between conception of design and production.

instance, had not considered CAD because its shortage was 'neither large nor persistent'.

The Impact of CAD on Labour Demand

At AES the introduction of CAD has caused a marked shift in the occupational structure. The relative demand for draughtsmen had declined and tracers had been eliminated, but the system created programming vacancies which absorbed much of the surplus labour from the drawing office. However, the labour saving in the drawing office came not solely from the use of CAD itself but also from the introduction of printed circuits which were made possible by CAD. It is difficult to disentangle the changes which arise from the system itself and those which are due to simultaneous developments in product technology.[45]

Hardware Ltd uses a similar system to AES for the production of printed circuits. The drawing office manager gave an illuminating indication of the effect of the change in technique. The design of a computer, he said, may require 2,000 mechanical drawings and 250 printed circuits. When the printed circuits were produced conventionally, there were roughly equal numbers of electrical and mechanical draughtsmen; with CAD there were four mechanical to every one electrical draughtsmen.

However, the applicability of CAD is constrained by the technology of a firm. The technique can be employed only in areas of the drawing office concerned with the design of parts which have been digitized.[46] Though the scope of CAD can be extended as programmes are worked out and as production techniques are adapted to NC machinery (such as by replacing casting with machine milling), the system is only viable in a firm which makes extensive use of NC machines and already possesses a large computer. There are also limitations on the type of product for which the CAD system is suitable. At present the system has major application only in electronics, mapping and architecture, and body designs for ships

45. Bell reports on a similar system: 'The system is planned to be used by design draughtsmen, responsible for detail design as well as drawing. The draughtsmen without design responsibilities will be almost entirely eliminated, thus greatly reducing numbers. It is planned that in ten years the drawing office staff will be reduced to no more than 30 per cent of present numbers. Draughtsmen will also no longer need to spend time on clerical functions such as drawing up parts lists, or consulting the standards book. Additional manpower effects will be the elimination of part programmers for NC machine tools' (1972:19).

46. Thus in AES, which is one of the most extensive users of CAD, there is one reader for every twenty draughtsmen, whereas full CAD would mean one reader between six draughtsmen.

169

Draughtsmen

and vehicles. A buyer would have to be a company which was continually reviewing its products, for the system to be economically viable.

The Union Stance on CAD

The national policy of TASS, exemplified in Cooley (1972), is not hostile to the introduction of CAD itself, but it is wary of the ways in which it might be used. In particular it is conscious of possible pressure for shift-working, the fragmentation of skills, and the intensification of work.

Because of the high capital cost of CAD equipment, employers will seek to increase its utilization and so introduce shift-working. TASS opposes the extension of shift-working. A survey of members quoted by Eastwood[47] indicates that the vast majority opposed shift-working and that as many as 60 per cent were prepared to 'stand and fight' the introduction of shifts. In AES, the TASS membership had ignored the introduction of shift-working for white-collar non-members, but the indication was that management would not find it easy or cheap to introduce it amongst TASS members.[48]

One effect of this system is to eliminate some of the most highly skilled jobs on the shop floor. A similar consequence may be felt in the technical areas through the fragmentation of skills:

In order to exploit their high capital equipment to the full the employers will want our members to specialise more and more. Once they have achieved a degree of specialisation the employers will insist that they remain in that particular job whilst they are still needed. Fewer and fewer of our members will be able to see in a panoramic way the end product of the job on which they are involved. They will see only a tiny part of it. The effect will be that job satisfaction will be eliminated from more and more of our members. (Cooley, 1972:78)

Where the essence of CAD is the elimination of routine work, a designer or draughtsman spends more time on actual design decision-making. While wasteful to the firm, the time spent on routine work is of therapeutic necessity to the designer. The stress put upon a designer who spends the major part of his time on decision-making

47. (1970); it is not clear whether he carried out this survey or whether he is quoting some other source.
48. TASS is concerned that it must organize all those involved with CAD. Firstly, it does not want to lose members as technology changes the occupational mix, and secondly the fear is that employers 'will seek either to introduce tame trade unions or anti-union collaborationist organisations such as UKAPE' (Cooley, 1972: 87). Cooley warns that firms producing programmes and software packages for design work are a threat equal to that of contract drawing offices.

can be enormous. Moreover, under CAD the machine-setting function is determined by the draughtsman at the reader rather than by the craftsman at the machine tool. This places greater responsibility on the draughtsman because there is no 'last check' on draughting errors.

Thus it is TASS policy that any CAD introduced should carry certain riders: no redundancy, the retaining of existing staff for the new process, realistic wage levels, no work measurement. The increase in stress and work tempo must be countered by a shorter week, longer rest periods, and longer holidays. A majority of union members agreed to these points in the survey, but how do individual office committees act in negotiations over CAD? At Carbits, the committee's action had been broadly in line with TASS policy. They had insisted on draughtsmen becoming the programmers and operators, thus giving TASS control of the equipment. Part shifts had been proposed by management and rejected, and overtime was only worked for time off *in lieu*, and redundancies were avoided.

In AES, the office committee had agreed to co-operate with the CAD programme because of management assurances about redundancy and retraining. The deal involved a moderate pay rise, and the question of shiftwork was not raised, but the committee came into conflict with TASS policy by accepting work measurement. Despite TASS's condemnation of this agreement, one can see that, even in a paternalist firm such as AES, CAD is a highly constrained adjustment instrument.[49]

It is clear from union policy and membership attitudes that any introduction of computer aids must be the subject of negotiation between TASS representatives and management. The use of this instrument does not fall, therefore, into the area of managerial prerogative.

Conclusion

This use of the computer in technical areas is a form of capital substitution and, as such, it becomes a possible adjustment instru-

49. The TASS (then DATA) representatives at AES were severely criticized by the union externally over their handling of CAD. In 1969, a productivity agreement, signed between AES and TASS members in the company, provided for the members' co-operation in introducing CAD and permitted the use of 'work sheet recording enabling information to be compiled for productivity assessment'. TASS was opposed to productivity agreements, and concerned that a precedent of accepting the AES system had been created which would make it difficult for the members in firms which bought the equipment to resist similar agreements. The TASS senior representative at AES said that management had assured them that they would aim to avoid redundancies and without that assurance 'we wouldn't have gone along with [CAD]'.

ment to various types of labour shortage. The constraints on its use in this way are severe. The nature of the product and size of firm limit its applicability and the administrative, training, and installation time make CAD a long-term adjustment only. It is more likely to be employed as an adjustment to a large projected shortage than a current one. The TASS office representatives, if they in any way reflect national policy, will tend to slow down the introduction, limit the degree of utilization of it by opposing shiftwork, and use it as an opportunity to secure a salary increase. CAD will be less constrained as an adjustment instrument where it is a case of *increasing* the number of automated devices, as the co-operation of the union members will already have been obtained and there will be trained staff ready to operate it.[50]

The major savings from CAD are not in the form of a reduction in the wage bill, but arise from the effects of shortening the time between the original design and the sale of the product. Thus the returns to the high capital cost of the equipment stem from a reduction in the cost of work in progress. Hence CAD can be an attractive investment for the type of firm described, even in the absence of a labour shortage.

Yet our evidence showed that on the whole the economic viability of a CAD scheme is a necessary but not a sufficient condition for its introduction. Partly because of union constraints, a serious labour shortage is usually required to spur the firm into a programme of CAD.

6. Recruitment

This section is concerned with the recruitment of trained draughtsmen from the external market. Although some firms rely heavily on the output of their own apprenticeship schemes, variations in the number of apprentices taken on play no more than a minor role in the adjustment to shortage or surplus.[51] This arises

50. Where contract office draughtsmen are employed by firms to overcome a heavy workload, they are usually given detailing work to do. One impact of CAD will be to make a peak load more easy to overcome internally. It is unlikely that many contract offices could afford to buy their own CAD.
51. In some plants the number of technical apprentices stays fairly constant while in others financial considerations dominate. Where need does affect the level of training intake, the effect of any adjustment will lag some four or five years behind the action. The important thing for a department which faces a shortage is to acquire a high proportion of the apprentices who come out of their time. In many firms the drawing office had failed to attract the number of apprentices it desired.

because the length of training exceeds the normal time-span for planning demand. The type of problem faced by the DES and the bus undertakings means that the employer can adjust by increasing the supply of teachers and bus drivers. The employer of draughtsmen, on the other hand, tends to direct his recruitment policy towards increasing his share of the numbers available. In doing so he may lower hiring standards, vary selection procedure, or alter his recruitment activity.

Hiring Standards

Since adjustments are defined as deviations from working norms, it is necessary to outline the normal standards which govern decisions to hire draughtsmen.[52] Firms expect to recruit draughtsmen who have served an engineering apprenticeship and who have some formal qualification such as an ONC. Sometimes the recruit will be expected to possess a certain amount of relevant experience, but this varies with the level at which he is to work. It was evident from our survey that aircraft and electronics firms normally recruited design and detail draughtsmen who had worked in the same industry. Firms in other sections of engineering required only their design draughtsmen to have relevant industrial experience. Any trained detail draughtsman could be recruited.

However, most of the firms in our survey had departed in some way from these working norms because of recruitment difficulty or labour shortage. This frequently took the form of an extension of the range of those recruited to include draughtsmen who had only worked in other industries. Sometimes a reduction in hiring standards was involved, but often such adjustments were accompanied by more intensive selection designed to ascertain an applicant's potential for adapting his skills. In the latter case the change in selection criteria was accomplished without any alteration in hiring standards.[53] Both forms of this adjustment were relatively

---

Other technical areas and craft occupations proved more attractive. This was often blamed on the erosion of the differential between the drawing office and the shop floor.

52. In Chapter 3 the recruitment section refers to three ways in which changes in hiring standards may be identified: by asking employers when their selection criteria have been changed, by looking at changes in the characteristics of recruits, and by assessing whether there have been any changes in the quality of recruits. In the case of draughtsmen, data on the characteristics of recruits were very poor if available at all.

53. For a fuller discussion of this see pp. 76–8.

unconstrained, particularly where selection criteria expressed preferences rather than requirements.

A few of the firms had made more positive reductions in hiring standards by training batches of recruits who displayed technical ability but who had not served an apprenticeship. The training involved formal instruction by senior draughtsmen and thus could be distinguished from a period of reorientation for someone with a different background. However, the magnitude of such an adjustment was limited both by the need to achieve some economies of scale in training and by the desire to avoid imposing too heavy a burden on the senior drawing office staff. Moreover, this adjustment required the involvement of a number of departments and the consent of the union. It depended also on a supply of suitable applicants when the market for trained draughtsmen was tight.

Although the union is keen to prevent any lowering of hiring standards,[54] the greatest resistance tends to come from the drawing office manager. Typically he is concerned with building up, or at least maintaining, the quality of the draughtsmen in his office.[55] This may explain why lowering of hiring standards has been restricted to the cases cited above. The conflicting goals within management are such that the choice between the alternatives of increasing pay, reducing hiring standards, or allowing the numbers employed to fall is not made by a single rational decision-maker but is the outcome of a highly political process involving a heterogeneous collection of decision-makers.

Selective Procedure

We have seen that a change in selection process can resemble a change in hiring standards and that some selection procedures permit the lowering of hiring standards without any explicit decision to do so.[56] Later it will be argued that the choice of recruitment style is to some extent dependent on the selection procedure adopted. It is

54. See, for instance, Mortimer's (1960) discussion of the union's resistance to wartime dilutees.
55. The drawing office manager at Carbits provided a good example of this. Ideally he would have liked to take seven outsiders for every three apprentices, but financial considerations and a large training school output prevented this. As it was, he tried to 'buy in talent from outside' and take the best of those available rather than recruit cheaply. If no candidate met the required standards he would reject them rather than lower those standards: 'I would rather send work out for six months and wait for the right man.' His insistence on maintaining these standards seemed to arise from a fear of being stuck with unsuitable people: 'The procedure to sack someone is so long that it would not be worth it.'
56. See pp. 76–7.

appropriate at this stage to examine the different types of selection procedure. Here we distinguish between three types: rank selection, qualifying selection, and exploratory selection.[57]

In *rank* selection the desire for quality takes precedence over any concern for swift or cheap recruitment. The employer aims to recruit the best-qualified or most experienced labour on the market, and though the salary that can be paid is subject to constraints, the cost of the recruitment process itself is unimportant. Applicants compete for jobs, and the interview is an integral part of this process. Such a selection procedure implies that the employer should make his vacancies known as widely as possible regardless of the state of the labour market. However, in firms which recruit draughtsmen the desire for quality on the part of the employing manager tends to be toned down by the personnel department which can satisfy the employing manager by supplying him with a shortlist of candidates of a certain quality. But the ability to draw up such a shortlist depends on the state of the labour market. Hence the recruitment method and intensity adopted will vary with the state of the external market.

Qualifying selection is essentially cheap and straightforward. The firm has explicit selection criteria, and it is the responsibility of the personnel department to identify whether applicants meet these criteria (be they formal qualifications, experience, or a satisfactory recommendation). Given the obligation, the personnel department will tend to minimize the time taken to recruit and the cost of doing so. Under this type of selection procedure an interview with the employing department may serve to check that an applicant meets the selection criteria, to sell the job to the applicant, to introduce him to the manager and the job, or simply to perform a ritual which re-asserts the authority of the employing department.

Exploratory selection is similar to qualifying selection but is more expensive and time-consuming. Selection criteria are less formal and the candidate's ability to do the job is assessed by interview and perhaps by performance at some test.[58] The rationale of this type of selection is that it produces a greater number of suitable recruits than

57. The distinction between qualifying and exploratory selection is implicit in the discussion of the selection process adopted for bus drivers (see pp. 80–81). An explicit distinction is made here, however, because rank selection is a third possibility in the case of draughtsmen.

58. When we talk of hiring standards — meaning the ability to perform the job satis-factorily after a certain level of training — these are distinct from the proxies for hiring standards (e.g. paper qualifications) which are used in selection. Doeringer and Piore distinguish between two types of error made in recruitment:

does the reliance on some explicit entry requirement. The number of applicants with which the personnel department will be required to supply the interviewers will be dependent on the probability of an applicant revealing that he meets the hiring standards at the interview. Again, if the personnel department is required to find applicants as cheaply as possible, subject to a time constraint, it will adopt more costly recruitment methods as the external market tightens.

Sometimes the selection procedure itself is varied with the market situation. At Autocar we saw a change from qualifying to exploratory selection as a labour shortage developed — the type of change described by Doeringer and Piore.[59] The recruitment manager described the adjustment: 'When there are a lot of good applicants, a good deal goes on the paper qualifications and written evidence of a man's experience. When there are a lot of mediocre people, selection tends to be in greater depth.' But this kind of adjustment is by no means universal. Some firms always sought the best people on the market, adopting rank selection, and this was reflected in the statement of one recruitment officer who said 'we always try to give the employing department a number of people to choose from.' In other cases the selection became more intensive when there was a market surplus — a firm would use qualifying selection when recruitment was difficult, but 'pick and choose' (rank selection) when a lot of qualified applicants came forward.

Thus, where selection procedure is changed in response to changes in the state of the market, there is a tendency to move from rank to qualifying to exploratory selection as labour becomes more difficult to find. However, no firm moved along the whole continuum, and some firms made no changes. The differences across firms can be explained to some extent by the relationship between the employing

---

'The type I error of rejecting a qualified candidate and the Type II error of accepting a candidate who is unqualified. For any given screening device, there is a trade-off between the two types of errors, and one can only be reduced at the expense of the other. The two types of error can only be reduced simultaneously by the introduction of more powerful, and generally more costly, screening techniques' (1971:103–4). The movement from qualifying selection to exploratory selection is an example of using a more powerful screening device.

59. 'The costs of Type I and Type II errors are affected asymmetrically by the business cycle. As the market tightens, and the enterprise has increasing difficulty attracting candidates, the cost of rejecting workers who actually meet its hiring standards is increased. Because of the pervasive fear of accepting unqualified workers, this tends most often to lead to the introduction of more sophisticated screening devices rather than a simple reduction in the levels of the existing criteria' (1971:104).

and the personnel department. Where the employing department is dominant, its insistence on maintaining the quality of staff may mean that rank selection is maintained in spite of the labour market. Where the reverse is true, the personnel department can ease its own problems by adjusting the selection procedure in accordance with the state of the labour market.

Recruitment Activity

The firm in its attempts to recruit labour may be forced to move away from the relatively cheap methods of attracting staff by relying on internal transfers, unsolicited applications, trade unions, and the DE's services, to the more expensive channels of advertising and the use of private employment agencies.[60]

But variation in recruitment activity is not merely a question of changing the recruitment channel. A firm may advertise in the press, in specialist journals, in cinemas, or on television. The coverage may be local or national. The number of advertisements placed can vary, and they can be displayed or classified. Indeed, in the firms visited or from the media itself we came across the use of all these recruitment methods, if not for draughtsmen, certainly for designers. These included one aircraft company advertising in the *Seattle Times*, some fairly large and frequent display advertising in the national press, and an electronics firm advertising on television peak-viewing time. TASS acted as a source of recruits fairly often, and some firms approached private employment agencies.

The implication of our discussion of the various selection procedures is that the recruitment style and intensity adopted will depend, *ceteris paribus*, upon the ease with which draughtsmen can be recruited from the external market. Moreover, any change in selection procedure may have an independent effect on recruitment activity. For instance, since rank selection implies a more intensive search for labour, a change from qualifying to rank selection may mean an intensification of search in spite of labour becoming more plentiful.

It is misleading, however, to assume that each vacancy is considered separately, as there are economies of scale in the use of many recruitment channels.[61] One personnel officer illustrated the

60. The introduction fees charged by private employment agencies vary between 4% and 10% of the employee's salary. The employer will usually be credited with this fee or a proportion of it if the employee leaves voluntarily within two or three months.
61. Private employment agencies tend not to give discounts for supplying more than one employee at a time and, if they do, these tend to be small relative to the economies of scale achieved in advertising.

influence of the stock of vacancies on the recruitment style, saying: 'When recruiting for replacement we usually use informal methods — by looking round the company or by personal recommendation. We would advertise when there is a batch to be recruited at the beginning of a contract.' Another summed up his attitudes to recruitment thus: 'The departments can live with wastage for quite a while, but once vacancies have built up we would make a splash [by press advertising].' Hence, the stock of vacancies as well as the flow of new vacancies and the state of the external market influences the type and intensity of recruitment activity.

However, there are a number of ways in which the choice of recruitment activity departs from the paradigm of economic rationality which has been described. Firstly, while contacting the TASS divisional office is a cheap and effective way of recruiting draughtsmen in periods of high employment, some firms were suspicious of this recruitment channel. CFE, for instance, feared that it might have to account to TASS for any applicants it rejected, and hence did not recruit through the union office.

Secondly, there were cases where the choice of recruitment activity did not reflect the interests of the firm as a whole, but fulfilled a political need for the personnel department which had to convince other departments of the efforts being made to recruit staff. Thus, commenting on two recent advertisements for draughtsmen, one recruitment manager remarked 'that was to make a show for the union', and 'we were forced to do that one by the old man [the personnel director].' In the former situation, the union was only prepared to accept sub-contractors or permit overtime working if it could see that serious attempts were being made to recruit permanent staff. In the latter case, the personnel director needed to convince the board that his department was performing the job required of it. The readiness of personnel managers to advertise in the national press for detail draughtsmen whose market they considered to be local is best seen in this light. Thirdly, the behaviour and attitudes of personnel departments suggested that they seek to perform their role satisfactorily rather than contribute to a collective goal of maximization. This involved pushing the bulk of the selection work over to departmental managers and toning down their expectations of the quality of staff that was available. Another work-saving technique in recruitment was to avoid internal advertising which brought forth a stream of unsuitable applicants who were looking for promotion or a transfer. But the personnel department also plays a role in persuading managers to take people who required some on-the-job training. The use or non-use of PER might be a reflection of the relationship between the employing and the recruiting departments. In Autocar it was possible to get the employing departments to give a detailed specification of the kind of person they wanted, whereas in Carbits the personnel department avoided using PER because 'the engineering departments want to do their own selection'.

One might expect the recruitment budget to act as a constraint on the choice of recruitment activity. In many plants, however, it was fairly easy to justify over-spending the budget and in one case it was said that there were so many organizational changes in the firm that the planned budget never ran its full term. In this case the recruitment officers were in a position to spend what they considered necessary on recruitment. In the absence of effective budgetary constraints, it is difficult to see how the relative costs of different types of adjustment instruments are taken into account in the choice of instrument.

Doeringer and Piore (1971:102) list recruitment activity as one of the least constrained adjustment instruments. Our study has found that this is broadly true in the employment of draughtsmen. There were a few relatively minor ways in which the choice from amongst the range of possible recruitment strategies departed from that predicted by a cost-effectiveness model. More significant was the lack of evidence that the choice between varying recruitment activity and other adjustment instruments was made on cost-effectiveness grounds.

7. Redundancy

Of the three occupational markets in our study, only in the case of draughtsmen had firms been faced with surpluses of labour. It is appropriate to complement the main subject of this study by seeking to explain the adjustments which have been made to surpluses of labour.[62] We approach this question through an examination of the redundancies which took place in the plants in our survey.

Types of Redundancy
The firm's demand for draughtsmen is derived from the amount it spends on research and development rather than directly from its product demand. Though some draughtsmen will be employed to

---

62. Surpluses of labour were also apparent in the external market for draughtsmen. These are discussed in Appendix C.

perform modifications for individual customers, the bulk of drawing office staff are concerned with product development. The important question is what determines the level of research and development which a firm undertakes.

In firms such as those in the aircraft industry which work on large contracts, the amount of research and development is determined mainly by the customer, and the demand for draughtsmen will tend to reflect product demand. However, firms which operate in a product market with a large number of customers determine themselves the amount of research and development to be undertaken and, though product demand and the demand for draughtsmen will be related, we do not expect the same association which characterizes contract-based firms.[63]

Where the market structure permits firms some autonomy over research and development programmes, the decisions which influence the demand for draughtsmen will be akin to investment decisions. Thus two main criteria are important in determining the demand for draughtsmen in such firms: a rate-of-return calculation will fix the optimal rate of product development, but this will be subject to the firm being in a satisfactory liquidity position. Hence, a surplus of draughtsmen may arise in two ways. Either the firm

---

63. Perhaps the most important factor in this distinction is the role of development in the manufacturing cycle. However, this is closely related to the structure of demand in the product market. Aircraft firms tend to face monopsonists, and here production, and to a lesser extent design, will be to contract. Thus the desired number of development staff will be determined by the quantity and the quality of the orders received. This exemplified Woodward's (1965) unit or small-batch production where the manufacturing cycle is:

Marketing ⟶ Development ⟶ Production

At the other extreme a firm whose demand is competitive determines for itself the amount of development which is done. In this large-batch or mass production the manufacturing cycle is:

Development ⟶ Production ⟶ Marketing

Between these two extremes are those firms, typically facing oligopsony, which themselves decide upon the main features of the product and the rate of product development, but which tailor the product to particular customer requirements (e.g. computers and machine tools). Here the manufacturing cycle is:

Development ⟶ Marketing ⟶ Tailoring ⟶ Production

Such companies will have a section of the drawing office which is employed on tailoring designs and whose draughtsmen are essentially direct labour.

decides that the return from its draughtsmen does not justify the cost of employing all of them, or the liquidity position is such that it is expedient to reduce current costs even if it means forgoing a future return.

It is necessary to distinguish between these two sorts of labour surplus because they give rise to two distinct types of redundancy. The distinction is best thought of in terms of the earlier discussion of demand and establishments. Establishments represent the economic level of requirements based on product demand or the optimal rate of product development, and employment in excess of this establishment is referred to as an 'economic' surplus. However, the demand for labour may be lower than the establishment because the firm has a liquidity problem. The excess of employment over demand, when it is below the establishment, is termed a 'liquidity' surplus. In our survey it was apparent that both types of surplus had arisen in the case of draughtsmen and had resulted in redundancies.

Seven of the ten plants in our survey had had redundancies in the early 1970s which involved draughtsmen. The majority of these were readily classified as being a response to either an 'economic' or a 'liquidity' surplus. The redundancies at UM and AES were the result of the ending or cancellation of government contracts. Thus an 'economic' surplus was created by a fall in product demand, and draughtsmen were affected in the same way as direct labour. Elsewhere, such as in AFP, Hardware Ltd, and Autocar, the redundancies were managements' way of cutting their indirect costs. Such redundancies were examples of a response to a 'liquidity' surplus and bore no relationship to the rate of return accruing to the firm from the employment of draughtsmen.

The CFE redundancy was essentially a cost-cutting one, but unlike the three firms mentioned above which faced competition on the demand side, here the major project was a government contract. There had been a lot of public criticism about the cost of the Atlas project which was underwritten by the government, and CFE felt it necessary to demonstrate that this was under control. The engineering manager explained, 'there is a temptation to create extra work if there is nothing else to be done. One tries to perfect an aircraft to a much higher standard than is necessary. We had to exercise discipline on this front. One gets Parkinson's Law operating if one doesn't watch it.'

GMT's redundancy was both a response to a decline in the product demand and a cut in indirect costs. In machine tools, draughtsmen are working both on product development and modifications for individual orders.

The distinction which we have drawn between 'economic' and 'liquidity' surpluses is important for two reasons. Firstly, it plays a role in the explanation of the movements in the overall state of the draughtsmen's labour market. This is dealt with in Appendix C. Secondly, the whole decision-making process and the alternatives to redundancy are different for the two types of shortage. It is to this question which we now turn.

Constraints on Redundancy

Constraints which impinge upon management's use of redundancy as an adjustment instrument can be general or specific. The way the union reacts to a specific redundancy proposal will constrain management to some extent. However, there were factors present at Helico, Carbits, and AES which dissuaded management from redundancies in general.

As Helico was the only significant employer of engineering trades in the local labour market, it regarded the provision of secure employment as necessary to attract and retain skilled labour. It therefore avoided redundancy partly by sub-contracting in cyclical upturns, rather than recruiting. Similarly, CFE learnt from experience that it was difficult to attract labour after a redundancy.

AES had given the union an assurance that no redundancies would result from its introduction of CAD. Indeed, in the long run CAD avoided the need for redundancies. At Carbits the situation was slightly different. Management had avoided redundancies partly because it thought they would be blamed on computerization, and TASS members had the power to stop the computer.

In a number of the firms, CFE, AFP, and Autocar in particular, the TASS office committee reacted in a similar manner when the proposed redundancy was announced. It disputed the need for redundancies, imposed an overtime ban, and suggested a shorter working week. In all cases a compromise was reached whereby volunteers for redundancy were accepted from any department and people transferred accordingly. The office committees pointed out vacancies and made sure they were filled internally. In some cases the committee vetted those accepting redundancy to make sure they had jobs to go to.

The effect of such a compromise is a rise in the quality of those accepting redundancy since the more highly skilled staff are in greater demand. Once management has lost control of the redundancy in this way, the economic utility of the redundancy — in terms of variable cost savings as against future fixed labour costs — is reduced.[64] However, the redundancy retains an organizational utility for the local management acting on the orders of a holding company, and provides a short-term financial gain.

In a number of cases a firm started recruiting within six months of the redundancy. Where this occurred, redundancy pay, and recruitment, and training cost offset a high proportion of the saving in wages. It may have been that the upturn in labour demand was quicker than expected, but we found no evidence of any management estimating the time lapse before the upturn in labour demand when considering a cost-cutting redundancy.

To offset the impression that a union can only hope to improve redundancy terms it is appropriate to give an example where a proposed redundancy was averted. Twice during 1971 Automative Products in Leamington tried to have a redundancy in the technical and other white-collar areas, which TASS members successfully resisted.[65] In the first attempted redundancy, the three white-collar unions involved acted together with TASS taking the lead. TASS members refused to accept the redundancy and, in addition to banning overtime and sub-contracting, they threatened to impose a four-day week if the company persisted with its plans, and a walkout if names were issued or notices served. After an unsuccessful meeting with a senior director, some two thousand staff walked out and reaffirmed the proposed action. The company was considerably embarrassed by this meeting and modified its firm line. Although there were some voluntary leavers, the terms were higher than originally proposed and the numbers leaving were considerably less than the size of the planned redundancy.

It could be argued that the threat to put the wages clerks and foremen on a four-day week was crucial in preventing redundancy through the impact it would have had on the shop floor. However, in the second attempt at redundancy, TASS was fighting alone and was just as successful. Solidarity amongst TASS members was important, as were the tactics adopted by the office committee to prevent this solidarity being broken by the issuing of names. To some extent TASS members were in a fortunate position because the company was trying to increase profits by cutting indirect costs while there was difficulty in getting work done in some of the technical areas. Another factor was that TASS was negotiating at company level where the decision to have a redundancy had been taken. If the

64. For a discussion of fixed and variable labour costs see Oi (1962).
65. For a detailed account of what happened at Automative Products see Kennell (1971).

local management had been acting on the orders of a foreign holding company the situation might have been different.

Alternatives to Redundancy

The need for redundancies is often averted by the policies pursued when there is a shortage. Carbits, for instance, had used sub-contracting fairly extensively when the workload was high and only employed permanent staff where they were required in the long term. LP and Helico were both able to shift work between plants and keep the numbers employed fairly steady.

But, apart from an ability to avoid a labour surplus, we must look at the adjustments open to a firm with a surplus apart from redundancy. In a situation of 'economic' surplus the firm has a number of possible adjustment instruments. Where, however, there is a 'liquidity' surplus some of these options are closed because only those options which save money can be considered as alternatives to redundancy. These are examined in Table 5.3.

A number of conclusions can be drawn from the information displayed in the table. Where transfers and early retirements are possible they tend to be preferred to redundancy because they are less highly constrained by the union and because less labour potential is lost for the same reduction in numbers. Apart from these, there are rarely any suitable alternatives for the firm which decides to cut costs by reducing its labour demand (though cost savings in other areas might be posed as alternatives). However, there is a wider range of alternatives to an 'economic' surplus. Shifting work between plants is acceptable, but short-time working is considered administratively inconvenient (and in this respect the treatment of draughtsmen differs from most direct manual labour). The choice between redundancy and hoarding can be seen as a rational economic one in which fixed costs and variable costs are considered. However, the timing of the expected upturn in demand will play a crucial role, and the effect of the union's opposition to redundancy will enter the picture as an additional cost on the firm if it decides on a policy of redundancy.

8. Conclusion

The draughtsmen's market, characterized by fluctuating demand, has exhibited both shortages and surpluses in recent years. Firms employing draughtsmen have faced a variety of problems: insufficient labour and excess labour, difficulty recruiting labour and difficulty retaining labour, temporary peaks in the workload and the

ALTERNATIVE ADJUSTMENTS TO REDUNDANCY

Instruments	In 'Economic' Surplus	In 'Liquidity' Surplus
Sub-contracting from other plants or firms	This is done whenever possible but is more likely to be inter-plant, intra-firm sub-contracting (e.g. Helico, LP, and UM)	Unlikely to have required effect of reducing costs, though one would expect to recoup labour costs quicker in this way than would be possible where employee is working for the firm
Hoarding and/or 'making' work	Tendency to hold those with design skills even when there is no work for them. GMT would hold a surplus for 3–6 months depending on time of year	Produces no savings
Inventory changes	In some drawing offices there is a lot of less urgent work that can be done	Produces no savings
Reducing hours per man	This has been tried by one or two plants but proved 'administratively inconvenient'	This would reduce total costs but hourly labour cost would rise. It does not give the same impression of savings to higher management
Transfer	Nearly always considered as an alternative	This is usually acceptable – it just means that jobs become redundant rather than men
Natural wastage	Redundancy will usually occur because this adjustment has proved too slow	This is an acceptable alternative if fast enough. It does not, however, have the same demonstration effect
Accelerating wastage	If this means lowering pay or worsening conditions to induce people to leave it is highly constrained by the union. Where it does operate is in the increasing of redundancy pay to induce more voluntary redundancy	
Early retirements	More acceptable than redundancy probably – always tried first 1. less future productive labour lost 2. considered more acceptable socially, if it is voluntary	

commitment to large projects which threaten to create shortages in the absence of remedial action. This chapter has considered the responses that have been made to these various stimuli.

Though in Chapter 2 we have listed a large number of possible adjustment instruments, the firm's definition of its problem and the circumstances it faces will tend to limit its range of choice considerably. Viewing shortages as problems to be solved is useful for understanding the adjustments which are made. Indeed, three main points emerged from this approach. First, a net outflow of labour is a more important stimulus than a stock shortage of labour. The former is much more likely to result in a pay increase. Second, shortages can be important in precipitating adjustments which would be economically viable even in the absence of a shortage. This was seen particularly in the case of CAD. Third, the problems created by temporary adjustments tend to diminish with use. Thus temporary adjustments such as the use of sub-contracting can become permanent.

The choice of adjustment instrument is affected not only by the way management defines its shortage problems but also by a variety of constraints which impinge on that choice. Thus, technology may rule out the use of certain instruments, and we have seen, for example, that CAD is only suited to a limited range of products. Other constraints do not prohibit the use of certain adjustments but merely make them less attractive to the firm. Perhaps the most important are the various constraints on adjusting pay. Where bargaining structures are such that the coverage of a pay adjustment is far wider than the areas of shortage pressure, a pay increase becomes a very costly way of adjusting to shortage.

The existence of these constraints can be integrated fairly simply into a model which predicts that the firm acts as a cost minimizer in selecting its adjustment instruments. However, this model is more difficult to sustain in the light of some of our other findings. In the process of recruitment we saw that the 'choice' of adjustment instrument often rested on the outcome of inter-departmental conflicts with, to indulge in oversimplification, the employing department aiming to improve or maintain the quality of its staff, the personnel department minimizing its own workload, and the financial department exercising some loose form of control. The actions of individuals or groups pursuing their own goals do not usually result in the situation predicted by the model of a single rational employer. Similarly, when it was a question of adjusting to a peak in the workload without engaging more permanent staff, the choice of instrument was in general the outcome of negotiation between the office manager and the union office committee rather than one individual selecting the most cost-effective device.

An example of the successful application of the cost-minimizing employer model is seen in the response to an 'economic' surplus. Typically, the firm would compare the expected savings of variable costs with the extra fixed costs, while the unions sought to increase those fixed costs by improved redundancy pay. However, this model was not applicable to situations where higher management cut overhead costs in response to a liquidity problem by reducing the number of design staff.

We have seen that in the case of draughtsmen the cost-minimizing model works in two respects. First, the adoption of a 'common sense' solution is often consistent with rational economic choice. The disinclination to recruit permanent staff to deal with a temporary problem is an example of this. Second, there were a number of instances where cost effectiveness was the predominant criterion in the choice between particular adjustments. The choice of recruitment channel tended to be made on these grounds. However, there was no evidence to suggest that instruments under the control of different departments were compared under economic criteria. It was not customary to consider whether a pay increase was more cost-effective than a reduction in hiring standards or an improvement in working conditions. An adjustment would be chosen because it met the conditions imposed by quasi-political forces rather than because it fulfilled any economic criterion.

6

Conclusions

1. Introduction

This final chapter presents an evaluation of the cost-minimizing model and draws some of the implications of our analysis. The preceding empirical chapters have been concerned with whether or not the broad framework of cost-minimizing behaviour as set out in Chapter 2 can usefully be applied to the problem of adjustment to shortages, and Section 2 of the present chapter offers an appraisal. We argue that provided one adds flesh to the skeletal framework, for example by explicitly taking account of the way bargaining structures constrain the choice of instrument through their effect on costs, then the cost-minimizing model is one of the principal foundation blocks in a theory of adjustment. There are, however, other building blocks, and we indicate how, in further developments of a theory of adjustment, they might be put together. In Sections 3 and 4 we discuss some of the theoretical and policy implications of the study.

2. The Cost-Minimizing Model

In Chapter 2 we posed three questions about the cost-minimizing model which formed the basis of our empirical studies, and now we attempt to answer these questions directly. The first is concerned with the notion of cost and asks how far constraints and objectives must enter the cost function. The second deals with the way in which firms go about choosing their adjustments and whether the search for alternatives is extensive or limited. The third considers whether those factors which are deemed to be important in the process of adjustment to shortage can be accommodated by the cost-minimizing model. The final part of this section suggests the directions in which future theorizing might profitably be developed.

Cost-Minimizing, Objectives, and Constraints

Most cost-minimizing models are concerned with the problem of finding the cheapest way of producing a given output. The model outlined in Chapter 2 differs from these models in that it includes in the range of possible adjustments the residual adjustment of producing less than the desired output. The output constraint is replaced by an exogenous value of desired output and the cost of producing less than this desired output is included in the sum of costs to be minimized.

The advantage of this approach is that it can accommodate firms with a variety of objective functions. This can be done by extending the notion of costs to include any departure a firm makes from its objectives. In this section we consider which objectives are important in particular circumstances and how these help to explain the choice of adjustments. Later in the section we consider how some of the more crucial constraints which are imposed on employers affect the adjustment process.

The study of the teachers' market has shown that there are other residual adjustments, apart from the loss of output, which must be considered as costly to the organization. In this market the main residual adjustment to labour shortage is that of allowing the teacher–pupil ratio to fall. On the face of it, this adjustment strategy is cheap because it involves no financial cost. However, our model predicts that if this were all, the residual adjustment would be used invariably. Although we have observed a heavy reliance on this adjustment for many years, we have also to explain why other adjustments which entail considerable financial cost were ever sought. We therefore include, under the notion of cost, the effect of a decline in the teacher–pupil ratio on the quality of education.

Although employers differ considerably in their objective functions, we can make a basic distinction between profit-maximizing firms and those organizations run on a not-for-profit basis, which can be thought of as satisficers or utility maximizers. Our assumption of a given level of desired output is somewhat unrealistic when applied to profit-maximizing firms. There the desired output is set by equating marginal cost and marginal revenue, and the adjustments highlighted in our model affect both marginal cost and marginal revenue. However, what is important from our point of view is how these two sorts of objective function are accommodated in the cost-minimizing framework. An essential difference between the profit-maximizing and the satisficing firm is that, whereas the unit cost of lost output for the profit-maximizing firm is the forgone profit per unit, the satisficing firm may value lost output more highly if it is particularly averse to failing to meet its output objective. This difference can help to explain some of the main contrasts between the private and the public sectors. Indeed, it is in these terms that we have compared the municipal bus undertakings which are reluctant to reduce services with the more profit-orientated company-sector undertakings.

Where desired minimum output and service quality are specified, there is a tendency for positive adjustments to take place on the supply side rather than on the demand side. This can be seen in the case of the markets for teachers and bus drivers where almost all the efforts have been concentrated on expanding supply rather than altering the demand for labour (though residual adjustments may take place on the demand side in the form of the failure to run scheduled bus services or having 'oversize' classes). Where a minimum output is a heavily weighted objective this point is obvious enough — there will be a disinclination to reduce labour input.[1]

The quality aspect is more interesting. In industries where the product is in the form of a personal service, the quality of labour will directly affect the quality of the product. Indeed reductions in the quality of labour may, through their impact on product quality, have detrimental effects on recruitment. In order to minimize such repercussions there will be a tendency to preserve hiring standards, and this instrument is therefore likely to be more highly constrained than in cases where there is not the same face-to-face contact between employees and consumers.

The elasticity of product demand with respect to quality is relevant here. Where this is low, then deteriorations in the quality of service may be more acceptable than where the elasticity is high. In the case of teachers this elasticity is probably low, because of the difficulty in defining and measuring education output, so that variations in quality of output are less easily detected. In the case of buses, quality variations are more readily apparent, and Chapter 3

---

1. This assumes that large-scale capital substitution, which would allow the same output to be produced with a much smaller labour input, is impossible. In the case of the bus drivers this was partly for technological reasons (bus size can only be altered to a limited degree and one driver is required per bus). In the case of teachers it was shown that as part of the quality considerations there was a desired labour–output ratio (teacher–pupil ratio), the existence of which clearly militates against reducing labour requirements in the face of a shortage.

argued that the travelling public were very sensitive to quality of service.

There are in addition to the desired quality and quantity a number of other objectives which can assume considerable importance in some markets. In the teachers' markets, norms governing the way in which the service should be provided are strongly adhered to. These explain why certain instruments, which would otherwise be feasible, and which are widely used as responses to shortages of teachers in other countries, are avoided in this country.

We have argued throughout this study that constraints play an essential part in the explanation of adjustment choice, and some of the more important ones are discussed here. It is apparent that, because most constraints increase the cost of making an adjustment, the cost-minimizing hypothesis is largely impotent without their explicit consideration.

Institutional constraints, in the form of union restraints on certain lines of action, were everywhere apparent: each of the chapters provided examples of them, and the interesting question is to explain why the pattern of union constraints varied so much over time and between plants. This variation was most clearly seen in the case of busmen where there were often considerable differences between garages in what instruments were most highly constrained.

Another institutional constraint is the bargaining structure, since this determines the degree of coincidence between the area experiencing any labour shortage and the area covered by any response made. This has been noted on a number of occasions in the empirical chapters and can have a major effect on the costs of adjustment. The less the coincidence the greater the marginal cost of adjustment will be, especially in the case of pay as an instrument. A plant which is concerned to increase inflows may decide to raise pay but it will normally have to raise the pay of the stock of workers already in employment as well as new recruits. The bargaining structure is important in determining just how great will be the marginal cost of raising pay for new entrants. Only in the case of a perfectly discriminating monopsonist would this problem disappear.

The teachers' market provides a striking example where uniform salary scales[2] have meant that the pay of, say, maths and science teachers could not be raised without raising the pay of the whole teaching force. In the case of bus drivers the formal structure of the

2. There may be a number of reasons for preferring a common salary scale to individual negotiations. See Metcalf (1973) for a discussion of some of these.

negotiating machinery in the 1960s was such that local undertakings were part of national agreements and those with severe shortage problems were forced to withdraw from the national negotiations or were expelled for consistently breaking the agreements. In the draughtsmen's market the recruitment activity of TASS amongst a wide range of technicians other than draughtsmen may have militated against the use of pay as an adjustment in their case.

The more precise the coverage of any instrument, the cheaper it will be, and attempts are therefore made to improve the coincidence of the areas of shortage pressure and the coverage of the response. A notable example is the move towards company-level bargaining in the bus industry. Similarly, in the teachers' market, the 1971 pay award introduced more flexibility in the distribution of higher-scale posts among teachers of different subjects. We also found some employers of draughtsmen attempting to isolate individual groups of workers to restrict the coverage of negotiated wage increases.

Apart from these institutional constraints, the state of the labour market and the product market will affect the cost and hence the choice of instruments. The product market influences the relative cost of instruments through the elasticity of product demand. Where a firm has to pass on the cost of a wage increase as a price increase, the effect of this on product demand must be considered as an extra cost which the firm has to bear. Thus, wage increases are, *ceteris paribus*, more costly to the firm with an elastic product demand curve. Conversely, an inelastic demand means that adjustments are less costly and this may lead to looser managerial control systems.[3]

The state of the external labour market will determine the elasticity of the supply of labour to the firm.[4] The level of unemployment in the market will affect the firm's flow balance since it is plausible to assume that the flow of voluntary quits and the flow of applicants are, respectively, negatively and positively related to the level of unemployment; these flows in turn affect the stock balance within the firm but, more importantly, the relative costs of different instruments will be affected. The higher the level of unemployment the more elastic the supply of labour and the less costly will be the pay instrument. The cost effectiveness of recruitment may also change with the level of unemployment. The relative

3. The argument here is similar to that put forward by W. Brown (1973) who found that wage drift was highest in plants where there were the loosest managerial control systems and these depended on the price elasticity of demand for the product.
4. The extent of monopsony or competition in the labour market is also relevant, of course.

cost of many instruments will vary over the cycle, and cost minimization may thus yield different solutions at different times, though all instruments are not similarly affected. There is, for example, no reason to suppose that the costs of job redesign are dependent on the state of the external market.

The general implication is that we would expect a preference for non-pay adjustments during a tight labour market. This tendency, however, may be offset by competitive bidding so that in times of full employment there is a kink in the supply curve.

If a firm believed that its competitors in the labour market would follow wage increases but not wage cuts, the supply curve to the firm would be elastic below the current wage level and inelastic above it as in Figure 6.1. A kinked supply curve of this nature would give rise to a discontinuity in the marginal cost curve. If the demand curve passed through this discontinuity as it does in the figure, then only very large shifts in the demand for labour would result in any pay change.

Such a model can explain why aggressive pay increases were rarely used in the bus industry but when they were used, as for example by Alphabus and Townbus, they were often very large indeed.

Apart from affecting costs of different instruments, the state of the external labour market will also affect the firm's expectations on the

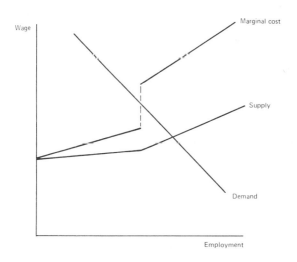

FIGURE 6.1. THE KINKED SUPPLY CURVE

193

duration of the shortage and hence whether temporary or permanent adjustments are appropriate. The matter is considered in the next section along with the broader question of how firms discover their cost-minimizing strategy.

The Search for Cost-Minimizing Strategies

Although the model which is developed in Chapter 2 is designed to explain how firms adjust to shortages of labour, it is broad enough to include all questions of labour acquisition and utilization even in the absence of shortage. The firm, it is assumed, will attempt to select that labour-force strategy which minimizes its discounted cost stream. In the absence of free information about the effects of alternative strategies, the firm will search the range of possible strategies in order to find a suitable one. This section is concerned with the question of how organizations actually search for the cheapest cost strategies. We will argue, firstly, that firms are more likely to change their current strategy in response to labour shortage than to other stimuli, and secondly that the choice of adjustment is made on the basis of a limited rather than an extensive search.

Labour shortage only enters the cost-minimizing model as a particular sort of cost, but it is apparent from our study that a labour shortage can act as a spur to action when other sorts of deviation from the cost-minimizing position do not. This is seen in the case of both computer-aided design and one-man operation. Even where these techniques were viable as cost-saving devices, the real spur to their introduction was often the appearance of a labour shortage. Furthermore, there were a number of instances where hiring standards could have been relaxed in order to reduce labour costs, but where such adjustments only took place in response to labour shortage. The reason why a labour shortage acts as this sort of stimulus is twofold. First, labour shortages create problems which require attention, whereas this is not always the case with other departures from the optimal position. Second, a labour shortage acts as a signal that there is a cheaper solution than the current strategy in which residual adjustments involve a cost to the firm. In either case the labour shortage will be an important stimulus to the firm which will start a search for an alternative strategy. The corollary to this is that the 'stopping-point' will tend to be a strategy which produces the desired quantity of labour rather than one which represents a strict cost-minimum.

Nevertheless, the principle of cost minimization was undoubtedly at work in the markets we studied. In the draughtsmen's market, for example, it was clear that the choice of which recruitment channel to use, and the decision of whether to work overtime, sub-contract, or take on permanent staff depended largely on the relative costs involved. Similarly, apart from situations arising from liquidity problems, the relative expenditure on fixed and variable costs was the crucial factor in deciding questions of redundancy. Cost minimizing was also apparent in the two public-sector markets. In bus undertakings the way the man–hours combination varied over time gave support for the cost-minimizing hypothesis, and the growing use of part-timers in the teachers' market must also be interpreted as a cost-minimizing strategy. Moreover, the importance of non-wage adjustments, which has been stressed in this study, can be explained only in terms of their costs relative to those of wage adjustments.

Thus, the cost-minimizing hypothesis appears to work to a limited extent. Where alternative adjustments are compared, the firm tends to select the one with the lower present value of the resulting cost stream. However, in none of the markets was overall cost minimization apparent. We could find no mechanism whereby such diverse adjustments as pay, capital substitution, and recruitment costs were compared as if they were alternative ways of achieving the same end. This was partly because the organizational structure limited the number of comparisons which were made — a point developed in the next section. But it was also because uncertainty as to the future market situation and about the effect of instruments resulted in a preference for temporary or familiar adjustments.

While some employers, such as those in the teachers' market, have responded to shortages by acquiring information through surveys,[5] the more common response in the face of uncertainty is to act cautiously, by trying out adjustments without committing the organization to their permanent use. Thus we observe firms employing temporary adjustments so as to acquire information through a process of 'learning by doing'. In such cases, as Dror has argued, 'if some of the information needed in an activity can be learned during the early stages of carrying out that activity, the more promising alternative ways to carry it out should be undertaken simultaneously, and the decision as to which is the best alternative

5. These are usually surveys of pay or potential recruits. Such surveys may of course give biased or misleading results and the firms will then be faced with erroneous information. The Pay Board (1974a:25) found this to be so in the case of several pay surveys. Where a market is highly atomized it may be more difficult to get information on potential inflows to the market as a whole.

should be delayed until information has been learned.'[6] There is therefore a tendency to adopt a mixed strategy, and this contributes to the explanation of the diversity of adjustments which we have observed.

Another implication of the lack of information is that, in addition to the adoption of many different instruments, there will be a preference for those instruments which are tried and familiar.[7] Such habitual behaviour may of course simply be the result of inertia, or the fact that the shortage problem is 'small' in terms of its cost implications for the firm as a whole, so that there is no incentive to change the pattern of adjustments adopted.[8] Apart from those considerations, however, habitual behaviour may represent a perfectly rational response by firms in an uncertain world, especially if the decision-makers are risk-averse.

Braybrooke and Lindblom[9] have put forward a model of decision-making which stresses the role of 'habit' and caution especially where the decision-making machinery is of a bureaucratic kind with regularized procedures. They see the decision process as being characterized by incremental decision-making with small changes from established procedure and a fragmentary and limited approach. The selection of particular instruments and the intensity with which they are used is based on what procedures are well known and have been customarily employed. Another feature of the Braybrooke and Lindblom model is that the decisions are made at many dispersed decision points and the whole process of limited and largely uncoordinated adjustments has therefore been labelled 'disjointed incrementalism'.[10]

6. (1968:142); there may also be a predilection for trying a whole battery of instruments rather than just one, where there is doubt over the principal cause of the shortage. There may be scope for learning by others' doing, e.g. taking note of other undertakings' experience with one-man operation or part-time working in the case of transport operators.
7. There were a number of instances where firms held entrenched assumptions about certain instruments, and their usefulness was dismissed with little consideration. London Transport always assumed, for example, that the use of part-time staff to cover weekend work was impossible because of union restrictions and an inadequate supply of suitable part-time labour. This may in fact be true though some surprise was felt when it was shown to be possible in other undertakings.
8. There were, on the other hand, examples of employers who in desperation made fairly radical changes in their employment strategy. The Alphabus productivity agreement was the prime example of this.
9. (1963); see Self (1972:171) for some criticisms of this model.
10. See Ehrenberg (1972: Chapter 2), for an empirical study where a model is specified which explicitly takes account of incremental budgeting by assuming that the desired employment level in any period is a function of the lagged employment level.

Explanation in terms of habitual behaviour sometimes seems to fit the facts well. The markets described in Chapters 3–5 showed many examples of ignorance, some attempts to overcome this, and widespread use of temporary and customary instruments. What we see therefore is an adjustment process characterized by slow adaptation to changing circumstances. Information acquisition and processing act as a powerful constraint on firms, and their behaviour thus departs from that of the rational, perfectly informed cost-minimizer.

We should be hard-pressed to argue, on the basis of the evidence in Chapters 3–5, that decision-makers continue appraising alternative adjustment strategies up to the point where the expected marginal benefits of extra search are equated with the marginal cost, but the broad argument of Chapter 2 that there will be a limited and piecemeal approach is confirmed.

Behavioural Considerations

The cost-minimizing model provides a useful starting-point in the explanation of choice of instruments and fits in well with traditional theory. Virtually all adjustments involve some sort of costs, the relevance of which has been noted in a number of previous empirical studies of firms' behaviour in response to shortage. There are obviously some difficulties in putting a cost-minimizing model into operational terms[11] but, provided we interpret the hypothesis in a sophisticated manner, such as taking account of the role and costs of information acquisition and the consequent 'learning by doing' which may lead to the use of several different instruments simultaneously, then we have a framework which can handle several important factors.

It can, for example, accommodate different objective functions and a variety of constraints. In reality the choice problem is often subject to many institutional and other constraints. These are not inconsistent with cost-minimizing behaviour but need to be taken into account if realistic insights are to be obtained.

However, one of the major shortcomings of the cost-minimizing model is that it ignores organizational considerations within the firm. Our empirical studies showed that these are often a major factor in understanding the choice of adjustment, and hence treating

11. If all non-financial costs including 'psychic' and 'political' costs were to be considered, this would provide a comprehensive theory but one which would be unfalsifiable since anything could be shown to be consistent with it if suitable monetary values were attached. We would only have empty tautologies.

the enterprise 'as if' it were a single rational decision-making organ may not yield accurate predictions. This is, in fact, a fairly general failing of the theory of the firm, as Cyert and Hedrick observed when they argued that

> the real world still escapes our models: our explanations remain at the aggregate level. The problem is clearly difficult but we wonder whether economics can remain an empirical science and continue to ignore the actual decision making processes of real firms. (1972:409)

The cost-minimizing hypothesis implicitly assumed that there are decision-makers empowered to implement decisions to eliminate shortages but this is not always so, as shown in the case of teachers. There it was apparent that, at the national level, the lack of a strong decision-making machinery in the early post-war years prevented any effective attack on shortages. Perhaps the lack of a capable decision process simply reflects the fact that the elimination of shortages is not a high-priority goal, and if the organization of decision-making were not appropriate to the goals then it would change. Whatever truth there is in this argument, there is sufficient evidence in the case studies to suggest that organizational form can have a decisive influence on the type of adjustment chosen.

Where there are different levels of decision-making, the discretion of individuals at the lower levels is often severely limited as when, in multi-plant firms or in local enterprises subject to strong national bargaining, there is little scope for raising pay to meet local conditions. A fragmented decision process, or — to use Braybrooke and Lindblom's term noted above — a disjointed process, seems characteristic of many enterprises. In such circumstances the control of different adjustments resides with different departments. Pay increases may, for example, be subject to an ultimate veto by the finance department, hiring standards controlled by the personnel department. Those with responsibility for dealing with labour shortages (and this responsibility may be split) seldom have control of all possible instruments, and so different firms react in different ways depending on the organizational structure.

Conflicts may arise within an enterprise which, in the short run at least, can affect the choice of instruments. In the draughtsmen's market, for example, such conflict was often noticeable in the process of recruitment, where personnel, finance, and design departments may all have slightly differing aims. The decision on how to go about recruiting extra staff was the outcome of negotiations between different interest groups within the firm, rather than the cost-minimizing strategy for the enterprise as a whole. This is probably typical of a much wider range of occupations.[12] Individuals in the personnel department may be concerned to minimize their workload or to give the impression of doing everything possible, and we observed instances, particularly in some large transport undertakings, where certain recruitment advertising or the employment of outside consultants may take place without much economic rationale.

These divisions within the firm mean that different groups have different goals and, equally important, different time horizons, so that the preference for temporary or permanent adjustments may vary with the particular decision-maker. It is evident that we need to draw on a behavioural theory of the enterprise, because behavioural models assume that it is individuals within the organization who act, rather than the organization itself. The objectives and the process of decision-making are both regarded as complex, and the decisions which do merge are the outcome of conflicting views held by various individuals and represent a workable consensus.[13] The way in which these individuals perceive and interpret situations is said to have a major bearing on the decisions which are taken.

This emphasis on the structure of the decision-making machinery and the recognition of conflict amongst different individuals and groups, each with their own goals, formal responsibilities, and authority, accords well with the attention given to these matters in our own and other empirical studies of adjustments which suggests that it is a profitable line for theory construction. There is, however, a danger that descriptive realism is achieved only at the cost of having a theory which is non-operational. Where the emphasis is on the 'internal' logic of the situation,

people assign meanings to situations and to the actions of others and react in terms of the interpretations suggested by those meanings. Thus they may respond differently to the same objectively defined stimulus. (Silverman, 1970:130)

This means that formulating laws of adjustment behaviour in response to shortages, whose objective characteristics are perceived

---

12. This idea of there being a split between those who recruit and others in the organization was put forward in Section 1 of Chapter 2, where it was stressed that personnel departments may be more concerned with the flow position whereas production departments may be more interested in the stock position. This idea is also found in the work of Shultz (1962) and Ehrenberg (1972:18).
13. See Cyert and March (1963).

by social scientists, may be quite misleading. We do not therefore have a theory offering predictions as to which particular adjustments will be chosen, as was the case with the cost-minimizing model.

Constrained Sub-Optimization

These ideas point the way to a synthesis of cost-minimizing and behavioural models. The two approaches are not necessarily incompatible and some of the explanations of adjustment choice which we have put forward have roots in both sorts of model. Basically, the process seems to approximate to a sort of constrained sub-optimization. That is, cost-minimizing behaviour provides an explanation of choice within limited areas. It is not helpful to assume that all organizational issues have been resolved.[14] The division of responsibilities and controls between departments, with their differing and perhaps conflicting goals, may narrow down the use of certain instruments but, if each department were regarded as a separate decision centre, then within its limited sphere and in pursuit of its limited goals it may well adopt cost-minimizing behaviour, subject to the various constraints.

The choice of operand, whether the firm is mainly seeking to adjust hours, inflows, outflows, or requirements, may also be governed by habit to a large degree or by the organization structure. But as one narrows down the choice problem, cost-minimizing aspects seem to play a greater part. For example, the selection of particular instruments such as whether to increase recruitment activity or reduce requirements may be strongly influenced by non-cost factors, but the choice of a particular recruitment channel is very likely to be determined on cost-effective grounds.

The outcome of these sub-optimization processes may differ from what would occur if the organization acted 'as if' it were a single entity cost-minimizing within the context of a well-defined objective function. In reality, taking the organization as a whole, it may not be optimizing anything at all.[15] What we observe in practice therefore is diversity between firms in apparently similar circumstances. Organization structure and constraints will differ, thus giving rise to a variety of responses to shortage.

A major feature of such a model of constrained sub-optimization

---

14. This is a major feature of the 'as if' approach of the traditional economic theory of the firm. See Horowitz (1970: 330–37).
15. This view has been expressed by Williams *et al.* (1974: Chapter 3), who show that in the case of universities there is no single unambiguous objective function, but it is probably true of a much wider range of organizations.

is that the adjustment process is thought of not as one where organizations instantaneously respond to secure a new equilibrium, but rather as one of slow adaptation to changed circumstances. Apart from the normal lags, such as in recruiting and training, there are costs of acquiring information, there is a learning process, and there may be constraints to be overcome such as altering the decision-making machinery if this is incompatible with organizational goals, and there may be an inertia factor. If such inertia creates a reluctance to change the approach to problems, then the choice of instruments will partly be governed by circumstances which were once thought to be important, and there may be no immediate tendency to conform to current 'best practice' techniques of adjustment. The process of adjustment will therefore be 'slow and strewn with errors of judgement' (Mackay *et al.*, 1971: 397).

Much of the argument which has been developed here is in line with that advanced by Doeringer and Piore. They found diversity typical. They also recognized that cost minimizing in a loose form may have some relevance and were obviously aware of organizational factors within the firm. Our empirical work confirms the general tenor of their implied thesis on adjustment choice but takes the argument further. In explaining the observed diversity of adjustments, Doeringer and Piore attach some weight to the view that this may be due to firms not forecasting, and therefore having to work on an *ad hoc* basis when faced with a shortage. This corresponds in part with our emphasis on the information problem. In other matters, our treatment of many factors has been more explicit than Doeringer and Piore, for instance on organizational factors, the objective function, the interdependence of instruments, and the constraints.[16]

The concentration on the firm level has in many respects revealed a confusing jumble of actions. This is understandable but it is of little use in advancing our knowledge of labour-market adjustment processes if we cannot make any generalizations. The following section explores the market level.

---

16. Our view of unions has been one in which they are seen only as a constraint on managerial action. This has been a useful perspective, though one which is not widely found in the literature, at least in quite such an exclusive manner. It is perhaps worth repeating here that we regard it as an entirely proper and often highly desirable function of a union to act in this way.

Conclusions

3. Market-Level Considerations

In analysing adjustments to shortage at the level of the firm, it proved necessary to account for the observed diversity of behaviour by adding more and more micro-level factors to the explanation. Thus the firm's current position, its norms and objectives, and the constraints it faces are all relevant in explaining the responses of a firm to shortage. However, when we consider the process of adjustment at the market level, we are interested not in the diversity of behaviour but rather in the broad patterns which can be used for forecasting and policy analysis.

In this section we consider how the market adjusts to shortages of labour, and compare the roles of wage and non-wage variables in the adjustment process, bearing in mind the prominence which economic theory normally gives to wage adjustments. We argue that the use of wage adjustments may be de-stabilizing.

The Role of Price Adjustments

In neo-classical economics there is no theory of the adjustment process. All that exist are some essentially *ad hoc* hypotheses appended to the Walrasian system. The dominant assumption is that price is the central variable in the adjustment process, and the speed with which price changes depends on the magnitude of dis-equilibrium. For example Arrow and Capron (1959) write 'the forces that induce price rises will clearly operate more strongly the greater the excess demand over supply. Hence we find it reasonable to accept the usual view that the rate of increase of price per unit of time is greater the greater the excess demand over supply.' Prices are assumed to provide incentives for transactors to alter their behaviour in such a way as to produce stable equilibrium, though there are price adjustment models which produce equilibrium with vacancies.[17] In this section we review the validity of this stress on the

17. See for example Arrow and Capron (1959), though their world is one in which there are no shifts in supply, and demand is treated as exogenous. There is continuous adjustment of wages but this is never sufficient to eliminate shortages. This situation implies that firms do not learn that their adjustment is insufficient to remove the stock imbalance. In practice other adjustments are likely to be tried. If firms do not make other positive adjustments then the residual adjustments, which necessarily occur, may become accepted as working norms. The shortage situation becomes ossified and firms learn to live with persistent stock deficiency. Equilibrium vacancies also occur in the monopsony model. In both this and the Arrow–Capron case the equilibrium is stable. This may not be so with a cobweb model where there may be non-convergence.

202

role of price adjustments and the stability of the adjustment process in the light of our findings. But first we must acknowledge some limitations of our study.

We have been concerned with the behaviour of buyers, though sellers will respond to shortages of labour by varying the controls they exercise in particular firms over recruitment, hours of work, and manning levels, and by changing their jobs or labour-force status, thereby altering the flows of new entrants to the market, withdrawals from the market, and quits from and applicants to particular firms. The emphasis in this study has been on the firm's response to its stock position. A related point is that aggregating up from firms' behaviour to the market level suggests that understanding the market position is simply a question of summing all the firms' responses. But such a view is misleading in so far as it plays down the interdependence between the state of the market and the state of the firm. Chapter 2 showed that the market position will influence the firm's flow position and hence its stock position. This occurs via sellers' actions as when excess demand at market level induces higher quits from individual firms or causes the quality of recruits to fall if there is a small flow of applicants. It also occurs through the impact of the market on certain adjustment instruments. The relative power of bargainers in central pay negotiations, for example, may be dependent on the state of the market and firms may thus find their pay levels varying even though there is no conscious attempt to use pay to eliminate a shortage.

Some of the actions of the firm which occur because of a shortage have no economic significance for the market. We have observed several instances, for example, of organizations engaging in advertising or the employment of consultants purely for internal political reasons, when some department's primary purpose is to demonstrate to others in the organization that it is acting vigorously, regardless of whether the action is effective in eliminating shortages.

In each of the markets studied there was some evidence of a price adjustment process at work, or at least the use of instruments which are wage-related, though it was clear that this was not always the whole, nor even the major, part of the adjustment story.

In the case of bus drivers a few undertakings had, on occasion, used the pay instrument aggressively and had raised earnings levels very substantially when faced with a shortage. But these were notable because they were exceptional. Typically, undertakings did not rely on increases in relative pay to solve their problems. The evidence discussed in Chapter 3 is not entirely clear-cut but strongly suggests that the only way in which pay was used as an instrument was in preventing deteriorations in the relative earnings position of drivers. Pay was kept in line with that in competing job opportunities (mainly semi-skilled) but no more. Some of the other instruments which are widely used throughout the passenger transport industry are related to pay and could therefore be construed as being part of a price adjustment process. There was widespread use of productivity agreements which raised both pay and productivity, heavy overtime working which raised weekly earnings, and one-man operation which raised drivers' pay.

Other instruments which are sufficiently common to have an impact on the market are reductions in hiring standards, which some may interpret as raising pay per efficiency unit of labour input. It is more interesting, however, to see this as a reduction in the quality of service provided, a point which is discussed below.

Other responses which have been characteristic of the market as a whole are mainly ones which have attempted to increase the supply other than by use of the wage instrument. Employing people previously considered unsuitable, such as women or those without previous driving or conducting experience, and improving the net advantages of the job through the restructuring of hours and reduction of uncongenial shifts, have been prominent features of the market in recent years. The latter has been associated in some undertakings with the employment of part-time staff. Adjustments of a non-price kind have also taken place on the demand side in the form of service cuts. This has occurred formally via cuts in the scheduled stage carriage services and a residual adjustment in the form of unscheduled reductions in service frequency. The consequent fall in reliability has been a major cause of consumer discontent and represents another manifestation of reduction in output quality.

The study of the teachers' market, like that for bus drivers, yielded some evidence of a price adjustment process but again this was not the dominant form of adjustment. Chapter 4 indicated a (rather weak) relationship between the rate of change of relative earnings and the level of excess demand, but much more important have been adjustments designed to affect supply, in particular the increase in the training capacity, redesign of the job (mainly restructuring hours to allow the employment of part-timers), and residual adjustments in the form of increasing 'productivity' through allowing the pupil–teacher ratio to rise above the norm. The latter represents a deterioration in the quality of output and in this respect has much in common with the position in the bus drivers' market where the market pressures were eased by permitting falls in product quality.

The two-tier system of decision-making in education, the DES and LEAs, produces an interesting variation of the monopsony model. Pay is set nationally at a value which produces what central negotiators regard as an equilibrium in the employment of teachers. There are, however, vacancies which decision-makers at a lower level try to eliminate.[18] They do not have power to alter pay and therefore seek to use non-wage adjustments, especially the attempts to recruit re-entrants and the 'temporary' acceptance of poorer-quality education in the form of 'oversize' classes.

Chapter 4 showed that there was continuous pressure in post-war years to improve the quality of education provided. The effect of teacher shortages has been to slow down the rate at which improvements could be made. Thus we do not always observe actual deteriorations in product quality but sometimes, as in the case of the delay in implementing the raising of the school-leaving age or the postponement of curriculum developments, merely a suspension of improvements in quality.

The market for draughtsmen differs from those for teachers and bus drivers in a number of respects. It has been characterized by surpluses as well as shortages, and there has been considerable use of sub-contracting which, though its main effect is to redistribute labour within the draughtsmen's market, tends to increase the pay of the marginal worker and thus increase supply. Direct pay adjustments have been used to a small extent and there has been a certain amount of overtime working which enhances weekly earnings. These price adjustments have, however, been sufficiently small or isolated to represent very little at a market level, and apart from sub-contracting there have been few adjustments which have made a market-wide impact, with the slight exception of changes in selection procedures[19] which may have had some effect in reducing hiring standards and enlarging the total supply in the market.[20] In individual firms particular adjustments such as the introduction of computer-aided design may have been dominant but they do not add up to much at the market level.

---

18. In the monopsony model, employment is set at the level where marginal labour costs are equated with the marginal revenue product. The wage rate will be less than the marginal cost of labour, since the supply curve is rising, but at this wage level demand exceeds supply and LEAs may attempt to eliminate this excess demand.
19. See Chapter 5 for a discussion of the change from 'rank' to 'exploratory' selection.
20. It should be remembered that the boundaries of the market for draughtsmen are much more fluid than those for other markets we have studied, and manipulating job titles and subtle changes in job design and job requirements more readily permit an extension of the market frontier.

Conclusions

This examination of the three markets leads us to question the emphasis of neo-classical economics on the price variable. There is clearly a limit to which generalizations can be made on the basis of studies of just three markets but the occupations we have covered are representative of many others,[21] and certain remarks about labour markets in general can be made with some confidence.

In none of the three markets did pay changes appear, at the market level, to be an exclusive or even dominant adjustment process. This is not simply a question of the constraints being imposed on this instrument but is partly due to the fact that it represents a more expensive strategy. There are in fact several reasons for supposing that wage adjustments are becoming more costly relative to non-wage adjustments.

Firstly, there has been a growing mismatch between the areas covered by labour markets and areas covered by pay adjustments. The effect is to raise the marginal cost of a pay increase which is designed to eliminate the shortage of a particular group of workers. This growing mismatch is due largely to the use of wider pay comparisons[22] and to the growth in the size of firms. Wider pay comparisons make it difficult to increase the pay of a single group without setting off pressure for similar increases from other groups. The growth in the size of firms tends to extend bargaining units over a wider range of labour-market conditions and to create internal labour markets, which increase the range of possible non-wage adjustments by permitting more internal training and mobility.

Secondly, external influence in the form of pressure from government agencies connected with incomes policies or growth promotion (the National Board for Prices and Incomes, the Office of Manpower Economics, the Pay Board, and Economic Development Councils) has been more intense since the mid-1960s. These bodies have laid emphasis on more efficient manpower utilization and argued that pay increases will not reallocate labour where labour shortages are general as they were in the 1960s. More recently, with higher unemployment this argument may be less applicable though the high rate of inflation and the persistence of pockets of labour shortage, especially for skilled trades, have not made pay adjustments any more popular.

21. About a fifth of the labour force is employed in occupations similar to those analysed in this study, including public-sector service workers and technicians and other white-collar pre-production workers.
22. For an account of the use of wage comparisons in wage determination see W. Brown and Sisson (1975).

Thirdly, the growth in public-sector employment has been faster than that in the private sector in the last decade. To the extent that public-sector employers fit the monopsony model, there will be apparent labour shortages but ones which put no pressure on the wage rate.

The suggestion that pay changes are not necessarily the major adjustment process confirms the conclusion of the well-known Organisation for Economic Co-operation and Development study that the allocative role of wages is small.[23] Their approach was to examine the supply side of the market by studying the influence of wages on labour mobility, whereas we have concentrated on the behaviour of employers. Thus prices do not deserve the primacy of place which they are usually accorded in neo-classical economics. We do not regard them as totally irrelevant, for as we showed earlier several of the responses observed are in fact wage-related and so could be loosely classified as price responses. We therefore do not deny that wages are determined by market forces or that wages have some allocative role and that wage signals need to point broadly in the right direction. But generally-applicable models which give them a highly sensitive role as an allocator of resources at the margin are unrealistic. Other adjustment variables are also at work.

Other Forms of Adjustment

The most interesting of these alternative adjustment processes apparent in our studies was quality variation. This is basically the variation in the quality of inputs but in the case of personal service industries it is equivalent to falls in the quality of output.

The reliance on this adjustment has stability implications. The price adjustment process is one where there is a self-correcting equilibrium, but quality adjustments may in some ways be destabilizing. In the teachers' market for example, if a major response (albeit a residual one) is to allow 'oversize' classes, then teachers face a more difficult task. Hard-pressed teachers find their colleagues' absence increasing and requiring them to forgo 'free' periods in order to cover. The childminding element in the job increases and the

---

23. See (1965). This study played down the allocative role of prices in the labour market though Turner (1966) has shown that their findings are still consistent with a threshold theory of wages in which people do respond to wage changes but only when they move outside certain limits. See Hunter and Reid (1967) and Parnes (1970) for reviews of other studies of wages and labour mobility. The weight of evidence seems to support the Organisation for Economic Co-operation and Development view though some studies show that income differences provide an incentive to move, e.g. Creedy (1974).

teaching element decreases, and there is a general decrease in job satisfaction. The image of the job deteriorates in line with reality and there is an adverse effect on supply which thus aggravates the shortage position. Stating the position in these terms is to over-dramatize so far as the teachers' market as a whole is concerned but it is scarcely an exaggeration of the situation in some inner-city schools in certain large conurbations. The same de-stabilizing influence may be at work in similar occupations such as the police and nursing. Where responses to labour shortage take the form of quality deterioration, the job becomes less attractive and this, in the absence of any other adjustments, results in persistent shortage.

The occupations mentioned in this context, teachers, nurses, and police, are those for which it is difficult to reduce labour require-ments. In the case of education, schooling is compulsory and, although private education services (and also private health and substitute police services) do exist, these form a comparatively small part of the market. There has also been a marked deterioration in the quality of bus services as a result of labour shortage, but in this case substitute products which do not draw on the same type of labour are available, and the growth in private passenger transport has been spectacular.

The form of adjustment adopted by individual firms will have an effect on the flows at market level. In the case of draughtsmen, part of the shortage was due to a mismatch between supply and demand. The problem in this case was amenable to solution by more efficient distribution of labour, especially across time and between firms, and the principal avenue for this change was via the sub-contracting which permits structural change in the way the market is organized. Employers of draughtsmen were often more interested in recruiting a larger share of the available numbers rather than recruiting additional trainees. This differs from the teachers' and bus drivers' markets where attempts were made to increase the total supply of labour to the market.[24]

Some of the factors relevant for understanding the choice of adjustment by individual firms, especially organizational factors such as who has control over what instruments and who has responsi-bility for dealing with shortages and how highly their elimination ranks in the corporate goals, are difficult to attach significance to at the aggregate level though they have the effect of giving rise to

---

24. This has different social consequences. The efforts to induce married women to re-enter teaching alters female labour-force participation rates.

diverse adjustments and hence, at the market level, to less prominence for any one form of adjustment.

The variety of adjustments we have described thoughout this study are not inconsistent with traditional economic analysis which does not specify an adjustment mechanism. Our findings do strongly suggest, however, that there has been undue emphasis placed on the price variable in the adjustment process, to the comparative neglect of other variables which are not necessarily part of a stable adjustment process.

4. Implications

Wage Structure

Much of the literature on the determination of wage structure is couched in terms of a conflict between customary and institutional forces on the one hand and market forces on the other.[25] Our stance is to treat employers as cost minimizers who are faced with a variety of constraints which affect the costs of different adjustments. Since both wage and non-wage adjustments can be important devices in the correction of a labour shortage, a wage structure can only be determined uniquely by market forces when the costs of alternative non-wage adjustments are known.

An early example of the relevance of non-wage adjustments to wage structure is shown by Reder (1955). He argues that skill differentials are likely to narrow during booms and widen during recessions, because of the tendency of employers to adjust to shortages of skilled labour by relaxing hiring standards. This approach can be applied to the impact of customary and institutional constraints. Where these constraints on pay as an adjustment instrument exist, non-wage adjustments become more attractive to the employer. Indeed, the greater the variety of non-wage adjustments at his disposal, the less likely is the employer to react to changing market conditions by an adjustment in wages. This is very much in line with the analysis of Doeringer and Piore (1971) who argued that the formation of an internal labour market protects the internal wage structure and the custom and practice rules from the impact of the external labour-market forces. However, we differ from Doeringer and Piore in two respects. First, we have found it necessary to elaborate on their distinction between less highly and more highly constrained instruments. Second, like W. Brown and

25. See for instance Phelps Brown (1962:147–53).

Sisson (1975) who examined the role of wage comparisons in the Coventry engineering industry and in Fleet Street, we consider the most important factor shielding the internal wage structure from the external market forces to be not the internal allocative structure but the bargaining structure.

Bargaining structures can act as a major constraint on the extent to which imbalances of supply and demand are translated into wage changes. Where the area of shortage pressure is narrower than the coverage of the bargaining unit, the cost of a wage adjustment can be considerable. This is often the case where a job evaluation system extends over a range of occupations or where coercive comparisons are used between different jobs. The teachers' market was characterized by a uniform national salary scale. In the busmen's market, drivers and conductors invariably formed a single bargaining unit, whilst national or company agreements extended over a variety of different local labour-market conditions. To a certain extent earnings did adjust to relative shortages in these markets through variations in hours in the case of busmen, and through differential speeds of promotion for teachers. However, in the draughtsmen's market the extention of TASS negotiating rights over a wide range of technical occupations made the adjustment of earnings for a single occupation particularly difficult.

If a wage increase has to be applied uniformly across a diverse bargaining unit, the extent of that increase is left indeterminate by market forces. This may be due to bilateral monopoly, but could also be because there is no single job or grade for which supply and demand must be equated by means of a wage adjustment.

The type of bargaining structure that has been described here is likely to result in rigidity of the internal wage structure. However, where a bargaining structure permits flexibility in wage adjustments between different jobs, our analysis suggests that the skill differential will behave in the way Reder describes. This is not because hiring standards are the most important variable apart from wages, but rather because there appears to be, *ceteris paribus*, a wider range of non-wage adjustments open to the employer with a shortage of skilled labour than there is when he faces a shortage of unskilled labour. However, since shortages of skilled labour arise more readily than shortages of unskilled labour, no clear-cut cyclical pattern of wage differentials can be forecast.

Incomes Policy

One important strand in the incomes-policy debate is the question of whether shortages of labour pose a threat to the maintenance of the policy. The *prima facie* case for supposing that such a threat exists is twofold. First, several of the groups which have been able to secure wage increases in excess of the incomes-policy limit, such as the miners and school teachers in 1974, have done so under conditions of severe labour shortage. Second, we have cited evidence in this study of cases where the Phase Two incomes policy was exceeded through union pressure associated with shortages of labour.

The question arises as to whether an incomes policy should be designed so as to allow shortage to be alleviated where necessary by a pay increase. Under some of the Prices and Incomes Board phases of incomes policy, one of the grounds for exceptional treatment was the need to reallocate manpower. Thus a pay increase above the norm could be granted if it was shown to be 'necessary and effective' for curing the shortage. Here the word 'necessary' creates problems. A strict interpretation of this condition would mean that an exceptional pay increase could only be granted if the shortage could not be alleviated in another way. However, as our study has shown, in the vast majority of cases the firm will have alternative adjustments open to it. If the firm is expected to make non-wage adjustments whatever their cost, these grounds for exceptional treatment will permit scarcely any exceptions at all.

A less rigid interpretation of this condition would allow pay adjustments only if the alternative adjustments were more costly to the employer. But it is only in these situations that the rational cost-minimizing employer would seek to increase pay, and hence, under this interpretation of the exceptions clause, it would serve no useful purpose. However, we have shown that there are ways in which the employer will not adopt the least-cost combination of instruments. The employer is, for instance, subject to various trade union constraints which dissuade him from a number of courses of action. Hence, the role of an incomes policy with an exceptions clause on grounds of shortage is to offset such constraints and force the employer to act as if he were an unconstrained cost minimizer.[26] This can be contrasted with an incomes policy without provision for such

26. It should be noted that an incomes policy with the shortage exceptions clause does more than just facilitate intervention to ensure that the full range of non-wage adjustments are considered. Through the requirement that the increase be effective in alleviating the shortage, the investigator must ensure that the wage increase can be made without consequential increases which would remove the redistributive effects.

exceptional treatment which acts as a constraint on wage increases *per se*.

One of the main problems experienced by both the Prices and Incomes Board and the Pay Board on this issue was that of measuring shortages in a reliable way. This problem is more acute than that created by the misleading use of establishment figures.[27] There are, as we have shown, a variety of circumstances in which the term 'shortage' is applicable. But even in the case of a straight-forward stock shortage there are problems of measurement. The accurate assessment of the extent of a shortage requires the identification of a set of values for working norms. For the policy-maker, the task of identifying these values will involve questions of whether they are 'right', 'efficient', or 'desirable'; the exercise becomes one akin to comprehensive manpower planning which, however desirable, is certainly not incomes policy.

Perhaps the safest rule for the policy-maker is to have no exceptions clause on the grounds of labour shortage or to allow an exception only when the alternatives have serious repercussions for the economy or society. Alternatively, it might be expedient to limit the manpower grounds for exceptional treatment to cases where there is a serious net outflow of labour. This policy has two main advantages. First, it avoids the problem of defining demand since concern is merely with the difference between wastage and recruitment. Second, it allows an outlet for the more acute economic pressures because, though an employer is required to live with an existing shortage, he may be permitted to avert a deterioration in the level of shortage by adjusting wages.

There may, of course, be political reasons for building such exceptions into an incomes policy, which override the arguments that are made here. However, these questions lie outside the scope of this book.

Wage Inflation

Many of the non-wage adjustments which the firm adopts in response to labour shortage will, once they work through to the aggregate level, cause increases in earnings. This is true of sub-contracting, the lowering of hiring standards, and some of the

27. Both the Pay Board and the Prices and Incomes Board made great play of the fact that establishment figures are not the same as labour demand, and they more or less conclude that shortages cannot be adequately measured. Our analysis of the concept of shortage shows that artificial establishment figures are not the real problem since one can easily recalculate them on the basis of working rather than formal norms.

changes that occur in the internal labour market. This makes it difficult to formulate a relationship between the rate of change of aggregate money wages and excess demand on the basis of the evidence presented in this study. What we can do, however, is make some tentative comments on some of the features of the recent literature on wage inflation.

We argue that the firm will respond to both stock and flow shortages. This implies that changes in wages will depend on the level of shortage in both the external and the internal markets. Hence, there is a *prima facie* case for including a measure of the state of the internal market such as labour hoarding, or hours worked,[28] alongside the measure of excess demand in the market. Alternatively, there may be a case for taking vacancies as the sole excess-demand variable on the grounds that it reflects the state of both internal and external markets — the usual reason for not doing so is the inconsistency of this variable over time.

Most wage equations, when translated into our framework, say that permanent adjustments (wage increases) are a function of previous residual adjustments (vacancies) and possibly temporary adjustments. The assumption is one of a constant relationship between these various sorts of adjustment. Our study shows that the degree to which, and the speed with which, shortages and temporary adjustments are translated into wage increases vary over time with a number of factors, in particular the expected duration of the current level of labour demand. Hence there is a case for including in the wage equation some indicator of firms' expectations of future demand. Moreover, we argued in the previous section of this chapter that in recent years wage adjustments have become more costly, relative to non-wage adjustments. If this is the case we are likely to observe a change in the relationship between wage increases and labour-market indicators.

One fairly definite conclusion that can be drawn from our results is that the firm's response to shortage is by no means symmetrical with its response to a surplus of labour. There are a number of reasons for this. First, the range of feasible non-wage adjustments

---

28. In recent years, wage equations have made increasing use of independent variables which measure the state of the internal labour market. See Hart (1973), J. Taylor (1974), and Peel and Briscoe (1974). It is not clear that hours worked is a particularly useful variable in wage equations. On the one hand, increasing hours per employee might be considered as an alternative to increasing pay; but on the other hand, as the demand for labour increases, the temporary adjustment of hours may be followed by a wage increase. These two tendencies will work in the opposite directions and the expected sign of the coefficient is unclear.

differs between shortage and surplus situations. Second, the unions are likely to support non-wage adjustments in times of surplus and wage adjustments in times of shortage. Third, a shortage creates a problem for the firm which requires action, but the problem of a corresponding surplus of labour, particularly if it is only in the external market, is never so acute. Thus a firm which experiences a labour shortage is usually under some pressure to raise its wages, whereas a firm faced with a surplus of labour on the external market may take advantage of the situation to raise its hiring standards but is unlikely to lower its wages. Neither is the firm with too much labour likely to correct the imbalance by a wage adjustment. It is more likely to declare part of its workforce redundant or hoard labour until it is reduced by natural wastage or required again.

Finally, we can draw some tentative inferences about the role of trade unions in the inflationary process. Most writers concerned with the effect of trade unions on inflation, particularly Hines (1964), have dealt with the pushfulness that unions exert on wages. Our study shows that unions act as constraints in the adjustment process, and thus contribute towards wage increases by opposing the use of non-wage adjustments to shortage. Hence, wage increases should be related not so much to the militancy of the unions' demands but rather to the unions' ability to channel shortage into wage increases.

Labour-Market Efficiency

One of the functions of any market is to secure an 'efficient' allocation of the goods exchanged within it. The test of market 'efficiency' is the ability to bring about changes in allocation swiftly so that shortages or surpluses are removed.[29] This definition of 'efficiency' cannot be thought of without some reference to the goals of the individual agents within the labour market. Some of the constraints which prevent swift market clearing and social efficiency may be of considerable value to the labour force or to management. The adherence to uniform salary scales in teaching, for example, which prevents the use of differential pricing to smooth out imbalances of different types of teacher, may be desired on such grounds as equity. It is evident that different forms of adjustment will have different implications for the speed of adjustment and

29. See Hunter and Robertson (1969:200), though this notion of allocative efficiency is debatable. Apart from the fact that second-best conditions prevail, some writers, e.g. Dougherty and Selowski (1972), have argued that allocative efficiency may not contribute much to increased output anyway.

allocation.[30] In this section we consider the question of whether, in the light of our study, labour markets can be considered 'efficient' or not.

The view that free labour markets are reasonably efficient has been advanced in the US by Freeman (1971) on the basis of his study of the market for college-trained graduates. He argued that price variables played a significant role in determining the allocation of workers among jobs. Doeringer and Piore, using a different line of argument, claim that free markets may be capable of making substantial adjustments to changes in demand and supply via well-developed internal labour markets. Our own study has shown that adjustment processes certainly are at work and these are frequently in an equilibrating manner, though we have shown that destabilizing quality adjustments in personal service markets are possible.

To the extent that labour markets do adjust without intervention, they probably do so most speedily where the shortage is unevenly distributed across firms or sub-sectors of the market. If the incidence of shortage between firms is very uneven then it is likely that there will be faster adjustment, taking the market as a whole, and hence a smaller shortage over time. This is because an individual firm's adjustments are likely to be faster the greater the shortage it faces and it may not bother to adjust at all if the shortage is small. There may be some minimum threshold which has to be crossed before a firm will adopt certain major instruments, and a given market shortage is therefore likely to produce a greater response the more uneven the distribution over firms.[31]

The alternative view, that labour markets are generally characterized by inefficiencies and failure to adjust speedily, has

---

30. Flemming (1975) noted, for example, that if the elasticity of output with respect to hours differs from that with respect to workers then the size of the multiplier may be affected depending on whether the adjustment is in the form of men or hours.

31. Structural characteristics may also have an impact on the type of adjustment. The size of firms in the labour market is difficult to comment on in *a priori* terms; smaller firms may be more adaptable but there may be some economies of scale in adjustment (e.g. in hiring, selection, and training) and larger firms will have a bigger base on which to apply actuarial methods, so that hiring can take place for anticipated quits etc. Bigger firms may also have a larger internal labour market on which to draw. Franke and Sobel (1970) found the structure of the product market relevant and argued that shortages were most severe in less competitive product markets and they argued that adjustments work best in a market-clearing sense, where the structure of the product market approaches perfect competition. It is, conversely, often in monopoly situations like much of the public sector where shortages persist.

often been argued. Evidence for this view is said to be the existence of substantial dispersion in pay for similar grades of worker and no clear tendency for this dispersion to narrow over time.[32] This may be partly due to the fact that different plants even within local labour markets respond in different ways to market conditions, for as we have argued there are likely to be different institutional pressures and constraints in different plants. In any event the price dispersion does support the view that the allocative role of prices may be limited.

It would be rash, however, to accept unreservedly the implication that labour markets are inefficient because of the existence of persistent wage dispersion. Such observed dispersion may be quite consistent with an 'efficient' labour market if there is incomplete information and high costs of search on the supply side.

There is also the point that if labour markets are to function at all as an allocative system, there must be a lack of capricious variation, and some regularity over time. In the case of wages, for example, Crossley has argued that, if expectations about relative wages are being cheated through continual variation, then job changes are unlikely to occur (1970:128). Similar arguments apply in the case of other instruments such as hours of work, hiring standards, and the length of training, since continual variations in any of these would have the effect of upsetting the employment relationship, the chief characteristic of which is that it is a continuing one.[33] The typical purchase and sale in the labour market is not a single transaction but is the establishment of a continuing agreement to provide labour for remuneration. This makes swift market-clearing less likely than in product markets.

A certain amount of sluggishness in the market may thus have some functional value, and this makes it difficult to comment on the degree of efficiency in labour markets.[34] But not all failure to eliminate shortage can be regarded as consistent with 'efficiency'. Studies of wage structures have shown for example that wage differentials which may at one time have had some economic rationale sometimes become fossilized by the forces of convention and inertia, thereby imparting a degree of rigidity to the market. This fossilization may also occur with non-wage instruments, and

---

32. See Robinson (1970) and MacKay *et al.* (1971).
33. This is one of the main distinctions between labour markets and product markets. See Rees (1971).
34. There is also the problem that shortages may arise from past misallocations based on insufficient foresight rather than from present or continuing misallocations; see Sattinger (1972).

indicate inefficiencies (in a narrow sense) in the labour market. One other characteristic of many labour markets which we have discussed repeatedly is the influence of institutional and organizational arrangements in matching the coverage of response and pressure. The nearer these two coincide the more 'efficient' markets are likely to be.

Whether intervention would be desirable, in the hope of improving labour-market 'efficiency', depends on which of the alternative views expressed above is the correct one. The implication of the first view is that labour markets are capable of adjusting satisfactorily, without needing what Freeman (1971) calls 'extraordinary non-market policy tools'. And Doeringer and Piore concluded that manpower planning underestimates the degree to which the free market can adjust through the use of internal labour markets. On balance, our study provides little evidence to suppose that manpower planning would make no contribution to improving the 'efficiency' with which labour markets operate.

Intervention by the government or by other outside agencies would however only be justified if their foresight and reaction speeds were superior to those of the direct market participants. This is very likely to be the case since firms seem to do little forecasting.[35] Monitoring the labour market and forecasting could help to fill some of the information gaps, and lessen imbalances which are due to a mismatch of vacancies and unemployed, though not all such mismatch problems could be solved by intervention. In the teachers' market the acute shortages in certain areas are mainly due to the administered rules which prevent price adjustments, and the solution here would be to remove constraints on such adjustments.

---

35. This was found by Doeringer and Piore (1971). It is probably true in this country too. Morley (1976), for example, found that when he was surveying firms in the north-east a third of his sample answered the question 'How far ahead do you plan your manpower policy in an approximate "give-or-take-10%" way?' by saying they did not plan at all or only up to a fortnight.

Appendix A

TABLE A.1
POSSIBLE ADJUSTMENTS TO SHORTAGE[a]

Instruments	Operand	Constraints	Side-Effects	Comment
1. Reduction of desired total hours				
Capital substitution	L^*	Union, technical	On demand for other types of labour, perhaps	
Increased productivity	L^*	Union, technical		May be residual (e.g. teachers)[b]
Sub-contracting	L^*	Union, technical, state of sub-contract markets		May be residual
Output curtailment	L^*	Organizational, government policy, union, technical		
Reduced stocks of finished goods	L^*	Technical	L^* in other periods increases	Residual perhaps. Includes any adjustment where work is done at a different time
Transfer of responsibility to another group	L^*	Union, technical, organizational, government	L^* in other groups increases	Including using trainees and moving location
2. Increase in average hours worked per employee				
Increased overtime working	H	Legal, supply, union	Increases average weekly pay	See 'pay' under type 4 operand below
Increased overtime payments	H	Government policy, union, organizational, employers' association, 'fairness'	Increases average weekly pay (if overtime is worked)	
Improved conditions	H			See also 'conditions' under type 4 operand below. Improved holidays would tend to reduce H

	H		
			directly but this may be offset by lower absenteeism and higher overtime working
Persuasion or compulsion		Union	Reduces attractiveness of the job

3. *Reduction of labour outflows (see also type 4 operands)*

	H		
Improved promotion opportunities	q	Technical	Involves loss internally
Relaxation of dismissals policy	s	Union	Output/quality may fall
Raising retirement age	r	Union	Output/quality may fall
Improved 'job satisfaction'	q	Union	e.g. by 'more appropriate training' or induction courses

4. *Increase in inflows of labour*

	H		
Reduce hiring standards	f_{5-8}	Union	Possibly lowering productivity, increasing q
Increased training capacity	f_{5-8}	Union, time	In order to recruit more untrained people
Increased training length	f_{5-8}	Union, time	In order to reduce the hiring standards of trainees
Relaxation of rules for taking outsiders	f_{2-4} f_{6-8}	Union, organizational	For a detailed discussion of allocative rules see Doeringer and Piore (1971: Chapter 3, and 99–101)
Job redesign	f_{5-8}	Technical, union	In order to reduce hiring standards without side-effects. See Doeringer and Piore (1971: Chapter 6) and Scoville (1972) for a treatment of job design in relation to the labour market

TABLE A.1 (continued)

Instruments	Operand	Constraints	Side-Effects	Comment
Permitted internal transfer	$f_{1,5}$	Organizational	On position elsewhere in the organization	
Breaking or rescinding a non-poaching agreement	$f_{2,6}$	Other firms, employers' association	q increases	
Pay	f_{1-8}, q	Government policy, union, organization, 'fairness', employers' association	Depending on income and substitution effects, hours supplied may increase or decrease	
Conditions	f_{1-8}, q			Greater impact on q than f as employees know more about conditions inside firm
Search activity	f_{1-8}	Image of job[c]		May be used for political reasons where it is not an ideal instrument. This instrument includes the reporting of job vacancies[d]
Selection procedure	f_{1-4}		f_{5-8} fall	More intensive selection shows more people who meet hiring standards[e]
Increasing hours	f_{1-8}, q	Union		As a means to paying more
Providing more convenient hours of employment	f_{1-8}	Technical, union	Impact on other hours adjustments	Particularly to induce people to join the labour force (i.e. on operands f_4 and f_8)
Forced or induced transfer of employees	$f_{1,5}$	Technical, union		

NOTES:

a. The following symbols are used: L^*, the desired labour services; H, the number of hours worked per man; q, the flow of voluntary quits; s, dismissals; r, retirements; f_{1-8}, inflows of labour as shown below.

| | | Source of Potential Inflows | | | |
		Employed by the Organization	Employed Elsewhere	Unemployed	Outside Labour Force
Meeting hiring standards	Yes	f_1	f_2	f_3	f_4
	No	f_5	f_6	f_7	f_8

b. We distinguish between residual and positive adjustments in Chapter 2, Section 3. Briefly, what we mean by 'residual' is the effect of shortage where positive action by the firm does not eliminate it.

c. The level of search activity is normally thought of as being one of the least constrained instruments. However, the *Guardian* (15 June 1973) carried a brief article on the shortage of priests. This led us to suppose that a church, because of the image of the job, would avoid the kinds of advertising that an industrial concern might indulge in. It has since been reported that one church has gone in for intensive display advertising for ministers. Nevertheless, we still feel the image of the job might be a restraining influence. See Vincens and Robinson (1974:111).

d. Doeringer and Piore (1971) list job vacancies as a residual adjustment. They do, however, admit that other residual adjustments will take place as well as job vacancies existing. For this reason we do not list job vacancies as a separate adjustment. It does not affect any of the operands.

e. Without altering hiring standards, the number of people in the potential inflows, f_{1-4}, may be increased by more intensive selection procedure. This adjustment would mean that there were less errors in the selection process. For a more detailed discussion of this instrument see Doeringer and Piore (1971:102–6).

221

Appendix B
Alphabus

This appendix outlines the way in which one undertaking, Alphabus, has adjusted to large and persistent shortages of labour. This case study is presented here to illustrate the complexity of the adjustment process and the unusual nature of this adjustment. Many undertakings have used piecemeal and marginal adjustments, but Alphabus made a sudden massive attempt to eliminate the shortage with little regard for the financial repercussions.

The Undertaking and Its Labour Position

Alphabus is one of the largest of the NBC subsidiaries. It has a fleet size of about sixteen hundred, and in 1973 about eight hundred of these were one-man vehicles. It serves a large area from its thirty depots and faces a variety of operating conditions ranging from quiet rural routes to congested conurbations. It also faces a variety of labour-market pressures throughout its territory. Alphabus has experienced the familiar pattern of a fall in passengers and mileage. Between 1970 and 1973, scheduled mileage fell by 12.6 per cent, though there have since been signs of an upturn in the number of passengers. Although some private hire, contract, and excursion and tour work is undertaken, stage carriage work accounts for about 90 per cent of the total driver hours.

A serious shortage was experienced in most post-war years, and by the end of the 1960s the gap between actual employment and establishment figures was about 20 per cent for drivers and over 20 per cent for conductors.[1] Various attempts were made to

1. These figures are for the company as a whole and conceal large differences between garages. In March 1970, for example, when shortages were running at very high levels they ranged from 3 per cent to 34 per cent in areas of widely differing local labour-market pressures. In general, those garages in heavy industrial areas were much worse-placed than smaller rural ones.

eliminate the shortages of platform staff during the 1960s though none had much success and the shortage persisted. Despite considerable advertising in the local press and on television and extensive bussing between depots with differing levels of shortage,[2] much mileage was lost because of staff shortage. The introduction of OMO had been started, and by November 1969, 25 per cent of the total hours paid were for OMO.

These and other efforts made little impact on the size of the shortage, and in 1970 a productivity agreement was signed which was designed to make major changes in working practices and earnings levels in a bid to eliminate the persistent shortage. It was based on the 'Guidelines for Local Productivity Agreements' set out by the NCOI in March 1969 but went far beyond them. It represented a marked change in the company's strategy for dealing with shortage by attempting radical changes in the use of some adjustment instruments and by introducing a number of new instruments.

The 1970 Productivity Agreement and Its Effects

The essence of the agreement was that increased rates of pay, which also consolidated many of the special rates,[3] were paid in return for agreement to the extension of OMO and changed working practices.[4] All Saturdays and Sundays became rest days with part-timers being used to cover much of the weekend work. This is obviously a gross simplification of what was a long and detailed agreement but it highlights some of the central provisions which are of interest for our present purposes. The agreement was signed at depot level and there were some minor variations between each depot, especially in the timing of subsequent supplementary agreements on further extension of OMO.

It is clear that the provisions of the agreement formed a package of instruments which was designed to deal with the shortage in several

2. This proved to be very costly since travelling time was paid.
3. Among the special rates and payments to be consolidated were Saturday and Sunday rates, spreadover penalties, early and late duty payments, public holiday rates, OMO acceptance bonus, urban bonus, stage carriage refreshment allowance, and additional annual holiday cash payment above the basic wage.
4. These included the elimination of restraints on the number of spreadover duties, acceptance of spreadovers up to ten hours, elimination of restraints on the maximum number of trips on any service, replacement of signing-on and signing-off time by a payment of five minutes at the start and end of each day's duty, no additional payment for washing, fuelling, and parking of buses, no unreasonable restrictions on the compilation of duty schedules, and no restrictions on working at other garages.

different ways. These various instruments are intricately linked, as indicated in the chapter. Many aspects of the agreement were conventional enough, but the *size* of the pay increase given represented a departure from the usual reliance on marginal changes. The major innovation was the use of Monday–Friday working with the use of part-timers to fill in on Saturdays and Sundays.

The effects of the agreement were dramatic. The level of earnings jumped by about 20 per cent overnight. Drivers' average gross weekly earnings rose from about £27 per week to about £33 per week. (It took almost another two years before a similar advance, in absolute money terms, was achieved.) Although earnings rose very rapidly during 1973, there was nothing comparable to the single increase in 1970.

The effect on employment was also sudden. About 250 extra drivers were recruited within 3 months following the productivity agreement. Over the subsequent 2 years, from mid-1970 to mid-1972, the total number of drivers employed fell and then levelled off at a little under 2,500. This fall, however, was in line with the fall in the establishment figure. Indeed the elimination of shortages was as much due to the fall in establishment, brought about through reduced scheduled mileage and improved scheduling, as it was to increased recruitment. An important element in the reduction of the establishment was the growth in the use of part-timers. Many of these were men already working for Alphabus as office staff or garage mechanics. At the time of our fieldwork about 200 part-timers were employed at weekends.[5]

The progressive introduction of OMO lessened staff requirements considerably, as the following figures show. In the three years following the agreement there was a drop of 27 per cent in scheduled

Percentage change in basic scheduled hours, May 1970–May 1973

OMO Drivers	Two-man Drivers	Total Drivers	Con-ductors	Total Platform Staff
+39.19	−49.70	−13.90	−49.61	−27.28

5. A considerable amount of weekend work is covered by rest-day working. Indeed, the average hours worked in 1973 were 54 per week. This is about as much as is consistent with the drivers' hours regulations. Hours had started to fall, as a result of these regulations, well before the 1970 productivity agreement. During the 1960s it was alleged that they averaged well over 60 hours per week.

hours. The OMO operation was regarded by management as a success, and plans for further extension were in hand. The principal factors working in its favour were the slow rate of introduction at each garage,[6] the low passenger boarding rate,[7] and the flexibility in the use of OMO buses and staff.

So far as the effect on the level of shortages is concerned, Table B.1 shows the result, comparing the situation in March 1970 (just before the agreement) with that three years later.

TABLE B.1
SHORTAGE AND THE PRODUCTIVITY AGREEMENT

	Drivers		Conductors	
	Establishment	Shortage (−) or Surplus (+) as Percentage of Establishment	Establishment	Shortage (−) or Surplus (+) as Percentage of Establishment
March 1970	3,268	−19.98	2,012	−21.52
May 1973	2,382	+ 1.68	836	+ 0.48

The distribution of shortages throughout the week was also affected by the productivity agreement. The introduction of a Monday–Friday week removed the shortage problem on these days since all rest days were at weekends. The whole of the shortage problem was shifted on to Saturdays and Sundays and this was dealt with in a number of ways. The employment of part-timers at weekends was one element in the strategy. On the demand side there was no differential pricing to discourage weekend passengers but it was clear that services, especially on Sundays, were greatly reduced. In January 1973, for example, the scheduled mileage on Saturdays was 93 per cent of the Monday–Friday average, and that on Sundays only 37 per cent. There is also a higher proportion of OMO at weekends, particularly on Sunday.

It appears, therefore, that the productivity agreement was highly successful in eliminating the persistent shortages of platform staff. But the costs were also great. There was a serious deterioration in the

6. This is partly governed by vehicle availability.
7. On many of the routes operated by the company, the passenger boarding rate per mile averaged 3 or 4 compared with about 8 in large towns and 11 in conurbations.

financial position after the agreement, and a critical cash-flow position seems to have developed. Four garages were sold, and the staff redeployed, and there was a marked cutback and centralization of the training facilities.

It is sometimes argued that the costs of adjustment rise at an increasing rate with the size of the adjustment made, in which case it would be cheaper to make a number of small adjustments rather than a single large one. During the 1960s, Alphabus made a number of small adjustments but they had little effect on the size of the stock shortage. When the major adjustment was made via the productivity agreement a full adjustment was achieved almost at once. This suggests there may in fact be some kind of cost threshold operating in the adjustment process, below which adjustment costs achieve very little, and above which substantial results are achieved.

The main constraints which have been operating on Alphabus's ability to adjust are the quasi-legal restrictions on formal output change, the budget,[8] and the union. The 1970 agreement was a complex instrument but there can be no doubt that one of its major purposes was the buying out of union restrictions. One other constraint is the existence of company-wide rates of pay despite local variations in labour-market pressures, and this means that if earnings are to match those prevailing locally then there must be substantial variations in hours.

Hours of Work

In 1973 virtually no garage in Alphabus had a shortage. But the average earnings necessary to preserve stock and flow balance at each garage depend on differing local labour-market conditions. Since there is a uniform company wage rate,[9] the earnings differences are produced by variations in hours worked. Figure B.1 shows that there is in fact a considerable range of earnings. The higher earnings are generally secured by working longer hours as indicated by the positive association between the two. Lack of data on local labour-market conditions, in areas corresponding to the recruitment areas of individual garages, prevents a precise test of the relationship between local earnings and local labour-market

8. In view of the already mentioned critical financial position which developed, it seems as if the actual financial obligations incurred were scarcely compatible with the cost constraint.
9. This needs qualifying slightly since different garages may be at different stages of the productivity agreement and the bonuses earned may differ, but the statement is broadly true.

conditions, but visual inspection of Figure B.1 shows, crudely, that garages in the tighter labour-market areas of the *A* and *B* divisions tended to have higher levels of earnings and hours than those of the less tight *C* and *D* divisions.

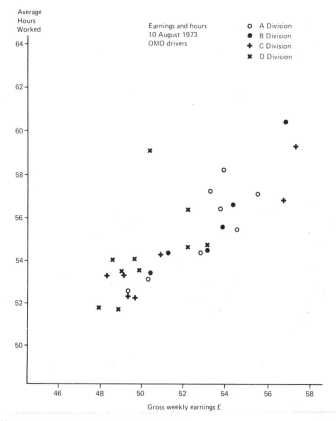

FIGURE B.1. EARNINGS AND HOURS IN ALPHABUS

This suggests, as argued in Chapter 3, Section 4, that hours are used as a means of increasing pay. But it was also argued that there are other determinants of hours, in particular supply-side factors and demand-side factors related to cost-minimizing combinations of hours and men. These considerations modify the precision of the relationship between earnings and local labour-market conditions. For example, some of the smaller garages may in fact operate with a slight surplus, in the sense of having a queue of applicants. Where this is the case, then hours worked are almost certainly greater than what are necessary to match local earnings levels.

Appendix C
The Market Position of Draughtsmen

In this appendix we examine the movements in the market for draughtsmen at the level of the occupation. It is apparent from published unemployment and vacancy data that draughtsmen suffered a sharp deterioration in their market position in the early 1970s. The reasons for this are considered in the light of the findings of the main chapter.

Unemployment and Vacancies

To assess the state of an occupational market over time, it is useful to examine movements in the unemployment/vacancy ratio (R). This measure has the benefit of demonstrating changes in the demand for labour without the necessity of estimating the employment level from scanty data.

Figure C.1 shows that for male draughtsmen the ratio has been very low compared with the ratio for all occupied males, indicating their relatively favourable position throughout most of the period, when vacancies for draughtsmen far outnumbered the unemployed. The ratios tend to rise in recessions because of the fall in vacancies and rise in unemployment. The 1962–3 recession seems to have been particularly severe for draughtsmen, as does the period since 1970. The relative position of draughtsmen can be judged by comparing the ratios for draughtsmen and for all males. Figure C.2 shows the behaviour of the ratio R_D/R_A where the subscripts D and A refer to draughtsmen and all males respectively. If the labour-market positions of draughtsmen and all males varied in exactly the same way we should expect similar proportionate changes in R_D and R_A and hence a stable R_D/R_A ratio. If, however, draughtsmen are a quasi-fixed factor of production, not subject to cyclical layoffs, we

229

FIGURE C.1. UNEMPLOYMENT/VACANCY RATIOS FOR
DRAUGHTSMEN AND ALL MALES

should expect to observe smaller variations in R_D than in R_A.[1]
The ratio R_D/R_A would fall in a recession and rise in periods of high
employment. Figure C.2 shows that R_D/R_A neither is stable nor
varies inversely with the unemployment level. Contrary to
expectation, it seems to rise in recessions (though it did not alter
during the structural shift of 1966).[2] This means that, although
draughtsmen appear to have enjoyed a relatively favourable position
(low R_D), their relative position deteriorates markedly during
recessions.

Here we hope to throw some light on the impact of the 1970
recession on the draughtsmen's market. To do this it is necessary to
examine the overall figures in greater detail, comparing the draughtsmen's position with that of the industries in which they are
employed, and assessing whether any other occupations have had

1. See Oi (1962) for a discussion of labour as a quasi-fixed factor. Strictly speaking
   we are interested in employment ratios, but such data are only annual and subject
   to the problems described in Section 1 of Chapter 5.
2. Referred to by Bowers *et al.* (1972), Gujarti (1972), and J. Taylor (1972).

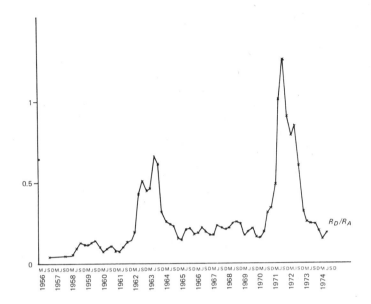

FIGURE C.2. UNEMPLOYMENT/VACANCY RATIO FOR
DRAUGHTSMEN RELATIVE TO ALL MALES

similar experiences.[3] What is required is a measure of the change in
the state of the market which can be compared with changes in other
markets. To continue using the unemployment/vacancy ratio is
dangerous,[4] and the shifts in the relationship between unemployment and vacancies warn us against adopting either of these as sole
measures.

To avoid this problem we can measure the absolute level of disequilibrium by the difference between vacancies (V) and
unemployment (U). But, to make this comparable across markets,
how are we to standardize it? The obvious denominator is

3. Toolmakers are compared with draughtsmen partly because they are the only
   occupation in which there was a greater percentage decline in the unemploy-
   ment/vacancy ratio, but also because many of our informants said that the
   deterioration in the draughtsmen's position was part of a trend which affected all
   pre-production workers.
4. If a change in demand is spread evenly in its impact between vacancies and
   unemployment this will give a greater change in the unemployment/vacancy ratio
   than if the distribution was uneven. (This is simply an application of the theorem
   that a square has a greater area than any other rectangle with the same perimeter.)

employment (E) or the size of the labour force (unemployment and employment). In this case the measure becomes the difference between the vacancy rate and the unemployment rate.

However, the measure $(V - U)/(E + U)$ is unsatisfactory on two counts. While it may be acceptable to assume a constant notification ratio for vacancies over time, to assume the same across markets is dangerous. Second, we are interested in the change in demand rather than in excess demand. Though the supply of men as a whole may be reasonably constant, the supply of draughtsmen and toolmakers will vary with the state of those markets. Both these factors are reflected by differences in the equilibrium level of unemployment (U^*) in a market.[5] The higher the statement ratio of vacancies, the higher the equilibrium level of unemployment will be. This will be lower, the greater the ability to escape from the market. We shall therefore measure changes in the demand for labour by $(V - U)/U^*$.

June 1966 is taken as a convenient base date. It is a minimum for unemployment and just before the shifts in the economy which have been attributed to the National Insurance Act, the Redundancy Payments Act, the July measures, and the wage freeze.[6]

The effect of industrial composition was assessed by calculating an average of the changes in industrial labour-market demand, weighted according to the distribution of draughtsmen. This is presented in Table C.1 together with the changes in demand for draughtsmen, toolmakers, all males, and engineering trades.

The table shows that draughtsmen suffered a greater decline than males as a whole and that only some of this difference is accounted for by their industrial deployment. Until September 1971 the change in the extent of disequilibrium was virtually the same for draughtsmen and toolmakers. This suggests that the question to be answered is why pre-production workers have fared worse than the average in the early 1970s.

---

5. The equilibrium level of unemployment is given by the equality of U and V. It is estimated from equations of the form,

$$\log U = \alpha - \beta \log V \text{ which implies } \log U^* = \alpha/(1 + \beta).$$

The equilibrium unemployment rates for these groups were:

All males	0.94%
Draughtsmen	0.57%
Toolmakers	0.18%

α and β were derived from a regression with DE quarterly data from 1961 III to 1966 II.

6. See Gujarti (1972) and J. Taylor (1972).

TABLE C.1

CHANGES IN $(V - U)/U^*$

	June 1966 to June 1971	June 1966 to September 1971	June 1966 to December 1971
All males	−3.15	−3.57	−4.16
Weighted average	−3.98	−4.39	−5.00
Draughtsmen	−4.95	−5.63	−5.56
Toolmakers	−5.04	−5.69	−6.81
Engineering Trades	−3.85	−4.33	−5.21

It is interesting to explore the change in demand over a longer period of time. The engineering trades group has been included in order to demonstrate that it can proxy a weighted industrial average. To compare the fortunes of draughtsmen relative to the industry where they predominate, we have the change in demand for draughtsmen and for engineering trades given in Figure C.3.

It is apparent from Figure C.3 that there was a greater decline in the industrial market in the early years of the post-1966 recession than in the draughtsmen's market. This is as one might expect, on the assumption that draughtsmen are a quasi-fixed factor of production and hence not subject to cyclical layoffs in the same way as manual workers. However, beginning in June 1970 there was a sharp decline in the draughtsmen's market which was faster than the decline in the industrial market. This caused a relative deterioration in the draughtsmen's position.

The Effect of Redundancy on the Market

One of the things that was stressed in our discussion of redundancies was the need to distinguish between 'economic' and 'liquidity' surpluses. This distinction has relevance not only for the alternatives to redundancy but also to the relative impact redundancy has on different sections of the labour force. If the surplus results from a fall in product demand, the direct occupations will be less secure than the indirect. Where the redundancy is a cost-cutting exercise, the designing and draughting staff, together with a range of other indirect employees, are hit more heavily than direct workers.[7]

---

7. In either case the designers are more secure than draughtsmen because the former are required to do work which is aimed at securing new contracts.

$$\frac{(U-V)_t-(U-V)_0}{U^*}$$

draughtsmen

engineering

FIGURE C.3. CHANGES IN THE DEMAND FOR DRAUGHTSMEN AND ENGINEERING TRADES WORKERS SINCE JUNE 1966

However, the likelihood of an 'economic' rather than a 'liquidity' surplus arising depends on the technology and market structure of the industry. Firms engaged in unit or small-batch production are rarely in a position to increase short-run profits by reducing their indirect labour costs, and hence 'liquidity' surpluses are unlikely to appear. Large-batch and mass-production industries, on the other hand, are quite likely to exhibit 'liquidity' surpluses of indirect workers leading to a greater reduction in indirect labour than in direct labour.

To assess whether the 1970–71 fall in demand for draughtsmen exhibited these features, we compare in Table C.2 the changes in

TABLE C.2
PERCENTAGE INCREASES IN EMPLOYMENT BETWEEN
MAY 1970 AND MAY 1971

Production Category	Industry	MLH	Percentage Increase in Employment between May 1970 and May 1971	
			Draughtsmen	All Males
Unit and small-batch	Shipbuilding	370.1	0.0	−0.6
	Aircraft	383	−0.4	−4.5
Tailoring	Machine tools	332	−15.7	−10.5
	Mechanical handling	337	−8.6	−0.5
	Other machinery	339	−8.3	−4.3
	Industrial plant	341	−12.5	−2.0
	Electrical machinery	361	−12.5	−7.6
Large-batch and mass	Motor vehicles	381	−4.6	+1.0

SOURCE: DE, 'L' survey.

employment of draughtsmen with changes in a total male employment between May 1970 and May 1971.[8] Industries are classified as unit and small-batch, tailoring, and large-batch and mass production.[9]

Thus, in those industries where the employer decides the level of research and development expenditure (i.e. tailoring and large-batch), the employment of draughtsmen declined more than total male employment. The demand for draughtsmen in aircraft and shipbuilding which is directly related to product demand does not appear to have fallen by as much as total labour demand.[10] Hence it is apparent that the fall in relative demand for draughtsmen was due largely to those firms which cut their overheads in response to the squeeze on profits.

8. During this period the 'substitution' of other technicians for draughtsmen referred to in Chapter 5, Section 1, was relatively small for the industries concerned, with the exception of electrical engineering.

9. The industries covered by Table C.2 were those with over 3,000 draughtsmen in the engineering sector by Minimum List Heading. Those industries which were not easily classifiable were the two residuals, 349 Other mechanical engineering, and 369 Other electrical goods, and 364 Radio and other electronic apparatus, which covers electronic systems for aircraft (small-batch), computers (tailoring), and domestic radio and television (mass).

10. Section 4 of Chapter 5 does, however, indicate that aircraft firms reduced their use of sub-contract draughtsmen during this period.

Possible Explanations

There is an intuitive appeal in explaining the relatively heavy unemployment amongst draughtsmen in recent years by reference to the concurrent rapid inflation. Firms faced with a slump in demand and rising labour costs will experience a fall in profits. Because of the organizational pressure to produce an annual profit, a natural response will be to cut back on development expenditure whose yield is realized only in the medium or long term.

However, attempts to derive a relationship between the demand for draughtsmen and the rate of wage inflation proved unsuccessful. Inflation may have had an impact on draughtsmen's demand after some threshold, but this reduces the theory's status to being merely *ad hoc*. Such a theory would have no superiority over others whose explanation lay in some feature peculiar to the early 1970s.

Most of the alternative explanations of the relative decline in demand for draughtsmen rely on the argument that draughtsmen have, or at least had, a relatively high degree of fixity and were therefore hoarded to a greater extent than the labour force as a whole during 'normal' slumps. In 1970–71, either demand was such that a high degree of fixity no longer ensured hoarding or there was change in the degree of fixity.

If the degree of fixity has remained constant, draughtsmen may have been dishoarded because of the longevity of the slump in demand. Hoarding, it is assumed, takes place because it is cheaper for a firm to pay variable labour costs over a short period than to lay off workers to save on these variable costs but then have to pay fixed costs both to reduce its labour force (redundancy pay) and to increase it again later (hiring and training costs). This being the case, hoarding will take place so long as firms expect demand to rise again in the not too distant future. A prolonged slump may depress expectations, with dis-hoarding as the result. The problem with this argument is that it is couched in terms of labour whose demand is derived from the demand for the product, and thus neglects the nature of the demand for draughtsmen described in this study.

While maintaining the assumption of a constant degree of fixity, but incorporating a more realistic demand theory, one might stress the depth of the slump rather than its longevity. The argument is similar to that which assumes development expenditure is reduced in the face of liquidity problems, but does not employ inflation as an explanatory variable. Firms' overheads, which include development expenditure, have to be financed out of the excess of sales over direct costs. If product demand falls, the firm is assumed to reduce its direct labour force, but in doing so its overheads are spread over a smaller output. In normal circumstances a firm might be prepared to allow its ratio of indirect to direct costs to rise, but if it becomes apparent that the fall in demand exceeds a certain level, overheads may have to be cut to restore the normal ratio. Furthermore, when in such circumstances overheads are cut, the firm may regard a drawing office as being *less* essential than other indirect areas and hence the impact may fall *more* heavily upon draughtsmen.

Alternatively, it might be argued that the degree of fixity itself changed. This could happen as a direct result of unemployment and thereby aggravate the problem. When unemployment in a certain sector rises, labour is more abundant, causing a reduction in firms' hiring and training costs and hence a fall in the degree of fixity. This, of course, will operate for any labour with a fairly high fixity and relies on an initial rise in unemployment. What may be more important in the case of draughtsmen is the effect of the growth in the number of contract drawing offices. They tend to pay higher wages and do less training than manufacturing companies, which makes their labour less of a fixed factor. Therefore little hoarding will take place in the sub-contract sector. Indeed, hoarding may be difficult or impossible in contract drawing offices simply because such companies do not have the resources to employ labour when there is no demand for its services. Thus the heavy unemployment amongst draughtsmen may have been due to redundancies in the sub-contract sector. It has been estimated that between 1969 and 1973 the numbers employed by contract drawing offices fell by half.[11] Hence, with the growth of sub-contracting the link between the demand for draughtsmen and the demand for their services became closer.

None of these explanations offers a general model of the demand for draughtsmen, but merely *post hoc* explanations of why the relatively secure position of draughtsmen changed. Moreover, not all of them explain the suddenness with which the demand for draughtsmen fell.

The argument that the reduction in the degree of fixity caused a relative decline in the demand for draughtsmen does not account for the sharpness of the rise in unemployment, and there seems no reason why firms should all respond together to the exceptional depth or longevity of the slump. The one common factor which might have influenced so many employers who independently determined their demand for draughtsmen was the onset of the wage explosion.

11. This estimate was made by the chairman of the FEDC. A survey carried out by the Federation in 1969 put the number of draughtsmen in the industry at 25,000 and his own impressions put the number at the end of 1972 at 12,500. This is not to say that the decline in numbers was spread evenly over this period.

Bibliography

Those works used purely as sources of statistical data are only cited at the point in the text where they are used, and are not included in the Bibliography.

Abraham, C., and A. Thomas, 1973. *Micro-Economics: Optimal Decision-Making by Private Firms and Public Authorities.* Dordrecht, Holland: D. Reidel.

Ahamad, B., and M. Blaug (eds.), 1973. *The Practice of Manpower Forecasting: a Collection of Case Studies.* Amsterdam: Elsevier.

Armitage, P., 1970. 'So when do we get the teachers?' *Higher Education Review*, II, no. 3, 41–7.

——, C. Smith, and P. Alper, 1969. *Decision Models for Educational Planning.* L.S.E. Studies on Education. London: Allen Lane, The Penguin Press.

Arrow, K. J., 1974. 'Limited Knowledge and Economic Analysis'. *American Economic Review*, LXIV, 1–10.

——, and W. M. Capron, 1959. 'Dynamic Shortages and Price Rises: the Engineer-Scientist Case'. *Quarterly Journal of Economics*, LXXIII, no. 2, 292–308.

Association of Education Committees, 1966. *Employment of Ancillary Helpers.* London: AEC.

Bain, G. S., 1970. *The Growth of White-Collar Unionism.* Oxford: Clarendon Press.

Balfour, C., 1972. *Incomes Policy and the Public Sector.* London: Routledge and Kegan Paul.

Bell, R. M., 1972. *Changing Technology and Manpower Requirements in the Engineering Industry.* Engineering Industry Training Board, Research Report no. 3. Brighton: Sussex University Press.

238

Bibby, J., 1970. 'A Model to Control for the Biasing Effects of Differential Wastage'. *British Journal of Industrial Relations*, VIII, 418–20.

Blank, D. M., and G. J. Stigler, 1957. *The Demand and Supply of Scientific Personnel*. New York: National Bureau of Economic Research.

Bowers, J. K., P. C. Cheshire, A. E. Webb, and R. Weeden, 1972. 'Some Aspects of Unemployment and the Labour Market, 1966–71'. *National Institute Economic Review*, no. 62, 75–88.

Braybrooke, D., and C. E. Lindblom, 1963. *A Strategy for Decision*. New York: Free Press of Glencoe.

Brechling, F. P. R., 1965. 'The Relationship between Output and Employment in British Manufacturing Industries'. *Review of Economic Studies*, XXXII, 187–216.

Bronfenbrenner, M., 1956. 'Potential Monopsony in Labor Markets'. *Industrial and Labor Relations Review*, XIX, 577–88.

Brooks, D., 1975. *Race and Labour in London Transport*. London: Oxford University Press.

Brown, R. M., and C. A. Nash, 1972. 'Cost Saving from OMO'. *Journal of Transport Economics and Policy*, VI, 281–4.

Brown, W., 1972. 'The Overtime Habit'. *New Society*, XX, 355–6.

——, 1973. *Piecework Bargaining*. Warwick Studies in Industrial Relations. London: Heinemann.

——, and K. Sisson, 1975. 'The Use of Comparison in Workplace Wage Determination'. *British Journal of Industrial Relations*, XIII, 23–53.

Bunting, R. L., 1962. *Employer Concentration and Labor Markets*. Chapel Hill: University of North Carolina Press.

Cain, G. G., W. L. Hansen, and B. A. Weisbrod, 1967. 'Occupational Classification: an economic approach'. *Monthly Labor Review*, LXL, no. 2, 48–52.

Cairnes, J. E., 1874. *Some Leading Principles of Political Economy Newly Expounded*. London: Macmillan.

Caplow, T. C., 1954. *The Sociology of Work*. New York: McGraw-Hill.

Chapman, C., 1965. 'Should Teachers Have Help?' *New Society*, V, no.137, 5–6.

Chiplin, B., and P. Sloane, 1974. 'Sexual Discrimination in the Labour Market'. *British Journal of Industrial Relations*, XII, 371–402.

Clegg, H. A., 1970. *The System of Industrial Relations in Great Britain*. Oxford: Basil Blackwell.

Cooley, M. J. E., 1972. *Computer Aided Design — its Nature and*

Implications. Richmond, Surrey: Amalgamated Union of Engineering Workers (Technical and Supervisory Section).

Corry, B. A., 1973. 'Some Aspects of University Teachers' Labour Market in the U.K.: Discussion'. *Essays in Modern Economics.* Proceedings of the conference of the Association of University Teachers of Economics, 1972. Eds. M. Parkin and A. R. Nobay. London: Longman, 212–14.

Creedy, J., 1974. 'Inter-Regional Mobility: A Cross-section Analysis'. *Scottish Journal of Political Economy*, XXI, 41–53.

Crossley, J. R., 1970. 'Theory and Methods of National Manpower Policy'. *Scottish Journal of Political Economy*, XVII, 127–46.

——, 1973. 'A Mixed Strategy for Labour Economists'. *Scottish Journal of Political Economy*, XX, 211–38.

Crowther Report, 1959. *15 to 18.* Central Advisory Council for Education (England). London: HMSO.

Cumming, C. E., 1971. *Studies in Educational Costs.* London: Chatto and Windus.

Cyert, R. M., and C. L. Hedrick, 1972. 'Theory of the Firm: Past, Present and Future: An Interpretation'. *Journal of Economic Literature*, X, 398–412.

Cyert, R. M., and J. T. March, 1963. *A Behavioural Theory of the Firm.* Englewood Cliffs, New Jersey: Prentice-Hall.

Davidson, P., 1974. 'Disequilibrium Market Adjustment: Marshall Revisited'. *Economic Inquiry*, XII, 146–58.

Deakin, B. M., and T. Seward, 1969. *Productivity in Transport.* University of Cambridge, Department of Applied Economics, Occasional Papers, 17. London: Cambridge University Press.

Deaton, D. R., 1975. 'The use of OMO as an Adjustment to a Labour Shortage: A Study of London Transport's Bus Drivers'. Coventry: University of Warwick, Industrial Relations Research Unit. (typescript.)

——, 1976. 'The Racial Mix of London Transport Recruits'. *New Community*, V, 316–19.

Department of Education and Science. 1970. *Output Budgeting for the DES.* Education Planning Paper No. 1. London: HMSO.

——, 1972. *Education: A Framework for Expansion.* Cmnd 5174. London: HMSO.

Department of Employment, 1972. *Classification of Occupations and Directory of Occupational Titles.* London: HMSO.

Devine, E. J., 1971. *Analysis of Manpower Shortages in Local Government.* New York: Praeger.

Doeringer, P. B., and M. J. Piore, 1971. *Internal Labor Markets and Manpower Analysis.* Lexington, Massachusetts: D. C. Heath.

Dougherty, C., and M. Selowski, 1972. 'Measuring the Effects of the

Misallocation of Labor'. Economic Development Report no. 210. Cambridge, Massachusetts: Harvard University, Center for International Affairs. (mimeograph.)

Dror, J. Y., 1968. *Public Policy Making Re-Examined.* New York: Chandler.

Duggan, E. P., and W. A. C. Stewart, 1970. *The Choice of Work Area of Teachers.* Keele: Sociological Review.

Dunlop, J. T., 1966. 'Job Vacancy Measures and Economic Analysis'. *The Measurement and Interpretation of Job Vacancies.* A conference report of the National Bureau of Economic Research. New York: Columbia University Press.

Eastwood, J., 1970. 'Labour Studies Research Project on Computer-Aided Design'. Oxford: Ruskin College. (typescript.)

Economist Intelligence Unit, 1970. *Remuneration of Young Teachers and the Effect on Recruitment and Wastage from the Profession.* London: Association of Teachers in Colleges and Departments of Education.

Ehrenberg, R. J., 1972. *The Demand For State and Local Government Employees.* Lexington, Massachusetts: D. C. Heath.

Engineering Industry Training Board, 1970. *The Technician in Engineering.* Research Report no. 1. Watford: EITB.

Fair, R. C., 1969. *The Short Run Demand for Workers and Hours.* Amsterdam: North-Holland.

Fidler, P. E., 1974. 'Passenger Loading Delays of OMO'. Discussion Paper 47. Bristol: University of Bristol, Department of Economics. (mimeograph.)

Fisher, M. R., 1971. *The Economic Analysis of Labour.* London: Weidenfeld and Nicolson.

Fishwick, F., 1970. 'OMO in Municipal Transport'. *Institute of Transport Journal*, XXXIII, 413–25.

Flanders, A., 1967. *Collective Bargaining: A Prescription for Change.* London: Faber and Faber.

Flemming, J. S., 1975. 'Wage Rigidity and Employment Adjustment: Alternative Micro-Foundations'. *Contemporary Issues in Economics.* Proceedings of the conference of the Association of University Teachers of Economics, 1973. Eds. M. Parkin and A. R. Nobay. Manchester: Manchester University Press, 80–87.

Folk, H., 1970. *The Shortage of Scientists and Engineers.* Lexington, Massachusetts: D. C. Heath.

Forrester, J. W., 1961. *Industrial Dynamics.* Cambridge, Massachusetts: MIT Press.

Fox, A., 1966. *Industrial Sociology and Industrial Relations.* Royal

Commission on Trade Unions and Employer's Associations, Research Paper 3. London: HMSO.

——, 1973. 'Industrial Relations: a Social Critique of Pluralist Ideology'. *Man and Organisation.* Ed. J. Child. London: George Allen and Unwin, 185–233.

Franke, W., and I. Sobel, 1970. *The Shortage of Skilled and Technical Workers.* Lexington, Massachusetts: D. C. Heath.

Freeman, R. B., 1971. *The Market for College Trained Manpower: A Study in the Economics of Career Choice.* Cambridge, Massachusetts: Harvard University Press.

——, 1972. *Labor Economics.* Englewood Cliffs, New Jersey: Prentice-Hall.

Goodman, J. F. B., 1970. 'The Definition and Analysis of Local Labour Markets: Some Empirical Problems'. *British Journal of Industrial Relations,* VIII, 179–96.

Gowler, D., and K. Legge, 1970. 'The Wage Payment System: A Primary Infrastructure'. *Local Labour Markets and Wage Structures.* Ed. D. Robinson. London: Gower Press, 168–214.

Gowler, D., and K. Legge, 1973. 'Perceptions, the "Principle of Cumulation," and the Supply of Labour'. *The Sociology of the Workplace.* Ed. M. Warner. London: George Allen and Unwin, 116–48.

Gujarti, D., 1972. 'The Behaviour of Unemployment and Unfilled Vacancies'. *Economic Journal,* LXXXII, 195–204.

Hamermesh, D. S., 1972. 'On Adjustment in Factor Markets'. Discussion Paper 39. Wivenhoe Park: University of Essex, Department of Economics. (mimeograph.)

Hart, R., 1973. 'The Role of Overtime Working in the Recent Wage Inflation Process'. *Bulletin of Economic Research,* XXV, 73–95.

Hines, A. G., 1964. 'Trade Unions and Wage Inflation in the United Kingdom, 1893–1961'. *Review of Economic Studies,* XXXI, 221–52.

Holt, C. C., 1970. 'Job Search, Phillips' Wage Relation and Union Influence: Theory and Evidence'. *Microeconomic Foundations of Employment and Inflation Theory.* Ed. E. S. Phelps. London: Macmillan, 53–123.

——, and M. H. David, 1966. 'The Concept of Job Vacancies in a Dynamic Theory of the Labor Market'. *The Measurement and Interpretation of Job Vacancies.* A conference report of the National Bureau of Economic Research. New York: Columbia University Press, 73–141.

Holt, C. C., C. D. MacRae, S. O. Schweitzer, and R. E. Smith, 1973. 'Manpower Policies to Reduce Inflation and Unemployment'. *Manpower Programmes and the Policy Mix.* Ed. L. Ulman. Baltimore: Johns Hopkins University Press.

Horowitz, I., 1970. *Decision Making and the Theory of the Firm.* New York: Holt, Rinehart and Winston.

Hunter, L. C., 1967. 'Income Structure and Labour Mobility'. *British Journal of Industrial Relations,* V, 386–98.

——, and G. Reid, 1967. *Urban Worker Mobility.* Paris: Organisation for Economic Co-operation and Development.

Hunter, L. C., and D. J. Robertson, 1969. *Economics of Wages and Labour.* London: Macmillan.

James Report, 1972. *Teacher Education and Training.* Department of Education and Science. London: HMSO.

Jay, L. J., 1966. 'The Mobility of Teachers'. *Education,* no. 128, 372.

Kaldor, N., 1972. 'The Irrelevance of Equilibrium Economics'. *Economic Journal,* LXXXII, 1237–55.

Kelsall, R. K., 1963. *Women and Teaching.* Ministry of Education. London: HMSO.

——, and H. M. Kelsall, 1969. *The School Teacher in England and the U.S.* London: Commonwealth Library of Technology, Engineering and Liberal Studies.

Kelsall, R. K., A. Poole, and A. Kuhn, 1970. *Six Years After.* Sheffield: Sheffield University, Higher Education Research Unit.

Kennell, K., 1971. 'Euphemistically — You're Sacked'. *DATA Journal* (May), 12–13.

Kerr, C., 1950. 'Labor Markets: Their Character and Consequences'. *American Economic Review,* XL, Papers and Proceedings, 278–91.

——, 1954. 'The Balkanization of Labor Markets'. *Labor Mobility and Economic Opportunity.* Ed. W. W. Bakke. Cambridge, Massachusetts: MIT Press, 92–110.

King, J., 1972. *Labour Economics.* London: Macmillan.

Koizumi, T., 1973. 'Adjustment Costs and the Laws of Demand for a Quasi-fixed Factor Input: a Comparative Statical Analysis'. Report 7310. Columbus, Ohio: Ohio State University, Division for Economic Research. (mimeograph.)

Latham, R. W., and D. A. Peel, 1974. 'The Wage Variable and the Phillips' Curve.' *Scottish Journal of Political Economy,* XXI, 289–94.

Leibenstein, H., 1965. 'Shortages and Surpluses in Education in Undeveloped Countries: A Theoretical Foray'. *Education and Economic Development.* Eds. C. A. Anderson and M. J. Bowman. Chicago: Aldine, 51–62.

Leijonhufvud, A., 1968. *Keynesian Economics and the Economics of Keynes*. New York: Oxford University Press.

Lester, R., 1952. 'A Range Theory of Wage Differentials'. *Industrial and Labor Relations Review*, V, 483–501.

——, 1954a. *Adjustments to Labor Shortage*. Princeton: Princeton University Press.

——, 1954b. *Hiring Practices and Labor Competition*. Princeton: Princeton University Press.

Levitan, S. A., G. L. Mangum, and R. Marshall, 1972. *Human Resources and Labor Markets*. New York: Harper and Row.

Lipsey, R. G., 1966. *An Introduction to Positive Economics*. 2nd edn. London: Weidenfeld and Nicolson.

Loveridge, R., 1972. 'Occupational Change and The Development of Interest Groups among White-Collar Workers in the U.K.: A Long-Term Model'. *British Journal of Industrial Relations*, X, 340–65.

MacKay, D. I., D. Boddy, J. Brack, J. A. Diack, and N. Jones, 1971. *Labour Markets Under Different Employment Conditions*. London: George Allen and Unwin.

MacKay, D. I., and R. A. Hart, 1974. 'Wage Inflation and the Phillips Relationship'. *Manchester School*, XLII, 136–61.

Martin, J. P., and G. Wilson, 1969. *A Study of Police Manpower*. Cambridge Studies in Criminology 24. London: Heinemann.

McCormick, B., 1959. 'Labour Hiring Practices and Monopolistic Competition'. *Quarterly Journal of Economics*, LXXIII, 607–18.

McGuire, J. W., 1964. *Theories of Business Behaviour*. Englewood Cliffs, New Jersey: Prentice Hall.

Metcalf, D., 1973. 'Some Aspects of the University Teachers' Labour Market in the U.K.' *Essays in Modern Economics*. Proceedings of the conference of the Association of University Teachers of Economics, 1972. Eds. M. Parkin and A. R. Nobay. London: Longman, 192–211.

Morley, R., 1976. 'Unemployment, Profit's Share, and Regional Policy'. *The Economics of Industrial Subsidies*. Ed. A. Whiting. London: HMSO, 159–81.

Mortensen, D., 1970. 'A Theory of Wage and Employment Dynamics'. *Microeconomic Foundations of Employment and Inflation Theory*. Ed. E. S. Phelps. London: Macmillan, 167–211.

Mortimer, J. E., 1960. *A History of the Association of Engineering and Shipbuilding Draughtsmen*. Richmond, Surrey: AESD.

Nadiri, M. I., and S. Rosen, 1973. *A Disequilibrium Model of Demand for Factors of Production*. New York: National Bureau of Economic Research.

National Association of Schoolmasters. 1965. *Ancillary Assistants in Schools*. Hemel Hempstead: NAS.

——, 1967. *Teachers' Aids, Helps or Substitutes*. Hemel Hempstead: NAS.

National Board for Prices and Incomes. (All, London: HMSO).

Report No. 16.   *Pay and Conditions of Busmen*. Cmnd 3012. 1966.

Report No. 50.   *Productivity Agreements in the Bus Industry*. Cmnd 3498. 1967.

Report No. 56.   *Proposals by the London Transport Board for Fare Increase in the London Area*. Cmnd 3561. 1968.

Report No. 63.   *Pay of Municipal Busmen*. Cmnd 3605. 1968.

Report No. 69.   *Pay and Conditions of Busmen Employed by the Corporations of Belfast, Glasgow, and Liverpool*. Cmnd 3646. 1968.

Report No. 78.   *Pay and Conditions of Busmen Employed by Rochadale County Borough Council*. Cmnd 3723. 1968.

Report No. 85.   *Pay and Conditions of Busmen Employed by the Corporation of Dundee*. Cmnd 3791. 1968.

Report No. 95.   *Pay and Conditions of Busmen Employed by the Corporation of Wigan*. Cmnd 3845. 1968.

Report No. 96.   *Pay and Conditions of Busmen Employed by the Corporation of Great Yarmouth*. Cmnd 3844. 1968.

Report No. 161. *Hours of Work, Overtime and Shiftworking*. Cmnd 4554. 1970.

National Union of Teachers, n.d. [*c*. 1967]. *The NUT View on Ancillaries and Auxiliaries*. London: NUT.

Newsom Report, 1963. *Half Our Future*. Central Advisory Council for Education (England). London: HMSO.

Oi, W., 1962. 'Labor as a Quasi-Fixed Factor'. *The Journal of Political Economy*, LXX, 538–55.

Organisation for Economic Co-operation and Development, 1965. *Wages and Labour Mobility*. Paris: OECD.

——, 1969. *Study on Teachers. Germany, Belgium, United Kingdom*. Directorate for Scientific Affairs. Paris: OECD.

——, 1971. *Training, Recruitment and Utilisation of Teachers in Primary and Secondary Education*. Paris: OECD.

Parnes, H. S., 1970. 'Labor Force Participation and Labor Mobility', *A Review of Industrial Relations Research*, vol. I. Industrial Relations Research Association. Wisconsin: University of Wisconsin, 1–67.

Pay Board, 1974a. *Relativities*. Advisory Report no. 2. Cmnd 5535. London: HMSO.

Pay Board, 1974b. *London Weighting*. Advisory Report no. 4. Cmnd 5660. London: HMSO.

Peel, D. A., 1973. 'Some Implications of Utility Maximising Firms: A Note'. *Bulletin of Economic Research*, XXIII, 148–51.

——, and G. Briscoe, 1974. 'Another Look at the Role of Excess Demand Variables in Determining Money Wage Inflation'. Discussion Paper 53. Coventry: University of Warwick, Centre for Industrial Economic and Business Research. (mimeograph.)

Pettman, B. O., 1973. 'Some Factors Influencing Labour Turnover: A Review of Research Literature'. *Industrial Relations Journal*, IV, 43–61.

Phelps, O., 1961. *Introduction to Labor Economics*. New York: McGraw-Hill.

Phelps Brown, H., 1962. *The Economics of Labor*. New Haven: Yale University Press.

Phelps Brown Report, 1964. *Report of the Committee of Inquiry to Riview the Pay and Conditions of Employment of the Drivers and Conductors of London Transport Board's Road Services*. Ministries of Labour and Transport. London: HMSO.

Plowden Report, 1967. *Children and their Primary Schools*. vol. I, Central Advisory Council for Education (England). London: HMSO.

Pratt, J., T. Burgess, R. Alemano, and M. Locke, 1973. *Your Local Education*. Harmondsworth: Penguin.

Raimon, R. L., 1953. 'The Indeterminateness of Wages of Semiskilled Workers'. *Industrial and Labor Relations Review*, VI, 180–94.

Reder, M. W., 1955. 'The Theory of Occupational Wage Differentials'. *American Economic Review*, XLV, 833–52.

Rees, A., 1971. *The Current State of Labor Economics*. Kingston, Ontario: Queen's University, Industrial Relations Centre.

Rees, A., and G. P. Shultz, 1970. *Workers and Wages in an Urban Labor Market*. Chicago: University of Chicago Press.

Reynolds, L. G., 1971. *The Three Worlds of Economics*. New Haven and London: Yale University Press.

Roberts, B. C., R. Loveridge, and J. Gennard, 1972. *Reluctant Militants: A Study of Industrial Technicians.* London: Heinemann.

Roberts, C. J., 1972. 'A Survey of Employment Models'. Discussion Paper 30. Coventry: University of Warwick, Centre for Industrial Economic and Business Research. (mimeograph.)

Robinson, D., 1968. *Wage Drift, Fringe Benefits and Manpower Distribution.* Paris: Organisation for Economic Co-operation and Development.

—— (ed.), 1970. *Local Labour Markets and Wage Structures.* London: Gower Press.

Rosen, S., and M. I. Nadiri, 1974. 'A Disequilibrium Model of Demand for Factors of Production'. *American Economic Review*, LXIV, 264–70.

Rothschild, M., 1973. 'Models of Market Organisation with Imperfect Information: A Survey'. *Journal of Political Economy*, LXXXI, no. 6, 1283–1308.

Routh, G., 1973. 'Incomes Policy'. *Scottish Journal of Political Economy*, XX, 179–87.

——, 1965. *Occupation and Pay in Great Britain, 1906–60.* National Institute of Economic and Social Research, Economic and Social Series XXIV. Cambridge: Cambridge University Press.

Royal Society, 1969. *The Shortage of Mathematics and Science Teachers in Schools.* London: Royal Society.

Salop, S. C., 1973. 'Wage Differentials in a Dynamic Theory of the Firm'. *Journal of Economic Theory*, VI, 321–44.

Sattinger, M., 1972. 'Manpower Shortages and Misallocations: A Review'. Stony Brook Working Paper no. 78. New York: State University of New York, Department of Economics. (mimeograph.)

Schultze, C. L., 1968. *The Politics and Economics of Public Spending.* Washington, D.C.: The Brookings Institution.

Scoville, J. G., 1972. *Manpower and Occupational Analysis: Concepts and Measurements.* Lexington, Massachusetts: D. C. Heath.

Self, P., 1972. *Administrative Theories and Politics.* London: George Allen and Unwin.

Shackle, G. L. S., 1966. 'Policy, Poetry and Success'. *Economic Journal*, LXXVI, 755–67.

Shultz, G. P., 1962. 'A Non-Union Market for White-Collar Labor'. *Aspects of Labor Economics.* National Bureau of Economic Research. Princeton: Princeton University Press, 107–55.

Silverman, D., 1970. *The Theory of Organisations: A Sociological Framework*. London: Heinemann.

Smedley, R., 1969. '25000 Draughtsmen at your Command!' *Engineering Materials and Design* (December).

Stigler, G. J., 1962. 'Information in the Labor Market'. *Journal of Political Economy*, XX (Supplement), 94–105.

Swann, D., D. O'Brien, W. P. Maunder, and W. S. Howe, 1974. *Competition in British Industry: Restrictive Practices Legislation in Theory and Practice*. London: George Allen and Unwin.

Taylor, J., 1972. 'The Behaviour of Unemployment and Unfilled Vacancies: Great Britain 1958–71'. *Economic Journal*, LXXXII, 1352–65.

——, 1974. *Unemployment and Wage Inflation*. Harlow, Essex: Longman.

Taylor, L. C., 1971. *Resources for Learning*. Harmondsworth: Penguin.

Tew, B., 1965. *International Monetary Cooperation 1945–65*. London: Hutchinson University Library.

Thomas, R. B., 1973a. 'On the Definition of Shortages in Administered Labour Markets'. *Manchester School*, XLI, 169–86.

——, 1973b. 'Postwar Movements in Teachers' Salaries'. *Industrial Relations Journal*, IV, 12–26.

——, 1975. 'The Supply of Graduates to Teaching'. *British Journal of Industrial Relations*, XIII, 107–14.

Thomson, A. W. J., 1971. 'Collective Bargaining under Incomes Legislation: The Case of Britain's Buses'. *Industrial and Labour Relations Review*, XXIV, 389–406.

——, and L. C. Hunter, 1973. *The Nationalized Transport Industries*. London: Heinemann.

Tinbergen, J., 1952. *On the Theory of Economic Policy*. Amsterdam: North-Holland.

Tinsley, P. A., 1969. 'On Optimal Dynamic Adjustment of Quasi-Fixed Factors'. Special Studies Paper no. 9. Washington, D.C.: Division of Research and Statistics, Federal Reserve Board. (mimeograph.)

Toder, E. J., 1972. 'The Supply of Public School Teachers to an Urban Metropolitan Area. A Possible Source of Discrimination in Education'. *Review of Economics and Statistics*, LIV, 439–43.

Turnbull, P., and A. Zabalza, 1974. 'Supply and Demand in the Labour Market for Teachers. A case study: Regional Differences, with special reference to London'. London: London School of Economics, Higher Education Research Unit. (mimeograph.)

Turner, H. A., 1962. *Trade Union Growth, Structure and Policy.* London: George Allen and Unwin.

——, 1966. Review of *Wages and Labour Mobility*, by Organisation for Economic Co-operation and Development, *Economic Journal*, LXXVI, 639–41.

Ulman, L., 1973. *Manpower Programs in the Policy Mix.* Baltimore: Johns Hopkins University Press.

Vaizey, J., 1963. *The Control of Education.* London: Faber and Faber.

——, 1969. 'Demography and the Economics of Teacher Education'. *Towards a Policy for the Education of Teachers.* Proceedings of the twentieth symposium of the Colston Research Society. Ed. W. Taylor. London: Butterworths, 75–95.

——, K. Norris, and J. Sheehan, 1972. *The Political Economy of Education.* London: Duckworth.

Vaizey, J., and J. Sheehan, 1968. *Resources for Education.* London: George Allen and Unwin.

Vickers. D., 1968. *The Theory of the Firm: Production, Capital and Finance.* New York: McGraw-Hill.

Vincens, J., and D. Robinson, 1974. *Research into Labour Market Behaviour.* Paris: Organisation for Economic Co-operation and Development.

Wabe, S., and O. B. Coles, 1975. 'The Short and Long Run cost of Bus Transport in Urban Areas'. *Journal of Transport Economics and Policy*, IX, no. 2, 127–40.

Williams, G., T. Blackstone, and D. Metcalf, 1974. *The Academic Labor Market.* Amsterdam: Elsevier.

Williamson, O. E., 1970. *Corporate Control and Business Behaviour. An Inquiry into the Effects of Organisation Form on Enterprise Behaviour.* Englewood Cliffs, New Jersey: Prentice-Hall.

Wilson Report, 1965. *Report of the Committee of Inquiry into the Causes and Circumstances of the Differences Existing Between the Two Sides of the National Council for the Omnibus Industry.* Ministry of Labour. London: HMSO.

Woodhall, M., and M. Blaug, 1968. 'Productivity Trends in British Secondary Education 1950–63'. *Sociology of Education*, XLI, 1–35.

Woodward, J., 1958. *Management and Technology.* Problems of Progress in Industry, 3. London: HMSO.

——, 1965. *Industrial Organisation: Theory and Practice.* London: Oxford University Press.

Zabalza, A., 1974a. 'A Labour Market Study: Teachers in England and Wales'. London: London School of Economics, Higher Education Research Unit. (mimeograph.)

——, 1974b. 'Supply and Demand in the Labour Market for School Teachers: Graduate Supply'. London: London School of Economics, Centre for the Economics of Education. (mimeograph.)

Index

Abraham, C., 31n.
adjustment
  asymmetry of, 27, 29
  classification by operand of, 17,
    18–19, 26–8, 37, 48, 52, 135,
    138, 152, 190, 200, 204
  constraints on, *see* bus industry;
    constraints; draughtsmen;
    school teachers
  disguising of shortage by
    temporary, 3n., 27n., 37, 43,
    152
  example of process of, 25–7, 28–9
  general theory of, 29–30 (*see also*
    cost minimization)
  interdependence of, 12, 20, 50, 60
  lack of a theory of, 12–13, 202
  model of, 4, 13, 25n.
  non-wage, 3, 16, 18, 193, 195, 205,
    209–10, 212, 214, 216–17
  permanent, 24–7, 37, 45–7, 63,
    138, 161–2, 166, 194
  precision of coverage of, 192
  price, 202–7, 209
  process of adaptation and, 195–6,
    201
  residual, 17, 24, 25, 26, 28, 31–2,
    35, 37, 189, 213 (*see also* school
    teachers)
  reversibility of, 24–5, 36, 79, 153
  stimulus to, 37
  temporary, 24–7, 36, 43, 45–6, 47,
    63, 79, 138, 161–2, 166, 186,
    194, 213
  time and, 17n., 25, 37, 48, 108
  uncertainty and, 195–6 (*see also*
    cost minimization;
    information acquisition;
    uncertainty)
  see also instruments of
    adjustment
Aero Electrical Systems Ltd (AES;
  pseudonym), 154–5, 164, 168,
  169, 170, 171, 181, 182
Ahamad, B., 1
aircraft industry, 145, 165–6, 173,
  177, 180, 235n.
Alphabus (pseudonym), 39n.,
  49–50, 57–8, 59–60, 64, 70–71,
  76n., 88, 193, 196n., 222–8
Amalgamated Union of
  Engineering and Foundry
  Workers (AEF), 145
Amalgamated Union of
  Engineering Workers (AUEW),
  9, 143
  see also Technical and
    Supervisory Section of the
    AUEW
Armitage, P., 113n., 119n.
Arrow, K. J., 36n., 49, 202
Associated Farm Products (AFP;
  pseudonym), 155, 156, 158, 181,
  182

factors affecting position of,
14–16, 37, 202
goals of, 38, 189
holding/parent company and, 5,
183–4
size of, 215
types of production and, 234–5
Fisher, M. R., 12
Fishport (pseudonym), 39n., 43n.,
65, 68–9, 74
Fishwick, F., 68n.
Flanders, A., 21n.
Fleet Street, earnings in, 210
Flemming, J. S., 215n.
flows, *see* labour market
Folk, H., 20n.
Fox, A., 2n., 59n.
Franke, W., 18n., 215n.
Freeman, R. B., 8n., 108n., 109n.,
215, 217

Gammabus (pseudonym), 39n., 44,
45, 73n., 82
General Machine Tools
(pseudonym), 160–61, 164n., 181
Goodman, J. F. B., 6n.
Gowler, D., 14n., 35n.
Granchester (pseudonym), 39n.,
67n., 86
Greater London Council (GLC),
40n., 89
Gujarti, D., 230n., 232n.

habitual behaviour, reasons for,
36n., 196–7
Hamborough (pseudonym), 39n.,
44, 57, 68, 74–5, 81, 90
Hardware Ltd (pseudonym), 164,
168, 169, 181
Hart, R. A., 3, 213
Hedrick, C. L., 198
Helico (pseudonym), 158, 168–9,
182, 184
Hines, A. G., 214
hiring standards, *see* bus industry;
draughtsmen; instruments of
adjustment; school teachers

Holt, C. C., 3n., 13n., 46, 150n.
Horowitz, I., 34n., 200n.
Hunter, L. C., 42, 59n., 91n., 207n.,
214n.

incomes policy, 2, 3, 49, 210–12, 232
see also bus industry; constraints;
draughtsmen; school teachers;
wage inflation
industrial action, 162n.
inflows, 14–16, 19, 27, 35, 103–5,
108, 117, 129
see also operands; recruitment
information acquisition, 33–4, 36,
105, 194
see also cost minimization;
uncertainty
Inner London Education Authority
(ILEA), 126n.
instruments of adjustment
capital substitution as, 17, 20, 27,
50, 190n., 195 (*see also*
computer-aided design;
draughtsmen; school teachers)
change in entry requirements as,
19, 127–30
dilutees as, 24 (*see also*
draughtsmen; school teachers)
dismissal policy and, 28, 83–4, 85
expansion of labour supply as,
18, 19
hiring standards and, 18, 25, 28,
187, 190, 204, 209, 212, 216 (*see
also* bus industry;
draughtsmen; school teachers)
hours of work and, 216 (*see also*
bus industry)
inventory changes as, 50
one-man operation as, *see* one-
man operation
overtime as, 19, 25, 27 (*see also*
bus industry; draughtsmen;
recruitment; school teachers;
trade unions)
part-timers and, *see* bus industry;
draughtsmen; school teachers;
trade unions

257

redundancy and, 183
re-engagement and, 79, 84
school teachers and, 108, 111, 119
selection criteria and, 76–7, 78–9,
  80–81, 83, 172–9
skill level and, 15n.
temporary staff and, 75–6
training and, 50n., 82–3, 172–3,
  178
trade union constraints on, 76,
  174, 177, 178
wage increases and, 73–4
Reder, M. W., 209, 210
Redundancy Payments Act 1965,
  232
Rees, A., 5n., 8n., 18n., 216n.
Reid, G., 207n.
research methods, 9–11
Road Transport Industry Training
  Board (RTITB), 51, 82
Robbins Committee, 102n.
Roberts, B. C., 142n.
Robertson, D. J., 214n.
Robinson, D., 4, 6n., 15–16, 18n.,
  20n., 35, 216n.
Rosen, S., 33n.
Rothschild, M., 13n.
Routh, G., 5n., 7
Royal Society, 130n., 134n.

Sattinger, M., 216n.
school-leaving age, 109, 112n., 130,
  133, 134
school teachers
  administered rules and, 108–10,
    134, 137, 217
  ancillary staff and, 106n., 132n.
  attraction of job and, 119–20
  capital substitution and, 109,
    131–2
  changes in age structure of, 122n.
  changes in situation of, 10–11,
    95–6, 98–9, 131–2
  characteristics of market for, 8–9,
    95, 96–7
  class size and, 98–9, 102n., 105n.,
    117, 134, 190, 207–8

components in supply of, 103–4
compulsory schooling period
  and, 132–3
constraints on instruments to
  increase supply of, 108–9, 127
decision-making and, 110, 114,
  128, 135–40
deferment of improvements and,
  108, 133–4
definition of shortage of,
  100–103, 105
demand for, 8, 11, 23n., 96, 98,
  99–101
dilutees and, 131–2, 135
Emergency Teacher Training
  Scheme and, 112
factor substitution and, 130–32
female, 96, 104, 114n., 115n., 118,
  119–21, 122, 135, 208
financial constraints and supply
  of, 100, 108, 133
flow of new, 111–12, 115–19, 121,
  126n., 127
formal norms and, 106, 111n.,
  117n.
graduate training requirement
  and, 106, 128–30, 135, 138
higher pay for scarce, 125, 135
hiring standards and, 107, 109,
  112, 127–30, 138
'immobile', 119
improvement in staffing
  standards and, 100, 112n., 116,
  118, 131, 135, 137, 138, 205
incomes policy and, 111, 123–5
inflows of, 105–6
in-service training and, 127
length of school day or year and,
  109, 133–4
lengthening of training course
  and, 116–17, 127–8, 138
local education authorities and,
  98, 99–101, 204–5
London allowance and, 126
maths and science, 108, 128n.,
  130n., 134n., 135n., 137, 191
national level of decisions about,